Adolescents, Cultures, and Conflicts

Michigan State University Series on Children, Youth, and Families
(Vol. 3)

Garland Reference Library of Social Science
(Vol. 1112)

Adolescents, Cultures, and Conflicts
Growing Up in Contemporary Europe

Edited by Jari-Erik Nurmi

GARLAND PUBLISHING, INC.
A MEMBER OF THE TAYLOR & FRANCIS GROUP
New York & London
1998

Library of Congress Cataloging-in-Publication Data

Adolescents, cultures, and conflicts : growing up in contemporary Europe /
    edited by Jari-Erik Nurmi.
            p.   cm. — (Michigan State University series on children,
    youth, and families ; vol. 3)   (Garland reference library of social
    science ; vol. 1112)
        Includes bibliographical references and index.
        ISBN 0-8153-2389-1 (alk. paper)
            1. Teenagers—Europe—Social conditions.   2. Adolescence—Europe.
    3. Social change—Europe.   I. Nurmi, Jari-Erik.   II. Series: Michigan State
    University series on children, youth, and families ; v. 3.   III. Series: Garland
    reference library of social science ; v. 1112.
    HQ799.E9A35   1998
    305.235'094—dc21   97–43496
                                                                CIP

Printed on acid-free, 250-year-life paper
Manufactured in the United States of America

Contents

Series Editor's Foreword

The publication of Jari-Erik Nurmi's book, *Adolescents, Cultures and Conflicts: Growing Up in Contemporary Europe,* marks the presentation of a valuable volume in its own right as well as the continued successful development of the Michigan State University (MSU) Series on Children, Youth, and Families. The Nurmi volume promises to be a seminal contribution to understanding the nature and character of contemporary European adolescence and, in turn, to the eventual development of community-based programs for addressing the unique and contextually influenced issues and concerns of adolescents in a changing Europe. In particular, the book addresses issues of adolescent development that have emerged in the face of the dramatic political and social changes in Europe in the 1990s, including the collapse of Soviet hegemony, migrations across national borders, and ethnic/religious conflicts. Furthermore, the scholarly work in the volume is a prime example of the creative emphasis on cutting-edge scholarship that the MSU Series represents—a focus on issues of social policy and practical application in relation to the needs of diverse groups of children, youth, and families in communities in the United States and around the world.

In addition, the Nurmi volume provides an exemplary illustration of the goals of the Institute for Children, Youth, and Families (ICYF) as an example of the relationship of outreach scholarship to essential issues of policy and program development which, in turn, has the potential for enhancing the lives of children, youth and families in diverse national and international communities. Likewise, the publication of this book offers evidence that the MSU Series, initiated by ICYF and well served by the commitment and intellectual leadership of Senior Editor John Paul McKinney with the able guidance of Marie Ellen Larcada of Garland Publishing, serves as a compendium of scholarly work reflecting the very best scholarship aimed at enhancing the life experiences of children, youths, and families. As such, both the Nurmi volume and the MSU Series provide further justification for the importance and feasibility of the mission of ICYF in integrating research and outreach.

The mission of the Institute for Children, Youth, and Families at MSU is based on a vision of the nature of a land-grant university as an academic institution with a responsibility for addressing the welfare of children, youths, and families in communities. More specifically, the mission of ICYF is shaped by an ecological perspective on human development that places the life span development of human beings in the context of the significant settings of human experience, including community, family, work, and peer networks (Lerner et al., 1994; Schiamberg, 1988). Historically, the ecological perspective has both been associated with and a guiding frame for colleges of home economics or, as they are more recently termed, colleges of human development, human ecology, or family and consumer sciences (Miller and Lerner, 1994). Using the ecology of human development as a conceptual framework, the Institute for Children, Youth, and Families continues to develop programs that integrate the critical notion of development in context with the attempt, indeed the necessity, of creating connections between such scholarship and social policy, program design, and evaluation.

The MSU Series is designed to provide a vehicle for the publication and transmission of research and outreach efforts characterized by a collaborative partnership between scholarly expertise and the community. The Nurmi volume represents the innovative research of authors who have been engaged, first hand, with the developmental circumstances of European adolescents, in a variety of countries, who must meld the normative changes of adolescence with the challenges of a dramatically changing context. In many ways the primary challenge confronting those who serve European adolescents and families is the same as that confronting American research scholars and practitioners—applying their resources to address a variety of critical social problems. The Michigan State University Series on Children, Youth, and Families is, itself, an example of the outreach scholarship which reflects the contextual and practical policy focus of the ICYF research program. The MSU Series publishes reference and professional books, including monographs and edited volumes, that appeal to a wide audience in communities as well as in universities, including such constituencies as scholars, practitioners, service deliverers, child and family advocates, business leaders, and policymakers. As illustrated by the scholarly effort of Jari-Erik Nurmi and his colleagues on the emerging character of European adolescents in a changing context, the MSU Series has substantial import and appeal to these constituencies primarily because of its focus on the integration of research and outreach and, as well, an emphasis on collaborative relationships between universities and communities.

The volume by Nurmi represents an outstanding contribution to this emerging outreach/research focus. The MSU Series editors, including John Paul McKinney, Amy B. Slonim, Linda Spence, and Lawrence B. Schiamberg, as well as the staff editor of the Institute for Children, Youth, and Families at MSU, Linda Chapel Jackson, are most pleased to have this innovative book on the emerging social and developmental issues of European adolescence as part of the MSU Series. We trust this book will be the first in a series of volumes which are part of the European Series on Children, Youth and Families.

References

Lerner, R. M., Miller, J. R., Knott, J. H., Corey, K. E., Bynum, T. S., Hoopfer, L. C., McKinney, M. H., Abrams, L. A., Hula, R. C., and Terry, P. A. (1994). Integrating scholarship and outreach in human development research, policy, and service: A developmental contextual perspective. In D. L. Featherman, R. M. Lerner, and M. Perlmutter (Eds.), *Life-span development and behavior, 12* (pp. 249–273). Hillsdale, NJ: Erlbaum.

Miller, J. R., and Lerner, R. M. (1994). Integrating research and outreach: Developmental contextualism and the human ecological perspective. *Home Economics Forum, 7,* 21–28.

Schiamberg, L. B. (1988). *Child and adolescent development* (2nd ed.). New York: Macmillan.

Preface

The idea for publishing a volume on European advances in adolescent research was raised by August Flammer and Richard Lerner in the context of an international workshop on Youth and Social Change held at Pennsylvania State University in the summer of 1991 and organized by the Pennsylvania State University and the International Society for the Study of Behavioural Development.

It was not, of course, an accident that the idea for the volume arose at the workshop, where senior and junior researchers from all over North America and Europe were gathered to discuss key issues related to youths and social change. During the discussions it became evident that some of the adolescent research being carried out in Europe might have an interest for audiences in the United States and other parts of the world. The present book is the fruit of this idea.

Given this background, it seemed a natural choice to concentrate on adolescent development in terms of diversity in developmental environments and the impact of social change. The chapters concentrate on aspects of adolescent development in various contexts of cultural, social, and institutional diversity, sociopolitical change, political violence, and acculturation. In addition, the book introduces a wide variety of paradigms and approaches typical of European developmental research.

However, the book is not meant to be a complete representation of growing up in Europe. Rather, it provides examples of different developmental environments. I hope that the diversity in adolescent development discussed here helps readers understand how the development of adolescents may vary across different sociocultural contexts and what happens when young people are faced with special challenges, such as rapid social change and even political violence.

Europe has recently faced numerous important sociopolitical and historical events, such as the change from socialism to market economies in eastern Europe, the recent unification process, several political conflicts, and an increase in immigrant populations. For several reasons, the contents of this book are meant to cover some of these recent changes. First, these types of development have been part of European history for centuries. Second, how these changes and conflicts influence adolescents is assumed to be something unique that European adolescent research might offer to international readers. Finally, volumes that concern current social change are not typical of developmental research, a field in which studies take a long time to be completed and reported. We hope that readers will find the analysis of the impact of recent social and political changes on adolescent development not only stimulating but also helpful for their own research and conceptualizations of adolescence.

As the reader will find out, there is a wide diversity in perspectives, theoretical approaches, and ways of writing among the authors. Although an editor often aims at consistency in this respect, there has been a conscious effort in this volume to preserve diversity.

Several researchers on adolescence have contributed to the preparation of the book. I would like to mention first August Flammer, who supplied ideas for its contents and personal support and advice in the course of the editorial process. I would also like to thank Peter Noack, who has given a helping hand at several stages in the preparation of the book. Several other scientists have also made contributions. For example, Françoise Bariaud, Luba Botcheva, Luc Goossens, Sandy Jackson, Petr Macek, Katariina Salmela-Aro, Anna Stetsenko, and Bruna Zani were involved in the editorial review process. To all of these named here and to others unnamed, my gratitude.

Adolescents, Cultures, and Conflicts

Chapter One
Growing Up in Contemporary Europe
An Overview

Jari-Erik Nurmi

Although adolescence itself is characterized by several common markers across different developmental environments, growing up in Europe can be described as a multifaceted process for several reasons. Compare a senior high school student in Switzerland doing well at school and aiming at university studies with a Bulgarian agemate living in a small town trying to find his or her way through the changes in educational and career options created by the recent transition from socialism to a market economy. Compare these two with a Vietnamese refugee in Finland trying to adapt to the new challenges, values, and norms of the host society. Finally, to take the most extreme example, imagine the situation of a Bosnian teenager facing the horrors of war.

Although the diversity in developmental environments makes it difficult to speak about "European adolescence," this volume represents a collection of viewpoints about what growing up in Europe is like. There is no attempt to provide a systematic comparison of adolescent developmental contexts (Hurrelmann, 1994) and thinking (Alsaker and Flammer, in press), as some recent works have done. The book as a whole provides a variety of examples of what might be described as special environments for growing up in contemporary Europe (see also Noack, Hofer, and Youniss, 1995). The chapters concentrate on discussing adolescent development in the contexts of cultural, social, and institutional diversity; sociopolitical change; political violence; and acculturation to a new society.

Research on and theories of adolescence often aim at describing general laws of development (Adelson, 1980). However, studies carried out in the United States and western Europe may sometimes give a far too simplified and abstract view when they do not consider the diversity of developmental patterns (Adelson, 1980; Van Hasselt and Hersen, 1987). Consequently, this volume may help to increase our understanding of some key developmental processes of this age period.

Common Features of Adolescence

There are, of course, several general processes in adolescent development that define and constitute this life period in various environments,
and also provide a basis for understanding it from cross-national and
cross-cultural perspectives. For example, the onset of adolescence is
marked by physiological maturation and the development of new ways
of thinking. These changes not only provide a basis for adolescents'
new orientation toward and interest in their social world (Brooks-Gunn
and Reiter, 1990), but they also influence the ways in which other
people, such as parents and peers, view and respond to them (Brooks-
Gunn, 1987).

The second general feature of adolescence across various environments is that it is a transition period from childhood to adulthood. This
socialization into major adulthood roles can be described in terms of two
major processes (Nurmi, 1993; 1997). On the one hand, adolescents are
faced with several challenges, demands, and problems related to the developmental tasks, cultural norms, and role transitions typical of this age
period. As suggested by Havighurst (1948/1974) several decades ago, these
include achieving mature relationships with peers, forming a sex-role
identity, preparing for a future family life, achieving emotional independence from parents, and preparing for an economic career, which also
includes educational planning. Although there may be variation in the
concrete ways in which these normative patterns are reflected in adolescents' lives (Hurrelmann, 1994), the key themes of these developmental
demands seem to be similar across cultures (Nurmi, 1991).

On the other hand, in order to meet these challenges successfully
and to become socialized into major adulthood roles, adolescents have
to construct individual goals that fit the developmental tasks, explore
related opportunities in their own environments, plan possible means
for goal achievement, and be committed to their decisions. In this process of directing their own development (Lerner, 1983; Nurmi, 1993),
young people end up constructing motives, interests, skills, and knowledge about their environments and attitudes toward themselves, all of
which have been described in terms of identity formation (Erikson, 1959)
or self-definition (Nurmi, 1997). The fact that most adolescents are involved in the major developmental tasks of this age period not only di-
rects their own future development but also provides a basis for the continuity of the culture: Young people's acquisition of major adult roles
reproduces the specific culture and related way of life.

Third, adolescent development takes place in certain interpersonal and institutional contexts. Parents typically provide their adolescents with support, advice, and role models for how to handle age-graded demands (Nurmi, 1997). Similarly, peer groups, which provide a natural setting for discussion, negotiation, and social comparison (Savin-Williams and Berndt, 1990), form another important context for exploring future options and related behaviors, and for evaluating personal success in goal achievement. Adolescents are also faced with several institutional transitions and related opportunities that direct their behavior, decisions, and commitments in the context of socialization into major adulthood roles (Nurmi, 1991).

Contemporary Europe

A few words need to be written about the cultural background and history of contemporary Europe in order to put adolescent developmental environments in different parts of the continent into perspective. Each of Europe's many countries has its own, although closely linked, history, culture, and institutional structure. Many European countries have several official languages, as in Belgium, Finland, and Switzerland, for instance, or several languages that are spoken by citizens as their mother tongues. The variety of languages is also related to differences in culture and history. Often, by traveling only 100 miles, one may cross several national borders, experience a variety of cultures, and be able to practice a number of languages.

In spite of all this diversity, there are also some similarities based on geography. From political, linguistic, and religious points of view, Europe can be divided along a north-south line. Northern European countries share a cultural atmosphere that is characterized by political liberalism, Protestant religions and related values, as well as Germanic languages. Southern and central Europe have quite a different cultural atmosphere, characterized by certain types of conservatism, the Catholic religion, an emphasis on family ties, and Romance languages.

Another important dichotomy is that between east and west. Whereas the western European cultural heritage is characterized by Catholic and Protestant religions, and Germanic and Romance languages, eastern Europe has its basis in the Slavic culture and languages and in the Orthodox religion. One additional factor that has divided these two parts of Europe is its political history. Western Europe has been part of the free market economy for a long time; eastern European countries have had socialist regimes for decades.

It is worth mentioning, however, that although there are differences between north and south, and east and west, the changes from one part of Europe to another in terms of culture, and even in language, are seldom sudden, and they often occur within national borders rather than at them. Moreover, there are several interesting exceptions that confuse the picture. Take Poland, for example, which can be described as a northern European country with a Slavic language and a Catholic religion.

One of the key historical events that shaped the development of contemporary Europe was the First World War, after which several new independent states were formed following the collapse of the Austro-Hungarian empire and the onset of the revolution in Russia. The Second World War changed Europe again. After the defeat of the Nazi regime in Germany and the victory of the Allied forces, Europe was split into two blocs and two political systems. The majority of Western countries became members of NATO and continued to be part of the world free-market economy, whereas eastern European countries formed the Warsaw Pact under the control of the Soviet Union. This situation continued until the late 1980s and changed only in the context of the "velvet revolution" in eastern Europe and the collapse of the socialist regimes.

Two different tendencies characterize the present situation in Europe. First, the collapse of socialism has created several politically independent countries in eastern Europe and in some parts of the former Soviet Union. Developments in these countries have been characterized by rapid societal, political, and institutional change and by an increased orientation toward the Western world and its ideology. It also seems that this course of historical development plays an important part in adolescents' values and belief systems in these countries.

At the same time, western Europe has been characterized by political integration aiming at the formation of a "Federal State of Europe" in the context of the European Union. This development is evidenced by tendencies to form joint markets, a common currency, and one foreign policy, as well as by the inclusion of new members in the European Union. In addition, several historical events can be assumed to have provided a basis for the values and belief systems typical of western European youths: The end of the Second World War initiated a strong anti-authoritarian attitude; the radicalism of the 1960s turned into political cynicism in the 1980s; and the environmental problems related to rapid urbanization led to the emergence of a "green" ideology. Each of these developments has played a part in the creation of a special set of values and beliefs, and a worldview, that characterizes western European adolescents' thinking.

Variation in Developmental Environments

As already stated, a substantial amount of diversity exists in adolescents' developmental environments across contemporary Europe. Adolescents grow up in societies that vary along several dimensions, such as timing and patterning of the life-course transitions, cultural beliefs and norms, the rate of social change, and the political tensions and violence they face.

Transitions

One source of diversity is the differences in the institutional careers available to adolescents and the life-course patterns that they face. Although youths in different parts of Europe use education as a way to adopt adult occupational and social roles, the key transitions and the forms of social stratification differ substantially.

For example, Scandinavian adolescents receive comprehensive education until the age of fifteen without any major streaming, after which they go either to senior high school or to a vocational school. Because most of them choose high school, the major decisions concerning their future education and subsequent entry into the social hierarchy are made relatively late, when they apply for higher education (Roe, Bjurström, and Fornäs, 1994; Nurmi and Siurala, 1994). In some other European countries, streaming based on academic achievement begins much earlier, at age ten in Germany, for example (Hurrelmann and Settertobulbe, 1994), and continues later in several more stages (see also Buzzi and Cavalli, 1994; Mauger, 1994).

There are also substantial differences in the age at which the majority of adolescents first experience occupational life. In Sweden (Roe, Bjurström, and Fornäs, 1994), for example, the majority continue onto senior high school, whereas in Switzerland a substantial proportion serve apprenticeships after age fifteen (Buchmann, 1994). There is also substantial variation in unemployment rates among European countries and within different regions in any one country. These differences have an impact on entry into occupational life and on gaining independence from the parental home (Hurrelmann, 1994).

All this provides a basis for the substantial diversity in the institutional careers available to adolescents and, consequently, in the patterns of entry into and selection for the social hierarchy. Social hierarchy refers here to a complex set of societal roles and occupational positions that are associated with particular levels of prestige, power, education, and income.

The timing and structure of major transitions in other domains of life also vary across contemporary Europe. For example, marriage is postponed until a relatively late age in western Europe, whereas in the eastern and southern parts, people marry earlier. In Sweden, the median age for the first marriage is about twenty-eight for females and thirty for males (Roe, Bjurström, and Fornäs, 1994), whereas in Spain it is about twenty-three for women and twenty-five for men. However, it seems as if a new family pattern has emerged in some western European countries in which cohabitation, starting typically in the early twenties, precedes marriage (Mauger, 1994; Nurmi and Siurala, 1994). This cohabitation, which is far less typical in southern (Buzzi and Cavalli, 1994) and eastern Europe (Mirchev, 1994), in fact means that the age when people start to live in a marriagelike relationship does not vary across Europe to the extent that statistics on age at the first marriage suggest.

There are also interesting differences in the patterns of life transitions in interpersonal domains. Although marriage is typically assumed to be a key transition that coincides in most parts of Europe with moving from the parental home (Hurrelmann, 1994), in some countries, such as Bulgaria (Mirchev, 1994) and Poland (Wlodarek, 1994), married couples often live with their parents for a few years—either separately or with their spouses. This is mainly because of the lack of available apartments, but it may also reflect some cultural values.

Social Change

Social change is a multifaceted phenomenon. It may consist of rapid urbanization, changes in the way of life and cultural beliefs, an increase in multicultural nature of the society, and changes in the political and economic systems that influence the major institutions of the society. Although political tensions do not necessarily mean social change, these two are often connected. In this book, political tensions and violence will be discussed in the broader context of social change.

Although all modern industrialized societies seem to be characterized by rapid social change, some European countries have recently witnessed unusually dramatic historical events. One of the major post–World War II changes took place in the context of the "velvet revolution" in 1989, after which the former socialist countries in central and eastern Europe, with their centrally planned economies, began a transition to pluralistic parliamentary democracies and market economies. These sociopolitical events have been reflected not only in the political and economic systems, but also in the variety of changes in the institutions, ideologies, and belief systems adolescents encounter. These include the restructuring of educational institutions, the broadening of opportunities, changes in standards of living, an increase in the role of the church and religion, and the movement toward western, individualistic values. Such changes can be expected to have long-term effects on adolescent development.

Together with the recession in the early 1990s, the abovementioned historical changes have deeply affected some western European countries, especially the former West Germany. Although the decrease in economic growth and related problems may look minor compared with the potential changes in the standard of living in the former socialist countries, people seem to feel threatened as a consequence of the changes.

Other political tensions based on centuries of conflict also influence adolescents' lives in contemporary Europe. One typical case is the situation in Northern Ireland, where political violence has been part of everyday life for decades. Although there have been periods of more peaceful developments, separate Catholic and Protestant subcultures and identities continue to provide a basis for political tension and violence among adolescents.

Immigration and Racism

Since the Second World War, European countries have experienced a vast movement of immigrants and refugees. During the 1960s and early 1970s, there was large-scale labor migration into industrialized western Europe. More recently, there has been an increasing inflow of other groups, such as refugees. The former socialist countries have also accepted labor migrants from the developing countries with which they used to have strong political ties. However, the proportion of immigrants varies widely. Countries with a colonial history and those like Sweden with a liberal policy have the highest immigrant populations. In addition, big cities have appealed to immigrants more than more remote areas.

This development has created two kinds of social problem in contemporary Europe. First, differences in cultural traditions, values, and family patterns have caused immigrant populations various problems in adapting to their new home countries. These include a low level of education and high unemployment (Aronowitz, 1984; Hurrelmann, 1994). Although some immigrant groups have lived in their new countries for generations, some of these problems persist.

Second, the incidence of racist attacks on foreigners has escalated in most western European countries in recent years. Although this violence is typically perpetrated by small militant groups of young males representing specific subcultures, such as "skinheads," the opinion polls have also shown more negative trends in attitudes towards immigrants. This development has raised concerns about political developments in Europe. Such concerns have only been strengthened along with the increase in right-wing parties in several European countries that openly proclaim their racist attitudes toward minorities.

This increase in openly racist attitudes may have influenced immigrant youths in terms of creating a threat of violence. However, more negative attitudes towards immigrants may also influence adolescents among the indigenous population by providing a basis for the formation of a racist world view and negative cultural stereotypes, which is typical of the new rightist youth subcultures. It seems that young males from working-class backgrounds are most inclined to belong to these types of groups, possibly since their prospects have recently worsened because of increasing unemployment and other social problems.

Contents of This Volume
Cross-National Differences

European adolescents grow up in environments that display substantial diversity in terms of institutional transitions, cultural beliefs and values, standard of living, and amount of social change. The first three chapters examine how some of these phenomena are reflected in cross-national differences in adolescents' well-being, future interests, and conceptualizations of societal and international issues.

In the second chapter, Grob reports findings from an extensive Euronet study (Alsaker and Flammer, in press) showing that, although the pattern of adolescent well-being is quite similar across 11 European countries (13 cultural contexts) and the United States, there are evident cross-national differences in levels. The findings suggest that the sociohistorical background of the countries, and how this is reflected in adolescents' developmental environments, seems to explain some of these differences. In most cases, youths living in western European countries show a more positive attitude toward life and a higher level of self-esteem than adolescents living in former socialist countries. Interestingly, this difference in well-being was smaller among the younger adolescents, possibly because they were still children under the previous political system and were, therefore, less influenced by it.

Motola, Sinisalo, and Guichard then report some findings from a study in which adolescents' future career plans and occupational interests were compared in two countries that differ substantially according to their educational systems, related transitions, and cultural beliefs. Typical of the French system is that the selection of pupils for different educational tracks starts at an early age and continues up several subsequent steps mainly based on mathematical competence. This system provides a fixed basis for the stratification of pupils into different types of higher education, occupations, and positions in the social hierarchy. By way of contrast, the Finnish school system postpones tracking until the end of comprehensive school when pupils are 15 years old. Because the majority of adolescents attend senior high school, the major selection for higher education occurs even later, in the early twenties.

The findings of Motola and his colleagues suggest that the cross-national differences in the educational and streaming systems are reflected in adolescents' career plans in several ways. The Finnish educational system, in which only a small proportion of senior high school pupils are admitted to university, is reflected in Finnish adolescents' reluctance to express their plans for a future career. In turn, because French adolescents experience rigid streaming and easy access to universities, they seem to be able to formulate clear future career plans.

The results of Motola and his colleagues' study also show that adolescents' career interests seem to be structured differently in France and Finland, and also seem to be associated with different independent variables. In France, educational streaming seems to be the major factor that provides a basis for adolescents' career interests: Studying in the "mathematical stream" is associated with an interest in highly prestigious, technology-oriented, and male-dominated occupations such as architecture, whereas the "language stream" is associated with an interest in humanistic and female-dominated occupations such as translation. In Finland, gender seems to be the key factor that orients adolescents' interests in different future careers. Although women have a long tradition of active participation in working life, adolescents' career interests seem to be structured on the basis of cultural stereotypes concerning typical male and female occupations. The second important dimension that was reflected in adolescents' career interests in both countries was the social status related to future occupations. This, however, was not associated with the adolescents' own socioeconomic background.

The fourth chapter presents the findings of Hakvoort, Hägglund, and Oppenheimer concerning differences in adolescents' conceptions of peace and war in two northern European countries, the Netherlands and Sweden. Overall, young people were found to conceptualize both peace and war on a concrete level of reasoning. This, however, was not found to be associated with their age. The authors also found some gender differences. For example, girls frequently described peace in terms of personal, individual, and social definitions, whereas boys more often emphasized social rules and justice.

Hakvoort and colleagues also report several cross-national differences. For example, Dutch adolescents seem to describe peace by referring to aspects of their own society, such as liberty and democracy. This "peace-keeping" approach is assumed to be typical of countries in which war has been part of recent history, as is the case in the Netherlands. In turn, Swedish adolescents conceptualize peace in terms of international cooperation and sending help to other countries. This "peace attainment elsewhere" is suggested to be a typical conceptualization in countries that have experienced peace as a normal situation for centuries.

Social Change and Political Conflicts

Europe has a history of dramatic historical periods that have also provided the basis for some of the recent political developments. The next four chapters report findings on the impact of these sociopolitical changes and conflicts on adolescent development.

Botcheva reports findings from a unique longitudinal study in which the development of adolescents' behavioral style, identification, values, and well-being was followed across the major political changes in Bulgaria between 1989 and 1992. Several interesting results emerged. First, changes in adolescents' thinking were not continuous and seemed to reflect the concrete political events taking place in the society. At the beginning of the transition period, such changes were more substantial than in the subsequent relatively stable period. Later on, when the sociopolitical changes became more intensive, this was again reflected in their thinking.

Second, changes in the ways in which adolescents view themselves and how they value these changes showed different patterns. Although they started to value more active modes of behavior during the first change period, they simultaneously began to see themselves as having less control over their lives and as being less independent. This development continued later on, and was also reflected in a decrease in well-being. Third, some of the changes in behavior seemed to be domain specific. Although there was an increase in the use of active behavioral modes in the cultural domain of life, youths simultaneously reported increased passivity related to politics.

In Chapter 6, Silbereisen and Schwarz report findings concerning the timing of young people's first romantic relationship in the former West and East Germanies. Their results showed both similarities and differences across the two environments. In both parts of the country, those who showed earlier physiological maturation seemed to establish romantic relationships and had sexual experiences earlier than the late maturers. Moreover, those who reported a higher frequency of stressful life events tended to establish romantic relationships and to have sexual experiences at an earlier age. However, there were also some differences between the two parts of Germany. More frequent creative and other playful types of behavior were positively associated with earlier interpersonal transitions in former West Germany, whereas childhood activities in preparation for consumer roles were more influential in former East Germany. This was possibly because such activities signal differences in family background and orientation to Western types of values.

Chapter 7 contains a report of the findings of Kracke, Oepke, Wild, and Noack on the impact of social change and parents' political opinions on adolescents' antiforeigner and rightist attitudes in the former West and East Germanies. The results showed that in both countries parental beliefs seemed to have a strong influence on their children's antiforeigner and authoritarian attitudes. Moreover, a lower school track was associated with rightist attitudes. It was further suggested that, although social change in terms of economic disadvantage and experience of uncertainty seemed to provide a basis for adults' rightist opinions in both parts of the country, it influenced adolescents' antiforeigner and national-authoritarian attitudes only in former West Germany.

In the next chapter, Roe and Cairns review the literature on the impact of political violence on adolescent development in Northern Ireland. They suggest that, contrary to the prediction of a negative impact of persistent political violence, most evidence indicates that adolescents in Northern Ireland have coped and adapted well. Although they undoubtedly have experienced short-term stress from political violence, little evidence was found of any serious psychological disorders. This may be due partly to the fact that only some of them have personal experience of political violence. Some findings do seem to suggest that youths who have experienced violent acts suffer posttraumatic reactions. However, several factors, such as an intact and supportive family, seem to buffer the negative consequences of such events.

Roe and Cairns also suggest that social-identity formation may be a key process that is involved in maintaining sectarian Protestant and Catholic identities and related violence. The existence of two separate groups that construct their cultural memories in terms of their own history and cultural symbols provides a clear basis for the development of social identity during adolescence. It also appears that, although interventions seemed to promote cross-community contacts and friendship at the individual level, they seemed to have little impact on the polarization of adolescent group identification.

Immigration, Acculturation, and Xenophobia

During recent decades, European countries have experienced a vast increase in immigrant populations. This development has led to problems related to the adaptation and acculturation of immigrant youths into the host society, as well as to an increase in hostile attitudes among the indigenous population. The final two chapters discuss these issues.

Liebkind and Kosonen describe their findings on the relationships between acculturation and stress among young Vietnamese refugees in their monocultural host society, Finland. The results show, first, that what happens to refugee children and adolescents after they enter a new host society has a greater effect on their mental health than what has happened before. Second, although the refugee adolescents seem to show rapid acculturation to the values of the host society, it appears to cause them increased stress and depression: The more they adopted Western values, the more they reported acculturative stress and mental health problems. The simultaneous adoption of Western family values favoring children's autonomy, and the rejection of family solidarity and hierarchy, seemed to be particularly problematic.

Two factors were found to buffer negative developmental outcomes. Intact families practicing their own cultural traditions seemed to protect young refugees from depression. Moreover, living in a close ethnic community, defined in terms of the density of co-ethnics nearby, decreases mental health problems among girls in particular. This finding is important because it suggests that the resettlement dispersal policy typical of some European countries may have a negative impact on the well-being of refugee youths.

In Chapter 10, Westin examines some of the recent changes in political attitudes toward immigrants and immigration policy in Sweden. This is a typical example of a Western European country with a relatively liberal immigration policy in recent decades. A comparison of surveys made in 1987 and 1993 shows that although the general public, and young people in particular, have become more decisively in favor of a restrictive immigration policy, there is no evidence of an increase in manifest xenophobia. Westin suggests that about 5 percent of the population seems to voice racist opinions, but the majority of criticism against immigration is based on other motives, such as concerns about the costs of the refugee reception programs and the tensions expected to arise from integrating refugees into society. As with Kracke and colleagues, Westin's findings show that lesser-educated working-class males have the most negative attitude towards immigrants. It seems, in fact, that the increase in racist actions among certain youth groups is largely a by-product of the problems these adolescents are facing when trying to integrate into the adult world.

Diversity in Frameworks

Alongside the differences in young people's developmental environments in Europe, there is diversity in the ways in which adolescence is conceptualized and in which the data are analyzed. This volume provides some examples of these diversities as well.

Most chapters follow an Anglo-Saxon paradigm that is typical among researchers in western and northern Europe and in the United States, and evidenced in the major scientific journals of these countries. Those written by Roe and Cairns, and Silbereisen and Schwarz, are good examples of this approach. Even so, the reader will notice more emphasis on theoretical issues than might typically be found in some American volumes. However, the book also includes examples of viewpoints that can be described as "European" in a very specific sense. The chapter written by Motola and colleagues is a good example of the French research tradition. It is based partly on Bordieu's (1984) theory of "habitus," one of the most influential theories in French sociology during the last decade. There is also a typical example of what might be described as "European youth research" written by Westin. In this framework, social and political concerns are emphasized more than is typical in Anglo-Saxon adolescent research.

To complement the diversity of theoretical frameworks, there are also examples of what might be described as uniquely European ways of handling data. Although diversity of methods may be the most characteristic feature of this "European" tradition, another might be emphasizing more the humanistic research tradition, such as qualitative data analysis, compared to the natural science paradigm that is more dominant in the United States. For example, Motola and colleagues use a statistical procedure called correspondence analysis. Although this method is sometimes overused in French research, it can provide new insights into how to handle complex categorical data. Note also that this method differs from others not only in terms of mathematical procedures, but also according to some basic statements concerning the use of statistics. The key idea of correspondence analysis is not so much to test specific hypotheses, but rather to provide a detailed description of the phenomenon under study.

References

Adelson, J., ed. (1980.). *Handbook of adolescent psychology*. New York: Wiley.

Alsaker, F., and Flammer, A. (in press). *The Euronet on adolescent study: A cross-cultural/ cross-national study*. Lawrence Erlbaum.

Aronowitz, M. (1984). The social and emotional adjustment of immigrant children: A review of the literature. *International Migration Review, 18*, 237–257.

Bordieu, P. (1984). *Distinction: A social critique of the judgment of taste*. Cambridge, MA.: Harvard University Press.

Brooks-Gunn, J. (1987). Pubertal processes: Their relevance for developmental research. In V. B. Van Hasselt and M. Hersen (eds.), *Handbook of adolescent psychology* (pp. 111–130). New York: Pergamon Press.

Brooks-Gunn, J., and Reiter, E. O. (1990). The role of pubertal processes. In S. S. Feldman and G. R. Elliott (eds.), *At the threshold: The developing adolescent* (pp. 16–53). Cambridge, MA: Harvard University Press.

Buchmann, M. (1994). Switzerland. In K. Hurrelmann (ed.), *International handbook of adolescence* (pp. 386–399). Westport, CT: Greenwood Press.

Buzzi, C., and Cavalli, A. (1994). Italy. In K. Hurrelmann (ed.), *International handbook of adolescence* (pp. 224–333). Westport, CT: Greenwood Press.

Erikson, E. H. (1959). *Identity and the life cycle*. New York: International Universities Press.

Havighurst, R. J. (1948/1974). *Developmental tasks and education* (3rd ed.). New York: McKay.

Hurrelmann, K., ed. (1994). *International handbook of adolescence*. Westport, CT: Greenwood Press.

Hurrelmann, K., and Settertobulbe, W. (1994). Germany. In K. Hurrelmann (ed.), *International handbook of adolescence* (pp. 160–176). Westport, CT: Greenwood Press.

Keating, D. P. (1990). Adolescent thinking. In S. S. Feldman and G. R. Elliott (eds.), *At the threshold: The developing adolescent* (pp. 54–90). Cambridge, MA: Harvard University Press.

Lerner, R. M. (1983). A "goodness of fit" model of person-context interaction. In D. Magnusson and V. L. Allen (eds.), *Human development: An interactional perspective* (pp. 279–294). New York: Academic Press.

Mauger, G. (1994). France. In K. Hurrelmann (ed.), *International handbook of adolescence* (pp. 146–159). Westport, CT: Greenwood Press.

Mirchev, M. (1994). Bulgaria. In K. Hurrelmann (ed.), *International handbook of adolescence* (pp. 77–91). Westport, CT: Greenwood Press.

Noack, P., Hofer, M., and Youniss, J., eds. (1995). *Psychological responses to social change: Human development in changing environments*. Berlin: Walter de Gruyter.

Nurmi, J.-E. (1991). How do adolescents see their future? A review of the development of future orientation and planning. *Developmental Review, 11*, 1–59.

Nurmi, J.-E. (1993). Adolescent development in an age-graded context: The role of personal beliefs, goals, and strategies in the tackling of developmental tasks and standards. *International Journal of Behavioral Development, 16,* 169–189.

Nurmi, J.-E. (1997). Self-definition and mental health during adolescence and young adulthood. In J. Schulenberg, J. Maggs, and K. Hurrelmann (eds.), *Health risks and developmental trajectories during adolescence* (pp. 395–419). Cambridge: Cambridge University Press.

Nurmi, J.-E., and Siurala, L. (1994). Finland. In K. Hurrelmann (ed.), *International handbook of adolescence* (pp. 131–145). Westport, CT: Greenwood Press.

Roe, K., Bjurström, E., and Fornäs, J. (1994). Sweden. In K. Hurrelmann (ed.), *International handbook of adolescence* (pp. 374–385). Westport, CT: Greenwood Press.

Savin-Williams, R. C., and Berndt, T. J. (1990). Friendship and peer relations. In S. S. Feldman and G. R. Elliott (eds.), *At the threshold: The developing adolescent.* Cambridge, MA: Harvard University Press.

Van Hasselt, V. B., and Hersen, M., eds. (1987), *Handbook of adolescent psychology.* New York: Pergamon Press.

Wlodarek, J. (1994). Poland. In K. Hurrelmann (ed.), *International handbook of adolescence* (pp. 309–321). Westport, CT: Greenwood Press.

Part One

Cross-National Differences

Chapter Two
Adolescents' Subjective Well-Being in Fourteen Cultural Contexts

Alexander Grob

Introduction

A number of international surveys have been conducted over the past two decades that have asked about the participants' satisfaction and dissatisfaction with their lives. These studies have typically been carried out in the Western world, and have included samples drawn from the population as a whole (Headey and Wearing, 1992; Veenhoven, 1990). Where the research has centered on adolescents, its concern has been with dissatisfaction and deviant behavior rather than satisfaction. The present study, unlike many of its predecessors, focuses on subjective well-being rather than psychological distress, compares eastern European (former socialist) countries to western European countries and the United States, and focuses specifically on adolescents.

Subjective Well-Being

The predominant focus of research in adolescent development over recent decades has been on variables associated with psychological distress (depression, norm-breaking behavior, eating disorders, etc.), which despite their importance relate only to a minority of the population. This study concerns itself with an index of normal everyday life that is of importance to every individual: subjective well-being (SWB). SWB is conceived of as a complex variable (Diener, 1984) that includes a lack of self-esteem and dissatisfaction on the negative side and happiness and satisfaction with life and oneself on the positive side.

Why is SWB important? First, it is self-evidently significant to people in their everyday lives. Asking a person how she or he feels as a way of starting a daily interaction is almost universal in Western countries. Second, SWB is an important global indication of psychological health (Taylor and Brown, 1988).

Third, SWB has a motivation component expressed through utility maximization, an axiomatic motivator of rational behavior. In everyday terms, if people feel bad, they usually try to change this state into a positive one; if they feel good, they try to maintain this state. To stay in a positive mood—caused and maintained by whatever means—seems one of the most general of life's purposes (Argyle, 1987; Diener, 1984). We note that the significance and meaning of happiness has been a matter of discussion at least since the time of classical Greek philosophy.

Fourth, and directly relevant to this research, is the question of the extent to which SWB may be influenced by people's cultural background, that is, by the sociohistorical and the actual economic conditions, and by cultural demands and resources. In each cultural context there may be different means that are more likely to lead to a positive state than others. From a developmental perspective, Havighurst (1948) identified the societal component of developmental tasks. Solving these tasks was defined as providing well-being.

The earlier arguments imply that SWB may be a cultural universal; the question of whether there is one or many roads to happiness is important for development and, indeed, for societal organization. A prerequisite for answering this question is to examine whether the structure and meaning of well-being across cultures can be treated as the same or whether it varies in important ways.

As to the structure of SWB, we assume that it is composed of two main components (Diener, 1984; Diener and Diener, 1995; Grob, 1995). The first refers to well-being as a cognitive experience, suggesting that people compare the actual situation with a desired or expected one, or with an ideal situation. Discrepancies between "actual" and "desired" states index well-being. If the discrepancy is either zero or positive, the person is experiencing satisfaction (Cantril, 1965). In addition, a recent formulation by Michalos (1985) regards satisfaction as flowing from a series of judgments about discrepancies between self-perception and peer perception, between self-perception and one's ideal self, and between generalized self-perception and one's actual experience.

The second process focuses on the affective side of SWB (Bradburn, 1969). Actual everyday experiences are always evaluated as emotionally positive or negative. Satisfaction is experienced if the resultant of emotionally positive episodes minus emotionally negative episodes is positive.

Taking into account these parallel cognitive and emotional processes, we proposed a series of indicators as relevant to and therefore constituting

SWB (Grob, et al., 1991): attaining socially defined values, adapting to and being supported by the social environment, achieving self-chosen and authority-imposed goals, successful handling of divergent goals, satisfaction of everyday needs, participating in interesting activities, meaningful use of time, positive evaluation of daily events, good health, and accepting oneself.

However, the question remains whether the measure of SWB reveals a similar structure in different countries. The answer to that question is not self-evident; we would, on the basis of the work of others, expect that it would (Diener and Diener, 1995; Little, et al., 1995). To investigate this question empirically, we included participants from fourteen different cultural contexts in this study. Of these, seven samples belonged to contexts of former socialist countries: Bulgaria, the Czech Republic, Hungary, Poland, Romania, Russia, and Transylvania, (the home of a Hungarian minority living in Romania). The remaining seven samples were recruited from traditional Western countries: Finland, France, Germany, Norway, Switzerland (separate French- and German-speaking samples), and the United States.

Choosing Countries for the Sample

Although a number of surveys of SWB have been conducted in recent times, few of them have been undertaken in socialist countries. Until very recently, the basis of social, cultural, economic, and political life in these countries was explicitly different from that of Western countries. Consequently, the factors influencing people's well-being in Eastern Europe might be assumed to be different from those influences in Western countries. The sudden change in the political and economic organization and goals of the countries in the Eastern bloc created opportunities by allowing the collection of data before reforms and change had really begun, while the anciens régimes still had a de facto existence in the daily lives of the populace.

In addition to the economic state, there is some evidence that the well-being level of a country depends on various societal factors such as the level of democracy, affluence, and equality (Headey and Wearing, 1992). The former socialist countries were much poorer than the Western countries (and still are). For example, the GNP in 1992 of the former socialist countries of this study varied between US$1,130 (for Romania) and US$2,970 (for Hungary), whereas it varied between US$21,970 (for Finland) and US$36,080 for Switzerland in the Western countries. In addition, the former socialist countries were less democratic (by any reasonable test of democracy), but perhaps more equal than Western countries. Certainly, their ideology was one of equality, while practices in the West reflect the view that some inequality is an important motivator for the *homo economicus.* The nature of equality may be important: Equality of opportunity may be as important as equality of outcome. If utility cannot be maximized, or the maximum is set externally, then one might expect that levels of SWB would be lower, but that the variances within a socialist society would be less. If utility can be maximized, but circumstances result in the maximum varying widely, the overall mean of SWB may be higher in the Western countries, and so will the variance.

This discussion of well-being assumes that well-being is similar in different contexts. But an argument can be made that as the culture of a country changes, so does the structure of well-being. There is very little survey evidence that concerns this question. Nevertheless, in a society in which self-esteem is closely related to achievement—as is the case in the Western countries—one would expect that items related to self-esteem and to achievement would cluster together, but in a society where individual initiative is regarded as less important, and what one achieves depends to a greater degree on factors outside one's control, one would expect that there might be two clusters of items identified.

These considerations lead to the assumptions that SWB has a one-factor structure in the former socialist countries, whereas the structure of SWB is at least a two-factor structure in the Western countries. Furthermore, that the SWB level is higher in the Western than in the former socialist countries, and that the variance of SWB in Western countries is greater than in the former socialist countries.

Adolescence

Most surveys select samples from the population as a whole. Following the same logic that lead us to focus on western and former socialist countries, we restricted this study to adolescents. Age is a proxy for many variables, not all of them specifiable, so to restrict the age range to adolescents makes the topic more specific, and focuses our attention on those whose futures were being affected dramatically by the changes in Europe.

In recent years development has been increasingly recognized as an interactive process involving individual processes, social conditions, and historical developments (Baltes, 1986; Bronfenbrenner, 1979; Lerner, 1982). This perspective is of special importance in adolescence because adolescents are facing choices that decisively form their pathways within the historical, social, and economic conditions in which they live. The literature has shown that during the second decade of life young people are concerned decreasingly with their families, but increasingly with extrafamilial interactions and personal life purposes (Fend, 1990). In addition, adolescents enter into cultural and political life, and adults expect them to integrate themselves into the existing structures.

However, sociologists have preferred to describe adolescents as being specifically sensitive towards societal structures. This might have to do with the fact that adolescents are less committed to traditional values, but nevertheless are faced with miscellaneous values and are not yet forced to defend their biographies—as adults often are. Therefore, becoming a productive member of society signifies different things for adolescents and adults. For example, adolescents most probably perceive themselves as having to adapt to an existing system with many rules, and conversely, adults think they have provided favorable conditions into which adolescents can enter without genuine effort. These opposed views of the process of becoming a productive member of society might have consequences for adolescent and adult SWB. Whether the consequences for SWB differ significantly due to the sociocultural context is to be investigated subsequently.

Preliminarily, we have two possible hypotheses. The first assumes that a secure future fosters actual SWB. In this respect, adolescents living in the western countries have a more secure base than their peers living in the former socialist countries. But on the contrary, if too many things are predictable and threaten to become too rigid, the adolescents' degrees of freedom are lower, which in turn leads to dissatisfaction (Bandura, 1994). In this respect, the adolescents living in the former socialist countries might profit from their uncertain future: Few things are clear; most societal routines have yet to be established. This might give them more control over their own pathways, which in turn leads to SWB. Of course, one might also argue that a minimum of security and economic stability are needed for well-being. If this argument is correct, one might assume that adolescents from former socialist countries experience less well-being than their peers in western Europe.

But what happens if both hypotheses work, that is, if adolescents from the former socialist countries report the same level of SWB as their peers from the western countries? In this case, we might have to investigate in more detail the underlying processes that lead to SWB, assuming that they are different. Therefore, the methodological assumptions that might lead to such results have to be reflected carefully.

Methodological Preliminaries

Cross-cultural psychology undertakes the systematic comparison of psychological variables and cultural conditions using equivalent methods of measurement in order to specify the antecedents and processes that mediate the emergence of behavior differences in different cultural settings. In general, this perspective treats culture as an antecedent or an independent variable, and the individual behavior as a dependent variable (Berry, 1980). Following this argument, general or universal statements about systematic causal relationships among variables can be asserted only on the basis of comparative analysis.

A prerequisite for an unequivocal cause-effect relationship is the comparability of the variables under study. That means that one should place two phenomena on a single dimension (for example, SWB) in order to judge them validly in relation to each other. However, the comparability is established only if the dimensional identity or common underlying processes are demonstrated. Equivalence of the phenomena is the prerequisite in cross-cultural research, but it is the variation in a phenomenon that gives cross-cultural comparison its unique flavor.

Conceptual and Metric Equivalence

To ensure the equivalence and comparison approach, we distinguish two levels of analysis, dimensional identity and cross-cultural variation.

Dimensional Identity

Dimensional identity may be demonstrated by considering universals from biology, linguistics, or anthropology. So-called *functional equivalence* exists when two or more behaviors in two or more cultural systems are related to functionally similar problems. *Conceptual equivalence* refers to the assumption that the meaning of the behavior, and by implication, the stimuli such as items on the questionnaires generating that behavior, must be the same before any valid cross-cultural comparison can be done. This may be sought, for example, by forward or backward translation of the stimulus material. Finally, *metric equivalence* exists when the psychometric properties of the sets of data from different cultural groups share the same structure. The metric equivalence can be shown by examining the patterns of the items that form the dependent variables in the different cultural groups before comparisons are done, and checking the similarities in the correlation matrices (Poortinga, 1975) or by its common factor structure (Irvine, 1966). Both metric approaches require behavior measurements that are structured in similar ways within the different groups.

To test conceptual and metric equivalence, the participants in the different cultures and their data have to share some common features; that is, comparable procedures across and within the cultures have to be adopted as, for example, their representativeness, the quasi-manipulation of the independent variable by a considered selection of specific cultures, and the stratification of the participants within the cultures.

Cross-Cultural Variations

The next step compares the variation in the dependent variable; in the present case, SWB.

The first step considers the factorial structure within each culture and compares the factor structure of SWB between the cultures. If similar patterns appear across cultures, the cultural differences can be conceived of as variations of the same structure, and the mean differences between cultures can be examined.

Therefore, our analyses progress as follows: first, we examine the within-cultural factor structure and the items' consistency; next we compare these at the cross-cultural level to examine whether the cultural context affects the structure of well-being. On an aggregate level, the effect of culture on SWB, which is operationalized by our selection of countries and populations within those countries, is examined.

Meeting these requirements is difficult. It requires at least five additional conditions, namely to study *similar subjects* living in *different cultures* with the *same instrument* and the *same procedures* at about the *same historical time.* These prerequisites are seldom guaranteed in cross-cultural research. Nevertheless, the "Euronet on Adolescence" study, from which the data presented here are drawn, satisfied all five conditions. Fourteen samples—seven former socialist, six western European, and one American—were examined employing the same instrument, the same sampling procedures, and the same protocol.

Method
Participants

In all, 3,844 adolescents were included in the study. Most (2,945) were examined between January 1992 and April 1992 in ten European countries (Bulgaria, the Czech Republic, Finland, France, Germany, Hungary, Poland, Romania, Russia, and the French- and German-speaking areas of

Switzerland) and the United States. During May 1993, two additional samples were added (305 Norwegian and 594 Transylvanian adolescents). Table 2.1 shows the number of participants per country differentiated by gender (male; female) and age (age ≤ 14.5; age ≥ 14.5). The mean age of participants was 14.8 years (*SD* = 1.3 years).

Table 2.1 Numbers of Subjects per Country Differentiated by Gender and Age

Country or Region	Girls	Boys	Age ≤ 14.5	Age ≥ 14.5	Total
Bulgaria	127	108	135	100	236
Czech Republic	106	142	91	157	248
Finland	100	107	58	149	208
France	106	74	66	114	180
Germany	164	102	125	141	267
Hungary	238	334	259	313	572
Norway	150	152	147	155	305
Poland	110	91	91	110	201
Romania	119	95	111	103	215
Russia	98	91	58	131	191
Switzerland (German-speaking)	128	105	112	121	234
Switzerland (French-speaking)	114	73	94	93	187
Transylvania	327	267	246	348	594
United States	118	85	71	132	206
Total	2005	1826	1664	2167	3844

Note: Thirteen subjects did not indicate either their gender or age or both. Therefore, the sum of gender and age does not correspond to the total.

Measuring Subjective Well-Being

The items concerning adolescents' SWB were selected from the Berne Questionnaire of Adolescents' Subjective Well-Being (BSW/Y) (Grob et al., 1991). The components of satisfaction that constitute the BSW/Y are positive attitude toward life, self-esteem, lack of depressive mood, and joy of life. This structure of subjective well-being was replicated with three large samples, each comprising more than 1,000 participants (Grob, Flammer, and Neuenschwander, 1992). The BSW/Y is reliable (rt(second order factors, two weeks) = 0.77) and valid; that is, satisfaction correlated positively with the well-being scale of the California Psychological Inventory (r = 0.38) (Gough, 1975), and the self-value scale of the Minnesota Multiphasic Personality Inventory ($r = .51$) (Hathaway and McKinley, 1977).

Additionally, in three different independent Swiss samples (1986: $n = 1,173$; 1988: $n = 937$; 1990: $n = 923$), satisfaction (as well as positive attitude toward life and self-esteem) correlated positively with general personal feelings of being in control (Grob, Flammer, and Neuenschwander, 1992). There was no significant correlation between the scales of the BSW/Y and the openness scale of the Freiburg Personality Inventory (FPI-R-O) (Fahrenberg, Hampel and Selg, 1984). Further information about the BSW/Y is reported in Grob and colleagues (1991; Grob, 1995).

Eight items of the positive attitude toward life scale and five items of the self-esteem scale of the BSW/Y were used in the Euronet study. The English version of the items is shown in Table 2.2. Answers were recorded on a four-point Likert scale ranging from 1 (totally false) to 4 (totally true).

Table 2.2 Items of the Positive Attitude toward Life and Self-Esteem Scales from the Berne Questionnaire of Adolescents' Subjective Well-Being (BSW/Y)

Positive Attitude toward Life
1. My future looks good.
2. I enjoy life more than most people.
3. I am not happy with the way my life plans have developed. (reverse coded)
4. I accept the things in my life that cannot be changed. (reverse coded)
5. Whatever happens, I can see the bright side.
6. I am happy to live.
7. My life has not enough meaning. (reverse coded)
8. My life runs on the right track.

Self-Esteem
9. I am able to do things just as well as other people can.
10. I feel less worthy than others. (reverse coded)
11. I have an overall positive attitude toward myself.
12. I feel alone, even when I do not want to be. (reverse coded)
13. Sometimes I have the feeling something is wrong with me. (reverse coded)

Functional and conceptual equivalence of the items was achieved in two steps. First, at the eleventh meeting of the International Society for the Study of Behavioural Development in Minneapolis in 1991, eleven of the fourteen researchers involved in the study agreed to survey adolescents in their countries with the same instrument. Functional equivalence was achieved by discussing and agreeing on the concepts that seemed to be important during social change. To describe these macrocontextual political and economic changes and their possible effects on adolescents' attitude and behavior, the Euronet questionnaire contained in total seven concepts—daily activities and time use, future expectations, daily hassles, coping reactions when confronted with difficulties, subjective well-being, intercultural attitudes, and domain-specific control beliefs. Most of the proposed items came from questionnaires of the researchers involved in the study. The final English version of the questionnaire was sent to the researchers, who translated it into their respective languages.

A second effort to improve the conceptual equivalence was made by discussing the items of the questionnaire during workshops of the Euronet members in 1992 and 1993. Concerning the BSW/Y, no significant semantic differences were identified. There were slightly different formulations, but the semantic content was the same in every language version.

Procedure

In each country researchers were asked to select at least 200 adolescents, half of them age fourteen, half of them age sixteen, half girls and half boys. Students were to be recruited from public schools. Schools were to be chosen so that they were representative of the schooling systems in the respective countries. The expected age of the students in the selected classes was used to achieve a spread of ages.

Data were collected in the adolescents' classrooms during an ordinary school lesson (forty-five minutes). The paper-and-pencil questionnaire was introduced to the students as cross-national research. The data collection was carried out by trained psychologists.

Results

First, the metric equivalence of the SWB items on both within-cultural and cross-cultural levels were examined by evaluating the respective factor structures and testing their similarities with explanatory and confirmatory factor analyses. Having established that the measures of SWB were comparable over the fourteen cultures, we examined the effects of culture, gender, and age on SWB.

The Factor Structure of SWB Due to Culture

We conducted principal component factor analyses separately for each cultural context, including the thirteen items. When we took into account the relative importance of the consecutive factors, we found that in twelve of the fourteen samples the scree test indicated a single-factor solution. In these samples, the first factor explained at least two-and-a-half times more of the variance than the second factor. Two samples (French and Romanian) did not meet this fact. The scree test indicated a four-factor solution for the French sample and a two-factor solution for the Romanian sample. Consequently, we submitted each covariance matrix of the fourteen different samples to a confirmatory factor analysis (Jöreskog and Sörbom, 1989). Based on fundamental psychometric theory, recent cross-cultural research (Diener and Diener, 1995), and the general theoretical models that underlie the instrument (Grob et al., 1991; Grob, 1995), we explicitly assessed the cross-group equivalence of the constructs' measurement structure. Therefore, we specified two models and evaluated the differences in their relative fit. In the first model, the expected measurement pattern was freely estimated in the fourteen groups, and in a second model, we equated the factor loadings and intercepts, but not the factor-level relations. Our models showed acceptable fit in the fourteen sociocultural settings, providing support for the comparability of the constructs across these diverse settings (details in Grob, Little, et. al., 1996). Because these models indicate a strong theoretical position regarding the expected structure of well-being, that the fit statistics were acceptable, and that the differences in fit between the invariant and the noninvariant models were negligible, we conclude that the two-factor constructs generalize across the adolescents in these fourteen sociocultural contexts. That is, we identified positive attitude toward life and self-esteem as representing SWB, as proposed in earlier studies (Grob, 1995; Grob et al., 1991) as well as very recently in a large-scale cross-cultural study by Diener and Diener (1995).

Although the correlation between positive attitude and self-esteem in eleven of the fourteen countries was quite high ($r = 0.82$), it was different from 1.0 ($z = 11.30$, $p < 0.001$). This outcome supports our theoretical model that two distinct dimensions underlie adolescents' subjective well-being. The U.S. and Russian samples had a higher correlation than the other cultures' (for both, $r = .95$), and the French-speaking Swiss sample showed an association ($r = 0.66$) that was lower than the majority of cultures. Overall, unique and reliable variance is associated with each of the two components of SWB across all fourteen sociocultural settings.

The Effects of Culture, Gender, and Age on SWB

Next, we were interested in the respective contributions of the participants' culture, gender, and age to well-being. To investigate this, we undertook two MANOVAs with the positive attitude items and the self-esteem items, respectively, as dependent variables. The three independent factors were *country or region* (Bulgaria, Czech Republic, Finland, France, Germany, Hungary, Norway, Poland, Romania, Russia, German-speaking Switzerland, French-speaking Switzerland, Transylvania, United States), *gender* (female versus male), and *age* (younger versus older adolescents,). Subsequently, we tested the respective scale means as well as the respective items using analysis of variance with the same factors and their interactions as described above.

Positive Attitude toward Life
In the MANOVA, two main effects—country ($F(104, 28\ 354) = 16.01$; $p < 0.001$) and age ($F(8, 3\ 546) = 2.73$; $;p < 0.01$)—and two interactions—country x gender ($F(104, 28\ 354) = 1.55$; $p < 0.001$) and country x age ($F(104,\ 28\ 354) = 1.64$; $p < 0.001$) reached significance. The strongest effect was due to country. The two significant multivariate interaction effects were negligible, reaching significance mainly because of the numbers of degrees of freedom. On the univariate level, only two of eight items were affected by the significant interactions.

On the scale mean level, positive attitude toward life was affected by country ($F(13, 3\ 771) = 20.42$; $p < 0.001$) as well as the subjects' age ($F(1, 3\ 771) = 14.57$; $p < 0.001$) and the "country x age" interaction ($F(13, 3\ 771) = 2.47$; $p < 0.001$).

With a Scheffè test we tested which samples differed from the others significantly ($p < 0.01$). The results are shown in Table 2.3 (upper part). The Swiss adolescents living in the German-speaking area reported the highest degree of positive attitude toward life; they did not significantly differ from the American, Romanian, Finnish, French-speaking Swiss, German, or Norwegian adolescents, but they reported a significantly higher degree of positive attitude toward life than the Polish, the French, Bulgarian, Transylvanian, Russian, Czech, or Hungarian adolescents. The American adolescents differed significantly in their level of positive attitude from adolescents living in the former socialist countries (except Romanian and Polish adolescents) and from the French adolescents. In general, adolescents living in western countries report a higher level of positive attitude toward life than adolescents living in former communist countries. Nevertheless, there were two exceptions: Romanian adolescents, in particular, and Polish adolescents reported a higher level of positive attitude toward life than their peers in the former socialist countries, and French adolescents did not differ either from their western or eastern peers.

Table 2.3 *Means and Significant Differences between the Countries/Regions for the SWB Scales "Positive Attitude toward Life" and "Self-Esteem"*

Positive Attitude toward Life

Country/Region	Switzerland (German)	United States	Norway	Romania	Finland	Switzerland (French)	Germany	Norway	Poland	France	Bulgaria	Transylvania	Russia	Czech Republic	Hungary
M	3.22	3.21	3.18	3.15	3.14	3.11	3.10	3.07	3.04	2.98	2.93	2.91	2.87	2.86	2.86
United States															
Romania															
Finland															
Switzerland (French)															
Germany															
Norway	X														
Poland	X	X													
France	X	X													
Bulgaria	X	X	X	X	X	X	X								
Transylvania	X	X	X	X	X	X	X	X							
Russia	X	X	X	X	X	X	X	X							
Czech Republic	X	X	X	X	X	X	X	X	X						
Hungary	X	X	X	X	X	X	X	X	X						

Self-Esteem

Country/Region	Switzerland (German)	Norway	United States	Germany	Finland	Bulgaria	Poland	Switzerland (French)	Russia	Hungary	Czech Republic	France	Transylvania	Romania
M	3.22	3.18	3.12	3.08	3.05	3.04	2.95	2.94	2.93	2.92	2.87	2.84	2.78	2.65
Norway	X													
United States	X	X												
Germany	X	X												
Finland	X	X												
Bulgaria	X	X												
Poland	X	X												
Switzerland (French)	X	X												
Russia	X	X												
Hungary	X	X	X											
Czech Republic	X	X	X											
France	X	X	X	X										
Transylvania	X	X	X	X	X	X								
Romania	X	X	X	X	X	X	X	X	X	X	X	X	X	

Note: X refers to the fact that the means for two countries differ at the .01 significant level when paired comparisons are made using the Scheffé test.

Overall, the Scheffè test indicates strong empirical support for the proposition that the adolescents living in the former socialist countries experience a lower degree of positive attitude toward life than adolescents from western European countries and the United States. To test this assumption, we computed a three-factorial ANOVA for positive attitude toward life with these factors: former socialist versus western European countries, gender, and age. The adolescents' positive attitude toward life was affected by country ($F(1, 3\,819) = 145.86$; $p < 0.001$), age ($F(1, 3\,819) = 24.52$; $p < 0.001$), and the country x age interaction ($F(1, 3\,819) = 6.70$; $p < 0.01$). The respective means are depicted in Figure 2.1 (left side). Both younger and older adolescents living in western countries report comparably high levels of positive attitude toward life. The two age groups do not differ from each other. But both differ significantly from their peers living in former socialist countries who reported lower levels of positive attitude toward life. Furthermore, the two age groups living in former socialist countries differ from each other: Younger adolescents living in former socialist countries reported higher levels of positive attitude toward life than their older compatriots (all reported simple main effects $p < .01$).

Self-esteem

The MANOVA of the self-esteem items revealed two significant main effects—country ($F(15, 18\,302) = 27.53$; $p < 0.001$) and gender ($F(5, 3\,662) = 16.37$; $p < 0.001$). The strongest effect was again due to country. On the scale mean level, self-esteem was affected by country ($F(13, 3\,818) = 26.82$; $p < 0.001$) and gender ($F(13, 3\,818) = 108.24$; $p < 0.001$). With a Scheffè test ($p < 0.01$) we investigated which samples differed from the others significantly (Table 2.3, lower part).

A clear pattern appeared for adolescents' level of self-esteem with regard to their macrocontextual background: Adolescents living in Western countries generally reported a higher level of self-esteem than adolescents living in former socialist countries. But importantly, the two French-speaking samples reported a comparably lower level of self-esteem than their peers living in former socialist countries. Nevertheless, they did not differ significantly from their Western peers.

Again, we tested the assumption that the eastern European–versus–western European distinction plays an important role with respect to adolescents' self-esteem. Applying the same rationale as mentioned above, a similar pattern appeared: The strongest effect originated from the Eastern-versus-Western comparison ($F(1, 3\,811) = 151.99$; $p < 0.001$). In addition,

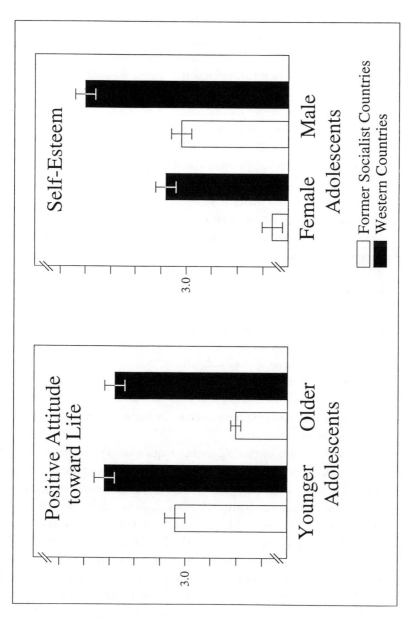

Figure 2.1. "Positive Attitude toward Life" differentiated by cultural context and age (left side) and "Self-Esteem" differentiated by cultural context and gender (right side).

there was also a statistically significant gender effect ($F(1, 3\,811) = 114.67$; $p < 0.001$). Analyzing the simple main effects (Figure 2.1, right side), all four groups differed significantly from one another: Male adolescents living in Western countries reported the highest degree of self-esteem, followed by female adolescents living in Western countries, followed by male adolescents living in former socialist countries and female adolescents living in these countries (all reported simple main effects $p < 0.01$).

Discussion

This study began with a simple question: Does the nature and amount of subjective well-being differ between different countries? In particular, are there differences between Western countries and former socialist countries? Broadly speaking, the answer is clear: there are no differences in the structure of SWB, but there are differences in its levels. In general, the adolescents living in western European countries are more satisfied than those living in former socialist countries. However, the structure of well-being was similar across the countries.

Structure of SWB

We had two alternative assumptions concerning the measurement space across these fourteen sociocultural settings. One was—as was actually shown in this research—that a metrically invariant pattern of positive attitude and self-esteem across all sociocultural contexts appears. The other was that the two-factorial pattern occurs only in the western countries, but not in the former socialist context. Contrary to the assumption and fortunately for the subsequent comparisons, the patterns were not different regarding the macrocontext.

In respect to the methodology, the unique solution of demonstrating a two-factor pattern is favorable because it indicates that problems such as translation errors and response biases were minimal and that making meaningful cross-cultural comparisons is allowed. Although the sociocultural uniformity of the correlational structure among these constructs may seem self-evident, this outcome is both veridical and important. Confirmatory factor analyses are quite sensitive to differences in correlations, particularly with the power of such a big sample (Jöreskog and Sörbom, 1989).

The within-culture pattern of individual-difference relations (i.e., the mental representations) among the well-being constructs was unaffected by the sociopolitical conditions. This result demonstrates an important intercultural similarity in the mental categories that adolescents employ when thinking about their own SWB: Across all the participating cultures, they distinguish a component referring to the self and another referring to life.

The two indices of well-being were related to each other. However, the distinctiveness of the two dimensions was also confirmed. Both constructs were highly and positively correlated, but were demonstrated as not being the same, indicating that unique and reliable variance is associated with each component of well-being. The distinctiveness was also demonstrated by the fact that the two dimensions showed differential correlations with other measures included in this research, that is, control expectancy and control appraisal (Grob, Stetsenko, et al., 1997).

Level of SWB

The high overall mean level of SWB confirms findings from other research (see, e.g., Diener and Diener, 1995; Headey and Wearing, 1992) that in general, adolescents show high well-being. In each context, the mean level of positive attitude toward life and self-esteem was above the theoretical average indicated by the scale. The adolescents report that their futures are favorable and that they are confident in their ability to do things as well as other people can.

However, differences between the countries exist, even though they are not large: The highest level of positive attitude toward life (German-speaking Switzerland) is only 15 percent higher than the lowest level (Hungary), and for self-esteem the difference between the highest and the lowest level reaches 19 percent (German-speaking Switzerland versus Romania).

The differences between former socialist countries and Western countries are nonetheless striking. Except for the French and French-speaking Swiss samples, every Western country is higher than every former socialist country. One may note that the people with the highest levels of well-being are the German-speaking Swiss, contrasting with their French-speaking compatriots with respect to their levels of self-esteem.

Is there any plausible account of these two seemingly anomalous cases? We can only speculate, but we note that the French sample comes from Brittany, an area that feels it does not enjoy the wealth and services that are available to the rest of France. But this finding also replicates a number of comparative studies within western European settings (Diener, Diener, and Diener, 1995; Near and Rechner, 1993) that have shown that French adolescents report lower well-being than their other Western peers.

In fact, we compared adolescents from two macrocontexts, the former socialist and the Western countries, which both prepare adolescents differently for life. In both macrocontexts, the younger adolescents were in elementary school when the Berlin Wall came down (assuming that this event was the "crossing of the Rubicon" with regard to the changes in eastern Europe), and the older adolescents were entering mid- and late adolescence at this time.

It might be that the older adolescents living in the former socialist countries experienced enough of their lives under socialism to be aware of what they were losing by the changes. Conversely, their younger peers might have been less affected by the changes due to the fact that they were children and did not appraise the advantages of the former system. And of course, the changes continue to take place in increasingly different ways in the former socialist countries: Youth unemployment continues to increase, and compared to the former situation, fewer jobs exist. In the western countries, the current political and economic changes are probably less dramatic for adolescents and barely affect their well-being. On the contrary, they live in a relatively predictable and secure environment.

It might be assumed that a too secure and stable future affects adolescent well-being negatively, due to the fact that few things are personally changeable and one seems to be on a fixed track, indeed with a lack of genuine personal control. However, the data show that security and economic stability favor SWB. But the data do not exclude an additional complementary working process which assumes that having personal control enhances SWB. This process has been demonstrated in another study where the determinants of SWB have been investigated (Grob, Stetsenko, et al. 1997): In a comprehensive model, background-type variables accounted for 22 percent of the explained variance in SWB (age and gender together 1 percent, macrocontext 4 percent, and strain 17 percent). In addition, three agentic-type variables (control expectancy, emotion, and action-oriented coping) added another 9 percent of explained variance in SWB. These data give support to the complementary hypothesis that both sociohistorical conditions and personal competencies affect SWB significantly.

Conclusions

The broad comparative framework has allowed escaping the confines of a one-society perspective. This approach is of special importance because self-related cognitions in adolescents, which serve as a prerequisite for their decisions about their future pathways, are under study. The impact of sociocultural factors might be particularly strong as this life period is characterized by growing demands and needs of integration into given societal, political, and economic structures.

First, the living conditions in eastern European countries differ from those in western European countries and the United States. But there is quite a strong variation within each of these two groups of countries on the same dimension. In addition, our sample of countries represents two different political organizations: an established Western-type democracy and a political system in transition from authoritarian command economies toward democratic and market institutions. The other dimension on which the countries in the sample differed was sociocultural orientation. This difference pertains to what has been conceived in cross-cultural literature as predominantly collectivist (i.e., eastern European countries) versus predominantly individualist-oriented cultures (i.e., countries of western Europe and the United States). Nevertheless, all the countries represented in the sample belong to modern societies in that they have comparable levels of industrialization, urbanization, family structure, and education. Given these culturally determined differences and similarities, the adolescents showed a similar structure of subjective well-being across all the cultures.

Second, sociocultural differences had a significant effect on subjective well-being. The general pattern was related to the former political frontiers: Adolescents who were living in former socialist countries reported a lower degree of well-being than adolescents living in the western European countries. In addition, younger adolescents living in former socialist countries reported a higher degree of positive attitude toward life than their older compatriots, and boys reported a higher degree of self-esteem than girls.

These results have sociopolitical implications. There is the question of how the well-being of adolescents who are living in the republics moving toward new democratic structures can be supported to establish a more positive life perspective. It is a matter of concern that adolescents living in former socialist countries and who are the "cutting edge" generation show a relatively lower level of satisfaction and optimism.

Notes

The research reported is part of a larger project run by the Euronet for Research on Adolescence in the Context of Social Change, chaired by August Flammer, Berne, Switzerland. In 1992–1993, researchers from eleven European countries and the U.S.A. conducted a survey study on living conditions and development during adolescence. The author thanks

Francoise D. Alsaker (Norway), Nancy M. Bodmer (Switzerland), Luba Botcheva (Bulgaria), Benö Csapo (Hungary), Erzsebeth Czachesz (Transylvanian sample), Connie Flanagan (United States), Nina Gootkina (Russia), Hanna Liberska (Poland), Aurora Liiceanu (Romania), Petr Macek (Czech Republic), Peter Noack (Germany), Jari-Erik Nurmi (Finland), and Colette Sabatier (France), who collected data in their respective countries.

This manuscript is a revised version of the author's keynote address at the 1994 International Conference on Youth Research Methods on Methodological Issues in Cross-Cultural Youth Research of the Social Psychology European Research Institute in Santiago de Compostela, Spain, May 21–22, 1994. I am very grateful to Alexander Wearing for the fruitful discussion we had and to Ursi Peter for the editorial support in writing the English manuscript.

References

Argyle, M. (1987). *The psychology of happiness.* London: Routledge.

Baltes, P. B. (1986). Theoretical positions of life-span developmental psychology: On the dynamics between growth and decline. *Developmental Psychology, 23,* 611–626.

Bandura, A. (1994). *Self-efficacy: The exercise of control.* New York: Freeman.

Berry, J. W. (1980). Introduction to methodology. In H. C. Triandis and J. W. Berry (eds.), *Handbook of cross-cultural psychology* (vol. 2) (pp. 1–28). Boston: Allyn and Bacon.

Bradburn, N. M. (1969). *The structure of psychological well-being.* Chicago: Aldine.

Bronfenbrenner, U. (1979). *The ecology of human development.* Cambridge, MA: Harvard University Press.

Cantril, H. (1965). *The pattern of human concerns.* New Brunswick, NJ: Rutgers University Press.

Czapö, B., Czachesz, E., Liiceanu, A., and Lazar, S. (1997) Being in a minority: Hungarian adolescents in Transylvania, Romania. In F. D. Alsaber and A. Flammer (eds.), *European and American adolescents in the nineties.* New York: Lawrence Erlbaum.

Diener, E. (1984). Subjective well-being. *Psychological Bulletin, 95,* 542–575.

Diener, E., and Diener, M. (1995). Cross-cultural correlates of life-satisfaction and self-esteem. *Journal of Personality and Social Psychology, 68,* 653–663.

Diener, E., Diener, M., and Diener, C. (1995). Factors predicting the subjective well-being of nations. *Journal of Personality and Social Psychology, 69,* 851–864.

Fahrenberg, J., Hampel, R., and Selg, H. (1984). *Das Freiburger Persönlichkeitsinventar* (The Freiburg personality inventory). Gottingen: Hogrefe.

Fend, H. (1990). *Vom Kind zum Jugendlichen* (From childhood to adolescence). Bern: Huber.

Flammer, A. (1988). *Entwicklungstheorien* (Theories of development). Bern: Huber.

Gough, H. G. (1975). *California psychological inventory.* Manual. Palo Alto: Consulting Psychologists Press.

Grob, A. (1995). Subjective well-being and significant life-events across the life span. *Swiss Journal of Psychology, 54,* 3–18.

Grob, A., Flammer, A., and Neuenschwander, M. (1992). Kontrollattributionen und Wohlbefinden von Schweizer Jugendlichen III (Swiss adolescents' attributions of control and subjective well-being). *Research Report Nr. 1992–4. Institute of Psychology.* University of Berne, Switzerland.

Grob, A., Little, T. D., Wanner, B., Wearing, A. J., and Euronet (1996). Adolescents' well-being and perceived control across fourteen sociocultural contexts. *Journal of Personality and Social Psychology, 71,* 785–795.

Grob, A., Luthi, R., Kaiser, F. G., Flammer, A., Mackinnon, A., and Wearing, A. J. (1991). Berner Fragebogen zum Wohlbefinden Jugendlicher (BFW) (Berne questionnaire on adolescents' subjective well-being). *Diagnostica, 37,* 66–75.

Grob, A., Stetsenko, A., Sabatier, C., Botcheva, L., and Macek, P., (1997). A model of adolescents' well-being in different social contexts. In F. D. Alsaker and A. Flammer. *European and American adolescents in the nineties.* New York: Lawrence Erlbaum.

Hathaway, S. R., and McKinley, J. C. (1977). *MMPI* (Manual). Bern: Huber.

Havighurst, R. J. (1948). *Developmental tasks and education.* New York: McKay.

Headey, B. W., Holmström, E. L., and Wearing, A. J. (1984). Well-being and ill-being: Different dimensions? *Social Indicators Research, 14,* 115–139.

Headey, B. W., and Wearing, A. J. (1992). *Understanding happiness*. Melbourne: Longman Cheshire.

Irvine, S. H. (1966). Toward a rationale for testing attainments and abilities in Africa. *British Journal of Educational Psychology, 36*, 24–32.

Jöreskog, K. G., and Sörbom, D. (1989). *LISREL 7: A guide to the program and applications*. Chicago: SPSS.

Lerner, R. M. (1982). Children and adolescents as producers of their own development. *Developmental Review, 2*, 309–333.

Little, T. D., Oettingen, G., Stetsenko, A., and Baltes, P. B. (1995). Children's action-control beliefs about school performance: How do American children compare with German and Russian children? *Journal of Personality and Social Psychology, 69*, 686–700.

Michalos, A. C. (1985). Multiple discrepancies theory. *Social Indicators Research, 16*, 347–413.

Near, J. P., and Rechner, P. L. (1993). Cross-cultural variations in predictors of life-satisfaction: An historical view of differences among West European countries. *Social Indicators Research, 29*, 109–121.

Poortinga, Y. (1975). Limitations on international comparison of psychological data. *Nederlands Tijdschrift voor de Psychologie, 30*, 23–39.

Taylor, S., and Brown, J. (1988). Illusion and well-being: A social-psychological perspective on mental health. *Psychological Bulletin, 103*, 193–210.

Veenhoven, R. (1990). *World databook of happiness*. Dordrecht: Reidel.

Chapter Three
Social Habitus and Future Plans
A Comparison of Adolescent Future Projects in Finland and France

Michael Motola, Pentti Sinisalo, and Jean Guichard

Introduction

As the twentieth century comes to a close, unemployment has become a crucial concern in Western societies, which have found themselves in the midst of unexpected socioeconomic turmoil that will affect a whole generation of youth. In France, for instance, the presidential election campaign in 1995 focused on the problem of "exclusion," which is the term used in France to define the increasing number of people excluded from society, which mainly means from working life. There are probably a greater number of children in Europe today than ever before whose parents do not work regularly. Young people, and especially the less qualified, are those most likely to experience exclusion. Even among adolescents with high school diplomas and university degrees job security is elusive. These adolescents, educated in an atmosphere of relative prosperity and well-being, are not prepared to deal with this kind of socioeconomic crisis (the unemployment rate among Finnish and French youth is about 25 percent).

It is not surprising that in such an atmosphere education is undergoing a reappraisal. Indeed, the role of education as the "great equalizer" and generator of major social transformation, as it has been considered since the Second World War is again being scrutinized. Studies made in recent years tend to show that education does not fulfill the hopes of democratization. On the contrary, there is evidence that education, especially higher education, has become a sorting and sifting institution in a Western society that is increasingly sophisticated and competitive (Husen and Tuijnman, 1992). If young people's vocational behavior has in the past been principally the concern of specialists, it has today become a vital challenge to all the actors in postmodern society.

Studies of vocational choices and career development can be roughly divided into two groups, the first with a psychological orientation and the second with a sociological view. The field of vocational psychology was for many years largely dominated by psychological concepts, such as aptitudes, interests, work values, and cognitive styles of decision-making. American sociologists, on the other hand, studying the field of education and work in relation to social classes, independently developed theories and analyses based on concepts such as status attaintment and occupational mobility. At the same time, the French sociologist Bourdieu observed the important role of education and vocational behavior in maintaining the reproduction process of the social structure (Bourdieu, 1980).

It seems that for many years psychologists have tended to avoid research on social factors, while sociologists have not used psychological concepts in their analyses. In the past three decades an increasing number of researchers have been trying to integrate sociological concepts and issues into psychological theories (Osipow, 1983; Nurmi, 1991; Gottfredson, 1981). In the same vein, Guichard (1994) in France adopted the concept of *habitus,* one of the key concepts in Bourdieu's theory, to study the spontaneous representations French students have of occupations and their future projects in general.

The theory of habitus is based on the assumption that during their lives people assimilate socially built-in schemes. Those schemes, the habitus, mold what can be called their life-styles. The habitus regulates everyday actions, perceptions, and choices, generally in a prereflective, unconscious way. Guichard's general idea is that the educational and career choices of students are mainly shaped by a complex interaction between their present experiences at school (school structure) and their social backgrounds (habitus).

The aim of this research is to study the impact of sociocultural factors on vocational behavior. We chose France and Finland because the two countries differ significantly in their cultures, educational politics, and institutional tracking. We focused on eleventh-grade students at secondary school because they have been influenced by the education process for a considerable period of time. We were particularly interested in examining the role of cultural and social habitus in this population.

The first section of this chapter is devoted to a short presentation of the theory of habitus and its relation to vocational behavior. In the second section, the main features of the French and Finnish systems of education are outlined. In the third section the research plan, method, procedure, and results are presented. The fourth section is devoted to discussion and commentaries.

Theory of Habitus

Habitus is the Latin translation used by Thomas Aquinas of the word *hexis*, which had been employed by Aristotle to designate a state or condition of the body and mind. The origin of "habitus" is in the Latin verb *habere*, to have or to be in condition. In his theory of perception and objectivization, Husserl describes the concept from a general perspective. According to him, in each of our perceptions, judgments, or decisions we employ, at least in a prereflexive manner, a prefabricated habitus that structures our interests and expectations; every experience is, in turn, deposited as a habitus (Héran, 1987, p. 405).

Bourdieu (1980, p. 134) purposely uses the Latin form of the word to emphasize that habitus is creative and inventive (within the limits of its structures) compared to the usual meaning of the word "habit," which suggests a repeated mechanistic and deterministic structure. Habitus is a structuring mechanism that operates within an agent. It is neither strictly individual nor in itself fully determinative of conduct. It is the strategy-generating principle enabling agents, that is, members of a specific group in society, to handle unanticipated and ever-changing circumstances. Integrating past experiences, it functions at every moment as a matrix of perceptions, appreciations, and actions, and makes possible the achievement of infinitely diversified tasks. In Bourdieu's work it also designates a manner of being, a habitual state (especially of the body), and in particular a disposition, tendency, propensity, or inclination (Bourdieu, 1992). In other words, habitus generates, practices, and supplies the perceptual framework enabling actors to classify given objects and practices. Habitus can been seen as the foundation of life-style.

According to Bourdieu, habitus can be changed (always within definite boundaries) by two main processes. First, change can be achieved by entrance into social trajectories, which are different from those existing earlier. Thus, for instance, students from working-class backgrounds attending a prestigious high school will have the opportunity to change habitus, that is, to change their tastes in art and cultural behavior, perhaps clothing, and other habits. Second, habitus can also be changed or controlled through the awakening of consciousness, a process Bourdieu describes in terms of socioanalysis.

The meaning of habitus cannot be understood unless it is relocated in relation to the concept of field. Bourdieu replaces the notion of "society" with those of field and social space. For him a differentiated society is an ensemble of relatively autonomous spheres of "play" that cannot be collapsed in a unique and conclusive way under an overall logic, be it that of capitalism, modernity, or postmodernity. Each field prescribes its particular values and possesses its own regulative principles. Nevertheless, it does not mean that, in a given society, each field is perfectly autonomous:

The question of the interrelation of different fields is an extremely complex one. . . . I believe indeed that there are not transhistoric laws of the relations between fields, and that we must investigate each historical case separately. Obviously, in advanced capitalist societies, it would be difficult to maintain that the economic field does not exercise especially powerful determinations. But should we for that reason admit the postulate of its (universal) "determination in the last instance? (Bourdieu and Wacquant, 1992, p. 109)

The field of education plays a fundamental role in the theory of social habitus. Its role is first to produce the interiorization of the perceptions, thoughts, and actions that make up a particular habitus. Thus, the education received by a given child (of a given sex, belonging to a defined social milieu) will lead him or her to produce a durable cognitive scheme that will enable him or her to organize in a certain way the representations of any particular object. Second, education imposes on everyone recognition of the legitimacy of his or her habitus. Indeed in the "Bourdieuan vision of society," education is the space where ruling groups in society impose their values and life-style upon the dominated groups. Therefore, cultural habitus inculcated at home passes through a special process of restructuring. The habitus of upper-class students, who feel at home in the new environment of high school, is reinforced. Lower-class students have to undergo a process of conversion (often with heavy sacrifices), or at least have to recognize the upper-class habitus as legitimate and their own as illegitimate. Consequently, the system of education provides the means for the dominant class to reproduce the social structure by adopting a neutral attitude that keeps this process hidden. Schools participate in this process of reproduction through the continuing action of teachers and professors, who, without really knowing or wanting it, impose the dominant habitus upon their students (Bourdieu, 1994, p. 46).

Future Plans and Life Trajectory
Bourdieu claims that

to try to understand life as a unique and self-sufficient series of successive events with no link other than the association with a "subject" is nearly as absurd as

trying to make sense of a route in the metro without taking into account the
structure of the subway network, that is, the matrix of objective relations be-
tween the different train stations. (Bourdieu and Wacquant, 1992, p. 208)

In consequence, if we consider the issue of vocational choices, the same
choice made by different people in different contexts must convey different meanings.

Bourdieu claims that the vocational behavior of families and adolescents—choosing subjects, study streams, schools, and so on—is not that
of passive particles subjected to external mechanical forces and behaving
under the constraint of causes, nor that of conscious agents acting with
full knowledge of the causes. People make decisions according to a practical sense, that is, their habitus. This practical sense, or preconceptual knowledge, enables people to act, and react, in response to the state of the field
(in this case the educational field). It enables them to outline the future
according to invisible hints perceived in the present. Bourdieu cites the
example of the soccer player who feels that his adversary is about to move
to the right, and so throws the ball to the left. He does not plan or conceptualize the action nor does he have a mental representation of it; he simply
moves according to embodied schemes that are the result of assimilation
of past experiences acquired under similar conditions. But this is not a
mechanical reflex, since the player has the relative freedom to choose one
of a number of possible strategies. Without behaving in a logical way,
people act in a sound way. Bourdieu suggests that, since a person is the
product of a particular class of objective regularities, the habitus tends to
generate all the "reasonable," "common sense" behaviors which are possible within the limits of these regularities, and which are likely to be positively sanctioned. Moreover, habitus tends to exclude all extravagances ("not
for the likes of us"), that is, all the behaviors that would be negatively
sanctioned because they are incompatible with the objective condition
(Bourdieu, 1990).

For Bourdieu, families are "corporate bodies" animated by a tendency
to perpetuate their social being with all its powers and privileges. Thus
they mobilize several types of reproduction strategies: fecundity strategies, matrimonial strategies, descent strategies, economic strategies, and,
especially and most relevant for our purposes, educational strategies
(Bourdieu, 1994, p. 39). Adolescents and their families moving in the
French system of education, with all its complexity, on the one hand, and
the clear "law of the game," namely intellectual excellence (measured mainly

by mathematical skills) on the other, must be very vigilant in order to take advantage of opportunities and to avoid traps. Families situated in different positions in the social field have different capitals (economic, symbolic, cultural, social). Bourdieu asserts that the structure of this capital, that is, the proportional weight of each type of capital, retranslated into a system of preferences (e.g., interest in economics or culture, money or art), is at the root of educational and social choice and embraces corresponding practices and opinions (Bourdieu, 1994, p. 46). In short, it is important to note the fact that adolescents and their families carry within themselves, namely in their habitus, the rule of their direction and their trajectory, the principle of their vocation, which will direct them toward a particular school or discipline.

A system of education is a field that has a certain degree of autonomy. But it is never completely independent in relation to the social organization of the country in which it is situated. Education reflects, according to its own structure, the specific features of the local culture. Thus, one can expect to observe similarities and differences in the educational organization between countries such as Finland and France, which are similar in some aspects (e.g., capitalist) but different in others (e.g., Protestant and Catholic).

Finnish and French Systems of Education
Finland

Education played a major role in the struggle toward independence and in molding the national character of Finland. The centralized and hierarchical administrative structure was established rather late. A central educational agency was created under Russian hegemony in 1869. The primary school *(kansakoulu)* was established at that time, and responsibility for elementary education was transferred from the church to the municipalities, which received state subsidies for maintaining them. Uno Cygnaeus, the "father of the primary school." aimed at providing a broad and basic primary education for children from all social classes. He emphasized that the goal of the primary school was to develop the whole personality of the child, and wrote in his program that the task of the school was to educate children to work diligently and seriously, to follow strict discipline, and to conduct themselves in an obedient manner. Later on, after Finland received its independence in 1918, the school played an important role in the process of building up a "national identity." Moreover, its role became even more important in the context of rapid change from an agricultural to an industrialized society after the Second World War.

Stream, Tracking and Selection

The comprehensive school, which was established in 1970, is compulsory for all children aged 7 through 16. All individuals completing the comprehensive school are provided with the same eligibility for further education.

Postcompulsory education is divided into general education, provided in the upper secondary school (senior high school), and vocational education, provided in vocational and professional institutions. Vocational education at the upper secondary level usually takes 2 to 3 years, and technical and professional education at the tertiary level, 4 to 6 years. Students must previously have completed either the comprehensive school or the upper secondary school. Some courses providing education for specialized professions are open only to matriculated students (senior high school diploma).

The upper secondary school is a three-year educational institution providing a postcomprehensive general education. The subjects in the curriculum are defined by law, and the government approves the number of hours devoted to each subject. Schooling concludes with a matriculation examination consisting of centrally administered tests that are identical for all upper secondary schools in the country, and complementary tests administered by the schools themselves. The matriculation examination provides the pupils with a basic qualification for higher education and other forms of education that require the completion of such an examination. Students must as a rule have matriculated before they can enter a university, although completion of a tertiary-level examination at a vocational and professional education institution provides them with the same eligibility as the matriculation examination. There are nevertheless only a few students who enter university via the latter route.

The selection process occurs for the first time at the age of sixteen, the age of the entry into the upper secondary school. The cohort is then split into four groups: those continuing to upper secondary school (52 percent in 1992), those entering vocational school (33 percent in 1992), those entering a voluntary tenth grade of the comprehensive school (5 percent in 1992), and those not entering any educational institution immediately (10 percent in 1992) (Education in Finland 1994, 1994). The explicit criteria for selecting either a vocational institution or a senior high school are school achievement (measured by a mean score of all subjects, each having the same weight) and interest. Those who choose the academic stream are, theoretically, more interested in longer studies, the vocational group being more interested in shorter vocational training. Each Finnish high school has a minimum entrance grade. Generally, this grade is about the same throughout the country, but there are differences between districts (depending on the number of available places in the district) or between schools (depending on the school's prestige and popularity).

Streams as they are known in other systems do not exist in Finnish high schools. Students choose disciplines "à la carte," for the most part, according to their interests. It is possible to distinguish between those who prefer mathematics (mostly boys) from those who prefer languages (mostly girls). This differentiation is not rigid.

All areas of university education have a fixed intake per year. Since the number of university applicants is far in excess of this intake, only one-third of them are admitted. This *numerus clausus* system in universities and the subsequent entrance examinations is one of the major concerns of adolescents at this age period. They are aware of the fact that most of them, even though they have passed the matriculation examination, will not enroll in a university that same year.

Socioeconomic Discrepancy

As is the case in most Western countries, the expansion of education in Finland has not eliminated the effect of background on the young person's selection of his or her future educational field. It is more common for children from highly educated, upper-class families to enter upper secondary school and go on to university than it is for children of families with a poorer educational background, while it is more likely that young people whose parents have a low educational level will choose a vocational school. The children of blue-collar workers are trained mainly for industrial occupations, and the children of farmers make their way into agricultural occupations, while children of white-collar workers are more likely to persist in the educational system, many of them aiming as high as possible. As a result, the latter become architects, physicians, jurists, graduate engineers, or economists, while the educational choices made by adolescents from agricultural and working-class backgrounds chzaracteristically show a rapid transition from education to employment. (Statistics Finland, 1991)

France

Two main principles that can be traced back to the French Revolution still prevail today: (1) The creation of a democratic political system required the active participation of free, educated citizens. Therefore the constitution of 1791 decreed the establishment of a common and public educational institution. (2) The regime did not seek to suppress social inequalities, but through education it aspired to prepare every individual for his or her place in society. These conceptions led to the institution of a dual educational network, one for the elite and the other for the ordinary people. The effect of these two contradictory streams can still be felt today in French society (Huteau, 1985).

It was not until 1975 that a unified school was created for all children up to the age of sixteen (the compulsory school age since 1959).

Stream, Tracking, and Selection
The first selection is made when students are about thirteen years old. At this point the tracking system begins its work. The most important criterion for selection is school achievement. Most of the pupils continue in the academic stream.

The second time students face selection is for entry into the upper secondary school. At this point they must either choose a stream from five academic or sixteen technical programs,[1] each leading to different final examinations (matriculation), or enter a vocational senior high school (unless they prefer apprenticeship). Each of these streams represents a different future perspective. In fact, a stream is considered by the students and all other social actors as a fate, a destiny. To have the best chance one must adapt her- or himself to the "rules of the game" and make the right choice, at the right moment, taking into account her or his record and abilities (especially in mathematics). Indeed, since the 1950s, mathematics, which was supposed to be socially unbiased, has supplanted the classical studies (Greek, Latin, French literature, and philosophy) in the role of "supreme judge" of pupils' qualities.

Selection to a stream is explicitly determined by two factors: grades in different school subjects and the interests of the pupil. Nevertheless, this streaming system produces cohorts of students that differ greatly in terms of the gender and social status of their parents. Let us focus on some examples. In the literature streams, there is a majority of girls (80 percent in 1991), and children from the upper classes are underrepresented (Dubet, 1991). There is no official selection during the three years of the upper secondary school program, and practically all students who begin in these streams reach the final examination stage, the Baccalaureate. Most of the students in this stream (74 percent in 1991) obtain the matriculation: 97 percent continue to university, three-quarters choosing the faculties of literature or human sciences. The most probable career for these students is teaching.

In the science streams the majority of students are boys (63.2 percent in 1991), and the upper classes are overrepresented (Dubet, 1991). In these streams students see themselves as participating in a competition. In fact, there is a selection in the second year of the upper secondary-school program that differentiates between the mathematics stream ("C" stream) and the biology stream ("D" stream). It is striking to observe that not every student in the biology stream is interested in biology. Some of them feel themselves to be failures and are sometimes perceived as such. The best students in all the fields are concentrated in the science streams. Half of the students in the mathematics stream continue to the Preparatory Classes for the Grandes Ecoles;[2] others choose science faculties, and a few choose technological institutes.

Selection continues at university. Although all students holding a matriculation can enroll equally in the faculties at the university, students from the upper level of society prefer longer studies like medicine (50 percent of medical students), while students from the lower class usually opt for shorter programs like technology. It seems that the faculties of law and medicine are the most socially discriminating, if we exclude the Grandes Ecoles.

Similarities and Differences between the Two Countries
Educational Achievements

Although we must be very careful in comparing statistics from different countries, we can observe striking similarities in the general results of education in France and Finland. About half of an age cohort passes the matriculation examination, a comparable proportion gets a university degree (15–20 percent), and a similar proportion leaves the educational system early and without any qualification (10–12 percent). Moreover, 10 percent in both countries have university degrees (compared to 24 percent in the United States and 5 percent in Portugal), 8 percent in Finland and 6 percent in France have higher education (nonuniversity) degrees, 43 percent in Finland and 36 percent in France have upper secondary education, and 39 percent in Finland and 48 percent in France have primary and lower secondary education or less (OECD, 1985).

"Stream Identity"

As we have seen before, there is a flexible definition of streams in the Finnish high school. This flexibility is a supple concept of the "subjects going together." For instance, it is possible to meet a good student who likes languages and who also has extensive mathematics courses but no courses in physics or chemistry. This is unimaginable in the French system, where the notion of "things going together" is much more rigid and rooted in the student's mind, reaching the point that permits Guichard (1993; Guichard et al., 1994) to speak of a "stream identity" for the French student.

Selection

The logic behind selection and transition from stage to stage is radically different. In Finland there is a basic differentiation between the academic and vocational trajectories, with a limited possibility of shifting from one to another. The vocational and technological student does not, in general, have a matriculation certificate and consequently cannot apply to university. In senior high school the curriculum is flexible and most of the students (85 percent) pass the matriculation examination. In France, as we have seen, the "logic of excellence" is the rule. Differentiation begins early, and students are kept in a rather rigid system of streams. There is less discrimination between the vocational and academic streams, in the sense that vocational students are entitled to get a matriculation degree and, theoretically, to enter university.

The two different ways of tracking and selecting students seem to reflect two different concepts of education. The French strive, as we have seen, to combine opposing values, the highest level of education for most of the population and the selection of the best according to a meritocratic logic. The Finns stick to a general separation of those "predestined" for an academic career and those heading for technological and professional areas. The idea of establishing a *numerus clausus* system in universities seems as odd and unnatural to the French as the proposal to open all universities to all students with a matriculation degree does to Finns.

Hypotheses

Based on the theory of habitus and the comparison of Finland and France according to their major cultural trends and institutional tracking, the following hypotheses were formulated for this study.

1. Since it was expected that the cultural beliefs and educational system are powerful factors influencing the future outlook of students, we expected to find differences in the manner in which students perceive their futures in the two countries.

2. On the basis of the theory of social habitus, it was expected that within a given society different individuals will have different expectations of

their potential occupational careers. This hypothesis indicates, for example, that two young men (or women) who differ in their cultural practices will not have the same degree of interest in a given occupation. Their expectations will be different because the schemes that structure their interests in occupations are linked more to general schemes structuring their visions of the world.

The theory of social habitus leads us also to postulate that the structure of the schemes determining young people's interest in the field of occupational expectations is homologous to the structure of schemes that determine their tastes and behaviors in other areas, such as sports activities, political opinions, and aesthetic preferences, among others, and more generally, the conceptions that constitute a successful life.

Study
Sample
Comparability of samples is both crucial and problematic in cross-national studies (Nurmi, Poole, and Seginer, 1995). The students for this study were chosen to be representative samples of the distinctive groups in the social sphere of each country.

The sample comprised 191 Finnish and 308 French students, 16 to 21 years old (in Finland $M = 17.9$, $SD = .33$, in France $M = 18.4$, $SD = 1$), attending the eleventh grade in senior high school. We tried to make the samples as representative of the entire population as possible and therefore chose thirteen schools in different areas of the two countries: the capital cities, the suburbs, and the countryside.

The participants in Finland were 106 girls (55.5 percent of Finnish participants) and 85 boys (45.5 percent), and in France, 192 girls (62.3 percent) and 116 boys (37.7 percent). The pupils followed different streams. Since the two countries do not have similar streaming systems, we chose to name the French streams as they are in France and to categorize the Finnish population in three groups: "pure" mathematicians, literature students with extensive language courses, and literature students with some mathematics courses. The distribution of the Finnish students in the streams was 113 (59.2 percent) in a literature stream with substantial mathematics, 32 (16.8 percent) in a literature stream with a substantial number of language courses, and 46 (24.1 percent) in "pure" mathematics. The French pupils came from the following streams: 27 (8.8 percent) literature with some mathematics, 64 (20.8 percent) literature with extensive language courses, 181 (58 percent) sciences and mathematics, 17 (5.5 percent) economics stream, and 19 (6.1 percent) in other professional and vocational streams.

In Finland the distribution of the students according to the fathers' level of education was 89 (46.6 percent) from a lower cultural background (fathers have achieved less than eleven years' schooling), 70 (36.6 percent) from a higher cultural background (fathers have had more than thirteen years of education), and an intermediate group of 20 (10.5 percent) students. Twelve students (6.3 percent) remained unclassified. In France the distribution consisted of 171 (55.5 percent) from a lower background, 88 (28.6 percent) from a higher background, 36 (11.7 percent) in an intermediate group, and 13 (4.2 percent) unclassified.

Measurements

Father's Level of Education

We asked the students about the professions and level of education of their parents. We chose to consider only the father's education as indicative of cultural capital. For the sake of convenience we will employ the initials SES (socioeconomic status) to represent the cultural capital of the students' families.

Professional Projects

Professional projects were examined first by asking the pupils which profession they aspired to (open-ended questions).

Second, they were given a list of thirty professions (see the list in Table 3.1) and asked to indicate on a scale from 1 to 7 chances of taking up a specific profession (1 = very unlikely, 7 = very likely). In creating the list of professions we tried to choose those professions that are relevant for academic upper secondary-school students. This question was created to provide an idea of

Table 3.1 List of Professions

Architect	Hairdresser	Public relations advisor
Army officer	Hotelkeeper	Reporter
Art critic	Lawyer	Rock musician
Artisan	Mechanic	Secretary
Author	Nurse	Shopkeeper
Bank employee	Physician	Teacher (high school)
Computer programmer	Politician	Teacher (primary school)
Economic consultant	Priest	Translator
Farmer	Psychiatrist	Travel Agent
Guidance counselor	Psychologist	TV producer

what possible occupations a person intuitively has in mind. In other words, we tried to portray the students' "habitus map" of possible careers.

Third, students were asked if they had thought about their professional plans. They had to choose one of the five statements (1 = No, because it is too early; 2 = Only vaguely; 3 = Yes, I have given it serious thought, but have not yet decided; 4 = Yes, I have given it serious thought and have a clear idea of the professional field; 5 = Yes, I have chosen my career).

Aesthetic Taste

Fifteen photos were presented to the pupils. They represented several types of material, such as photos of men and women in stereotypical situations (pregnancy, with babies, with family, in study etc.) or photos with a powerful suggestive atmosphere (woman musician, men in war, horse and man in nature, auto crash). One photo was "purely" artistic; it was a surrealist photomontage. We expected that pupils would react to the photos according to their gender and to their cultural capital. The students had to answer the following questions: (1) Which photo is the most beautiful? (2) Which is the most repugnant? (3) Which is the most interesting? (4) Which best reflects "tension?" (5) Which is the most insignificant? (6) Which best expresses the future? (7) Which best expresses your own future? (8) Which do you like the most?

We then grouped the positive and negative assessments into two groups in order to create a dichotomized variable (1 = have a positive attitude toward the photo, 0 = have a negative attitude).

Of all the photos, five were chosen in the actual study for their discriminative power: (1) a horse and a man in a field ("man and horse"), (2) two men with an electronic microscope ("study"), (3) a woman playing the cello ("music"), (4) a couple and a child ("family"), and (5) the surrealist photomontage ("surrealist").

This technique of asking people to evaluate photos was used by Bourdieu in his study on distinction (1984). Bourdieu states that photography has a special place between "noble" practices with universal claims such as music, literature, and painting and "vulgar" practices that include activities like cookery, decoration, and other everyday aesthetic choices. In spheres similar to photography Bourdieu places jazz, cinema, and chansons, a special type of French popular music. We used the photos to reveal patterns in aesthetic taste that might characterize different groups.

Procedure

Gathering data in France and in Finland was carried out by the first author and a research assistant during normal school hours. At the beginning the participants were informed about the study and then asked to fill in a questionnaire that included all the questions just mentioned.

The French students filled in a French version of the questionnaire, and the Finns, a Finnish one. The French questionnaire was developed first and was then translated by a bilingual person into Finnish. The Finnish version was translated back into French for comparison with the original version.

A pilot study was conducted with twenty-five students in Finland and fifteen students in France; this enabled us to revise and improve the first version of the questionnaire.

Results

Cross National Comparison

The results showed that the most striking difference between the two countries was the fact that Finns were more hesitant about their plans concerning career and/or studies while for most of the French pupils there was little doubt about their intentions (Table 3.2).

Table 3.2 Differences between Finnish and French Pupils' Ideas about Occupational Choice

"Have you been thinking about the profession you wish to take up in the future?" (%)	Finnish pupils (n = 191)	French pupils (n = 308)
	%	%
No, too early	6.3	2.3
Only vaguely	41.0	9.7
Yes, but have not yet decided	30.9	29.2
Yes, I have a clear idea of the field	15.2	38.3
Yes, I have chosen my career	4.2	19.8
Professional choices[a]	%	%
Army/Police	6.3	8.4
Art	12.0	5.2
Business	22.5	10.1
Education	24.1	37.0
Humanities/Media	12.6	12.4

(continued)

Table 3.2 *(continued)*

Professional choices[a]	Finnish pupils (n = 191) %	French pupils (n = 308) %
Languages	7.3	7.5
Medicine	17.8	19.5
Social Care	8.4	7.5
Science	23.0	27.0
Service Sector	5.2	10.4

[a]Every student could have more than one choice. The first three choices mentioned were counted.

Almost 50 percent of Finnish pupils had only vaguely considered, or had not even considered, their future careers at all, while only 12 percent gave this response in France. This is in accord with another finding which suggests that 12.6 percent of Finnish students are uncertain as to whether they will continue studying, while in France 3.9 percent of the students produced this response (Motola 1994).

The students were also asked to name the professions they would like to enter in the future. The first three choices were categorized into ten classes. The results showed that the French pupils were more interested in teaching than the Finnish adolescents, who expressed greater preferences for other careers (Table 3.2).

Career Plans in Two Countries

In addition to the impact of national culture we wanted to study the influence of social and cultural background on the vocational behavior inside each country. Moreover, we wanted to verify whether there are some structural similarities or differences between the two countries. To examine this, data from each country were analyzed separately by means of a correspondence factor analysis (CFA).[3] The dependent (active) variables were the likelihood of taking up certain careers. Before the final analyses, the variables were dichotomized. The following variables were projected in the factorial plan as supplementary (independent) variables: streams, gender, socioeconomic status (SES), and aesthetic taste.

Finland

The CFA results for Finnish adolescents are described in Figure 3.1 (see Table 3.3 for statistics describing the factors). The factorial solution of the two first factors are shown in order to provide a general view of the field.

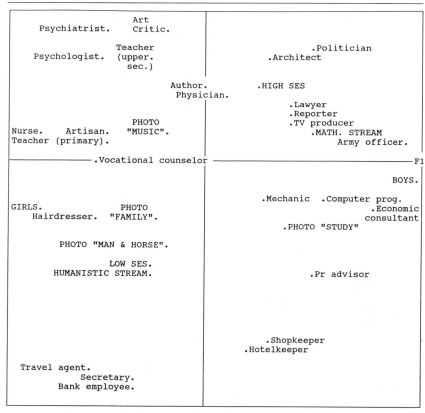

Figure 3.1. Graphic representation of modalities on the first two factor axes of CFA, i.e., Likelihood of taking up a profession: Finnish students. Factor 1 (horizontal): Inertia = 0.386, explained = 25 percent. Factor 2 (vertical): Inertia = 0.307, explained = 19.8 percent. The modalities in uppercase type are the supplementary modalities.

The factorial solution in Figure 3.1 explains 44.8 percent of the total variance. The first factor (horizontal) distinguishes "feminine" (nurse, teacher, etc.) and "masculine" professions (army officer, economic consultant, etc.). The second factor (vertical) separates choices of professions related to high culture and high prestige (art critic, psychiatrist, politician, etc.) from those of tertiary levels and business careers. The projection of the supplementary variables permits us to associate the first factor with the gender system categorization of professions, and the second with the differentiation of the field of careers according to the cultural capital of the family.

If we take a closer look at the top we see prestigious careers that range from the feminine, altruistic domain of psychology, through the domain of art (art critic, author), to the field of power and politics, which is more masculine. Close to politics we find other prestigious careers such as medicine, law, and the media. The army and the sciences are shared by all of the boys, while the career of shopkeeper is more favored by lower SES boys. Around the area designated as low SES we find the various service professions. Further on, we see the caring and teaching areas mostly dominated by women.

The examination of the supplementary variables shows that the only independent variable that seems to explain the choices of the Finnish pupils is gender (see Table 3.3). ("Boys" has a contribution of 0.143 in the first factor and Girls 0.137, respectively.) All other modalities have much less explanatory power; the contribution of the mathematics stream (which is linked with "Boys") is 0.033, and the contribution of the humanistic stream (linked with "Girls") is 0.028.

Table 3.3 Description of the First Two Factors of CFA: Likelihood of Taking up a Profession among Finnish Pupils

Modality	Factor 1		Factor 2	
	Co-ord	Ctr[*]	Co-ord	Ctr
Active variables				
Nurse	−.193	.096	.020	.001
Teacher (primary school)	−.153	.061	.013	.001
Hairdresser	−.151	.059	−.036	.004
Psychologist	−.138	.049	.112	.041
Guidance counselor	−.138	.049	.007	.000
Psychiatrist	−.122	.039	.127	.053
Artisan	−.120	.037	.024	.002
Secretary	−.106	.029	−.218	.154
Travel agent	−.095	.024	−.191	.119
Bank employee	−.066	.011	−.209	.142
Mechanic	.065	.011	−.023	.002
Reporter	.070	.013	.041	.006
Architect	.071	.013	.105	.036
Shopkeeper	.079	.016	−.171	.096
Lawyer	.112	.032	.059	.011
TV producer	.115	.034	.029	.003
Computer programmer	.135	.047	−.019	.001
Public relations advisor	.134	.047	−.096	.030
Politician	.139	.050	.123	.049
Army officer	.213	.117	.013	.001
Economic consultant	.218	.123	−.030	.003

(continued)

Table 3.3 *(continued)*

Modality	Factor 1		Factor 2	
	Co-ord	Ctr[*]	Co-ord	Ctr
Teacher (high school)	−.043	.005	.107	.038
Hotelkeeper	.062	.010	.180	.105
Author	.006	.000	.077	.019
Art critic	−.058	.009	.131	.056
Supplementary variables				
Boys	.235	.143	−.012	.000
Girls	−.230	.137	−.033	.004
Low SES	−.064	.011	−.081	.021
High SES	.069	.012	.074	.018
Mathematics stream	.112	.033	.019	.001
Humanistic stream	−.104	.028	−.086	.024
Photo "family"	−.060	.009	−.041	.005
Photo "man and horse"	−.054	.007	−.062	.012
Photo "study"	.100	.026	−.049	.008
Photo "music"	-.062	.010	.027	.002

Note: Factor 1: Ctr = 0.386, explained = 25 percent. Factor 2: Ctr = 0.307, explained = 19.8 percent.

[*]Ctr = The modality contribution to the composition of the factor, the total of the CTR of active modalities being equal to 1.000. Modalities of the active variables with a CTR less than .010 in the two factors were omitted.

SES does not give a very good explanation for the choices expressed by pupils. This is true even in regard to the second factor, which distinguishes high-status expectations from low-status anticipations. Of course, low SES goes with low status projects and high SES with those of high status. Nevertheless, the contributions attached to these modalities are not very strong (0.021 and 0.018 respectively).

The same could be said about the judgments concerning the photos. Positive judgments about the photo "study" (contributions: 0.026 in factor 1, 0.008 in factor 2) are more common among boys considering a job like "economic consultant" or "public relations advisor," whereas high appreciation of the photo "man and horse" (contributions: 0.007 in factor 1, 0.012 in factor 2) is more often expressed by girls, who are considering becoming hairdressers, for example.

France

The first and second factors account for 38.4 percent of the variance (see Table 3.4 for statistics describing the factors). The first factor (horizontal) opposes the choices of "science professions" (physician, computer programmer, architect) and the choices of occupations that could be called "verbal occupations" (translator, teacher, travel agent). The second factor distinguishes between professions "in relation to others" (psychologist, psychiatrist, teacher) and occupations in the domains of trade, services, and enterprises (hotelkeeper, travel agent, bank employee).

The examination of the supplementary variables (Table 3.4) shows that two variables have an important explanatory power concerning the choices of the French pupils. The strongest one is the school stream, especially the mathematics stream (its contribution in factor one is 0.147; the contribution of the language stream is 0.072). The preference of scientific professions seems to be explained here, above all, by the pupil being in the scientific stream, whereas the choice of verbal occupations is linked to the language stream.

Gender is also connected with these choices. The mathematics stream is more masculine, and the language stream, very feminine. But gender here also appears to have a certain impact on the distinction revealed by the second factor. The interest in professions "in relation to others" (caring, helping, teaching), and lack of interest in the domains of trade and enterprise, is more feminine (contribution of girls 0.054, of boys 0.019).

SES does not seem to explain the choices expressed by pupils (contribution of high SES 0.005 in the first factor, 0.008 in the second factor; contribution of Low SES 0.006 and 0.001, respectively). The same could be said of the judgments of photos. Only one photo, "family," seems to have a certain relation with choice of occupations. Students, mainly girls in the language stream, who like the photo "Family" express positive interest in professions in the fields of teaching and psychology.

In figure 3.2 we find a distribution of career choices according to gender and streams. At the top are the caring and teaching careers. The teaching careers are situated on the left in attraction to the feminine pole and literary stream, while the medical professions are situated on the right side in attraction to the masculine pole and the mathematics stream. At the bottom are careers related to the sciences, trade, and services. The area limited by "boys" and "mathematics stream" attracts masculine occupations, such as computer programmer, army officer, architect, and politician. The lower part of the figure is the "trade and services area." We find here more masculine professions such as bank employee, and to the left, more feminine ones such as secretary and translator.

Table 3.4 Description of the First Two Factors of CFA: Likelihood of Taking Up a Profession among French Students.

Modality	Factor 1		Factor 2	
	Co-ord	Ctr[*]	Co-ord	Ctr
Active Variables				
Translator	−.256	.132	−.084	.014
Teacher (high school)	−.226	.103	.238	.113
Teacher (primary school)	−.205	.085	.196	.077
Travel agent	−.199	.080	−.185	.068
Secretary	−.144	.042	−.122	.030
Guidance counselor	−.132	.035	−.005	.000
Public relations advisor	−.094	.018	−.021	.001
Politician	.078	.012	−.015	.000
Army officer	.093	.017	−.046	.004
Psychiatrist	.092	.017	.255	.131
TV producer	.109	.024	−.107	.023
Architect	.190	.073	−.003	.000
Computer programmer	.266	.143	−.095	.018
Physician	.282	.161	.118	.028
Hotelkeeper	−.024	.001	−.210	.089
Bank employee	.042	.004	−.177	.063
Shopkeeper	−.060	.007	−.159	.051
Artisan	.057	.007	−.074	.011
Nurse	.066	.009	.196	.077
Psychologist	−.017	.004	.286	.164
Lawyer	.044	.004	.089	.016
Supplementary variables				
Girls	−.199	.080	.164	.054
Boys	.192	.075	−.098	.019
Photo "family"	−.088	.016	.097	.019
Photo "man and horse"	−.062	.008	−.013	.000
Photo "surrealist"	−.017	.001	.038	.003
Photo "study"	.046	.004	.045	.004
High SES	.047	.005	.063	.008
Low SES	−.057	.006	.026	.001
Languages stream	−.189	.072	.025	.001
Mathematics stream	.270	.147	.050	.005

Note: Factor 1: Ctr = 0.494, explained = 19.1 percent. Factor 2: Ctr = 0.499, explained = 19.3 percent.

[*]Ctr = The modality contribution to the composition of the factor, the total of the Ctr of active modalities being equal to 1.000. Modalities of the active variables with a Ctr less than .010 in the two factors were omitted.

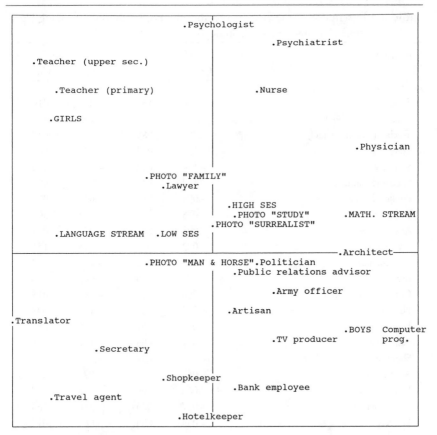

Figure 3.2. Graphic representation of modalities on the first two factor axes of CFA. Likelihood of taking up a profession: French students. Factor 1 (horizontal): Inertia = 0.494, explained = 19.1 percent. Factor 2 (vertical): Inertia = 0.499, explained = 19.3 percent. The modalities in uppercase type are the supplementary modalities.

To summarize the Finnish and French maps of professions we can say that in the Finnish map of occupations we find a net polarization of masculine and feminine occupations on the one hand and prestigious versus nonprestigious occupations on the other. Gender has a strong impact on the distribution of the choices, whereas SES seems to have a weaker one. This map of choices is similar to the cognitive map of occupations described by Gottfredson (1981): The girls imagine themselves in feminine careers, and the boys, in masculine ones. The more privileged pupils have more ambitious plans than the less privileged ones. In France the situation is different. The impact of the stream system is fundamental. The choices are shaped by the trajectory of the students in the rigid French system of streams. These preferences are also strongly influenced by gender. In such a context, the impact of SES cannot be clearly discovered. In any given stream there are some prevailing prototypes of the occupational future that can be expected. These expectations can, to some extent, be independent of the social origin of the pupils. Nevertheless, one must remember that no stream is representative of the entire population of pupils. We have seen, for example, that the mathematics stream is masculine and more bourgeois.

Discussion

It has been suggested that cultural features, educational policies, and institutional tracking play an important role in the way students perceive their futures (Nurmi, 1991; Guichard, 1993). Moreover, some recent studies in the field of vocational counselling have demonstrated that future planning can be integrated into the more general concept of habitus. Indeed, it seems that there is a connection between the way adolescents perceive their futures and their "life-styles" or "worldviews." In order to explore these hypotheses, adolescents' future projects, professional commitment, and cultural tastes were studied in the two national settings.

National Impact

The results showed that the Finnish pupils were very hesitant in comparison to their French counterparts about their future professions. To interpret these findings we must follow Bourdieu's (Bourdieu and Wacquant, 1992) suggestions about studying the objective structure of the field, which in our case is the field of education in general and institutional tracking in particular. As we have shown earlier, the Finnish and French populations are comparable in their levels of education, but very different with regard to their streaming policies. Because of the *numerus clausus* system it seems that the Finnish adolescents are more confused at the time of senior high school. Since they have only a 30 percent chance of enrolling in a faculty of their choice, they cannot afford to make a serious commitment to one particular domain, but have to remain open-minded about other possibilities.

The French, on the other hand, facing a rigid system of streams that obliges them to make crucial choices at an early stage, have a rather different attitude. Indeed, they consider tertiary education as the normal continuation of high school, and since there is no *numerus clausus* or entrance examination for most of the French faculties, they can express choices that have a high chance of being realized. In consequence, they can express their choices with greater confidence. However, for many of them the feelings of confusion and frustration are only postponed until a later stage, either when failing during their first or second year in college, when the rate of failure is very high, or when they discover that the degrees they have gained are not valued in the labor market and cannot assure their futures. Thus, national policies concerning university enrollment have far-reaching consequences for social stability. This was demonstrated during the 1968 revolt in Paris, when the national policies on university enrollment may also have provided a basis for confusion and frustration among young people.

It was found here that the adolescents in the Finnish sample show a high level of interest in business, whereas the French prefer education. This may be explained by the particularities of the two samples. As we have already mentioned, there is no streaming in Finnish schools. This situation probably has the following consequences: Senior high school pupils do not see themselves stuck in a track conducting them to some particular curriculum in tertiary education. This is not the case in France. In the present study the French sample was very particular. It mainly comprised students in the literary stream (29.6 percent) or in the scientific one (58 percent). Pupils in the economics stream accounted for only 5.5 percent, and the administration and bookkeeping curriculum was not represented at all. Nevertheless, these two streams are among the most important if we consider the percentage of pupil enrollment. For example, in 1989 17.1 percent of the matriculated high school pupils came from the economics stream, and 19.1 percent, from administration and bookkeeping. It is very likely that if students coming from these two streams had been questioned about their potential occupations, they would have displayed a much greater interest in business. The main reason for the huge preference expressed by French students for careers in education and their weak interest in business must be found in the particularity of the French sample, which almost completely excluded pupils in economics, administration, and bookkeeping. Can this completely explain the differences between Finland and France?

Only assumptions can be made. Nevertheless, we must recall that Wach (1992) found earlier in France that education was the most popular choice among adolescents. The Finnish interest in business might be connected with the general enthusiasm this field has aroused in Western countries in the 1980s. In Finland, as in a number of other countries, many new business schools opened their doors to numerous students eager to find the key to wealth. Indeed, in many Western countries the students in faculties of business, administration, and social affairs accounted for about one-third of all students in 1990. It would be interesting to study the specific representations people wishing to embrace these careers have of this field. Can this trend be related to Finnish values favoring diligent labor and respect for time and other values connected to the "Protestant work ethic"?

Education in France is closely associated with humanist studies. One of the most prestigious diplomas in France, *l'Agrégation*, is a graduate degree for teachers, and the *Agrégation de Philosophie* is one of the most difficult to earn. The *Agrégés* form a kind of highly respected caste in the educational world in France. Furthermore, statistics (Debizet, 1990) show that more students in France choose the faculties of humanities and literature than in other Western countries (e.g., 30 percent in France, 10.6 percent in the United States). A common way of making a living from such studies is to become a teacher. Can we infer from these observations that there is a kind of "cultural atmosphere" in France that makes the teaching profession one of the most attractive, despite the fact that it is not the most prestigious (Wach, 1992)? Or it may be that many lower-class girls are worried about unemployment (Motola, 1994), and becoming a teacher (a state civil servant) provides social and economic security.

The preceding interpretations can in fact be integrated into a more general theory of habitus. The results analyzed earlier have shown that the ways in which students perceive their future, their choices, and their commitment are connected to the national educational context and cultural milieu as well. The experience of growing up in a particular system of education molds our perception of reality in a specific, national manner. This national way of perceiving and classifying reality becomes natural for us, and only cross-national comparison can reveal its arbitrary and contextual character.

Affiliation to a Social Group: Gender System and Cultural Capital

We expected that within a given society different individuals tend to have different expectations of their possible occupational careers. We also expected to link these interests with gender, socioeconomic background, school stream (in France), and aesthetic tastes toward photographs. We focused our analysis within each country in an attempt to identify sub-groups that share similar representations of their future careers. The results showed that the most striking variables were gender (in both samples) and school stream (in France). The gender system is one of the most basic modes of categorizing reality. According to Bourdieu it is the form par excellence of symbolic violence of all forms of domination. The "male order" imposes itself as natural upon both men and women. In Bourdieu's words, ". . . men and women acquire different attitudes towards the social games that are treated as the most important. In Kabyle society these are the games of honor and war favoring the exhibition of manly virtues; in class-differentiated societies, the most highly valorized games are those of politics, art, science, etc." (Bourdieu, 1900b). This perspective may help us to understand the consistent results of many research studies that have revealed the gender differences of professional choices (Guichard, 1993; Häyrynen, (1970); Sinisalo, 1993; Motola, 1994; Gottfredson, 1981). Häyrynen (1970) found that women students stressed more heavily the intrinsic rewards such as creativity and working with people, compared with male students, who appreciated such rewards as status and income. These findings are in line with our results showing the net tendency of women toward caring and service careers, while men incline towards the sciences, politics, and economics.

Women in the Western world have dramatically increased their participation in education and in working life over the last twenty years. While the number of economically active men in the OECD countries has increased by 25 percent in the last thirty years, the comparable figure for women has been 74 percent. Women now form the majority of those gaining the matriculation; they are the majority in the universities, and their numbers are increasing in the labor market. The problem is that, despite their better achievements at school, women are not to be found in the stream leading to more prestigious careers; those in the labor market generally occupy low-level positions in professional life. Girls in our research follow the same path. They focus their choices in the fields of social and health care and of education. They exclude themselves from the sciences. This process of self-limitation is of great concern in many Western countries nowadays. Although there seem to be achievements, girls tend to underestimate their abilities in mathematics vis-à-vis boys. For example, it has been found that boys explain their failure in a mathematics test by saying that the test was too difficult, while girls in the same situation said that they were not good at mathematics (Amit and Moshevitz-Hadar, 1989). Only social learning experiences inscribed in a long tradition—in other words, the forming of social habitus—could create this kind of deeply instilled social conception. Should we wish to transform these basic social representations perpetuating male dominance in the social field, greater determination and more vigorous methods than those thus far employed would be required.

In France the main factor that seemed to influence occupational choice was a particular school stream; this is generally associated with gender and family cultural capital. This could be explained by the school organization in France, whose system is much more rigid than in Finland. Thus, the perception of things going together (in our case, the expectations of pupils of any possible occupational career) seems to be tied, first, to the student's "stream identity," and second, overdetermined by gender. (Gender in all probability is already a component of stream identity, at least implicitly.)

In the Finnish sample occupational expectations differ from one another along a dimension of prestige (Figure 3.1, factor 2). This opposition was not found in the French sample. It is possible that Finns facing an explicit system of selection (and social segregation) are more aware of their "place in society" than the French. In France the situation is more ambiguous in students' eyes. Bourdieu claims that

the diversification of streams, associated with procedures of selection becoming more and more precocious, tends to establish soft exclusion practices . . . which are not perceived either by those who apply them or those who suffer from them. The soft elimination, continuing in the long run, provides those who experience it with the possibility of deceiving themselves, and even of lying to themselves about what they are really doing. In that sense, the most crucial "choices" must be made earlier than before (at the upper secondary school and not, as in the past, after the Baccalaureate or even later) and the scholar's fate is sealed more precociously. But, in another sense, the consequences of these choices are more and more delayed. It is as if there were a conspiracy to persuade students to postpone the moment when they must face the truth and discover that the time they spent in school was a dead time, a wasted time. (Bourdieu and Champagne, 1992, p. 75)

One possible explanation for these differences could also be a degree of bias in our samples. It is possible that our Finnish sample was more polarized along the social dimension. Indeed, we had a large number of students from one of the most prestigious schools in Helsinki, but access to the most prestigious Parisian school was not possible. One must, nevertheless, remember that even in the Finnish sample socioeconomic status was not a good explanation of the high-prestige and low-prestige preferences expressed by pupils. Is it because of the operationalization of the SES variable? (SES was formed solely on the basis of the level of the education of the father and had only two modalities.) Or does the answer lie in the fact that in late adolescence the level of family education has a lesser impact on the adolescent's future orientation than the cultural practices that he or she is currently engaged in with his or her friends? Some findings gathered in France (Guichard et al., 1994) could support such an interpretation.

One of the essential hypotheses related to the habitus theory is that people who belong to social groups situated in analogous positions in different social fields will express judgments that are homologous in each of these different fields. Our modest attempt to study this hypothesis[4] leads us to consider the links between the individual expectations about occupational career (in the field of social positions) and his or her preferences among the photographs (in the fields of aesthetic judgments). This endeavor was partly successful. Indeed, only three kinds of occupational projects appeared to be linked to certain preferences in regard to the photographs. In the Finnish sample the attraction of the photo "study" appeared to be more typical among students (mainly boys) dreaming of professions like physician or architect. Such a choice is opposed by a preference for the photo "man and horse" chosen by pupils (mainly girls) thinking of their future careers in terms of jobs like hairdresser or travel agent. In the French sample the photo "family" was preferred by students (mainly girls) thinking of their future in terms of becoming a teacher. Of course, the modest contributions of these modalities could suggest that these aesthetic preferences are not strongly related to occupational interests.[5] Nevertheless, one can see that these three observations fit together well. They stress differences between boys and girls—in Finland and France both—in their expressed occupational projects and in their tastes for the photographs. This suggests that the question of the choice of an occupation is much more sophisticated than the approaches—in terms of "vocational interests," "work values," or "career decision making"—would imply. Some of these schemes leading to an appreciation or a rejection of an occupation appear to be related to schemes that lead to "liking" or "disliking" objects of a completely different nature.

Such a conclusion is consonant with the habitus theory. Bourdieu claims that convictions and beliefs are not chosen that are independent of any conditioning; they are, rather, embodied within individuals through a long historical process and in specific sociocultural contexts. Habitus can enchain us and restrict our future perspectives (as we have seen with vocational plans). But habitus can be transformed. It is through education, psychotherapy, and socioanalysis that new representations and practices can be created. But first we must free ourselves from the illusion that we are free and independent from all social influences, since, as Bourdieu (1990a, p. 15) has asserted, "Freedom is not a given but a conquest, a collective one."

Notes

We acknowledge with gratitude the assistance of Maarit Kankaanpää in the gathering of data, and of Xinhua Zhao and Jianzhong Hong for their comments on a draft of this article.

1. As a result of a recent reform, changes have occurred in the definition of the French Baccalaureate. The eight streams are now grouped into three major academic streams (literature, the sciences, and socioeconomics). The pupils participating in the present study were still working under the old system.

2. The Grandes Ecoles, created in the eighteenth and nineteenth centuries to train engineers and senior state executive employees, continue today to overshadow the universities (entry into the former was, and still is, highly selective) and contribute heavily to the elitist reputation of the French educational system.

3. CFA in its geometric form was created by the French statistician Benzécri in 1973. The French term "correspondence" was used to denote the "system of association" between the elements of two sets, generally the rows and columns of a rectangular matrix. The main idea of CFA is to replace a complex table of data with several variables with another table, which includes only a few "theoretical variables" and which still fits the first table in statistical sense (compare factor analysis). A simple example is the formula $A^2 - B^2$, which can be replaced by the product of two factors $(A + B) \times (A - B)$. The two expressions are identical, but the second presentation is more useful for later calculations. CFA is, in fact, the treatment of the deviance from the independence (between a system of rows and columns) expressed by the chi-square method. The algorithm of CFA extracts several factors that best fit the original matrix of rows and columns. Each factor is defined by its inertia and the percentage of the total variance explained by it. (The "inertia of a factor" is the amount of information with which the factor is loaded. The total inertia is known as the "Pearson mean-square contingency coefficient," which is the chi-square of a contingency table.)

During the processing, CFA differentiates two kinds of variables, the *active* and the *supplementary*. The former are mathematically processed during the analysis and contribute to the creation of the factors, while the latter are projected only after the mathematical analysis and therefore make no contribution to the creation of the factor and have no "mass." Generally the independent variables that describe the subjects are chosen as supplementary. What has contributed most to the success of this method is the possibility of representing the results of the lines and the columns graphically and simultaneously. When we deal with a large number of independent variables that describe participants and a large number of dependent variables that describe attitudes (as in our study), CFA creates a graphic figure where participants with a similar profile of attitudes will share the same space in a two-dimensional field.

In order to interpret the CFA figure it is important to bear in mind that there are three main relations between two points:

a. Conjunction—when the angle between two vectors (one representing a line and the other a column) is zero or less than ninety degrees. This case represents the attraction between two points (modalities of a variable).

b. Quadrature—when there is a angle of ninety degrees between the two vectors. In this case the two points (modalities) are independent.

c. Opposition—the angle between the two vectors is more than ninety degrees. It represents a state of repulsion between two points (modalities).

Cibois warns us of the danger of the "homothetic effect.""Indeed, CFA reveals the structure of deviations from independence but not their intensity. Thus we risk making a savant interpretation where the deviations from independence are so minimal that they might just as well be due to chance" (Cibois 1991, p. 123).

d. For a profound and far-reaching analysis, see Bourdieu's seminal study entitled *Distinction* (1984).

e. In fact, only a postfactorial analysis using a technique like Cibois's (1993b) PEM could allow us to be either more affirmative or more skeptical about the strength of these relations.

References

Amit, M., and Moshevitz-Hadar, N. (1989). Gender differences in attribution causes of success and failure in mathematic studies. *Megamot, 32*, 372–391.

Benzécri, J.-P., et al. (1973). *L'analyse des données* (Data analysis). Paris: Dunond.

Bourdieu, P. (1980). *Questions de Sociologie* (Sociology in question). Paris: Les Editions de Minuit.

Bourdieu, P. (1984). *Distinction: A social critique of the judgment of taste*. Cambridge, MA: Harvard University Press.

Bourdieu, P. (1987). What makes a social class? On the theoretical and practical existence of groups. *Berkeley Journal of Sociology, 32*, 1–7.

Bourdieu, P. (1990a). *In other words: Essays towards a reflexive sociology*. Cambridge, MA: Polity Press.

Bourdieu, P. (1990b). La domination masculine (Male domination). *Actes de la Recherche en Science Sociales, 84*, 2–31.

Bourdieu, P. (1992). *An invitation to reflexive sociology*. Chicago: University of Chicago Press.

Bourdieu, P. (1994). *Raison pratique* ("Practical reason"). Paris: Seuil.

Bourdieu, P., and Champagne, P. (1992). Les exclus de l'interieur (The inner-outcasts). *Actes de la Recherche en Science Sociales, 91/92*, 71–75.

Bourdieu, P., and Wacquant, L.J.D. (1992). *An invitation to re-flexive sociology*. Chicago: University of Chicago Press.

Cibois, P. (1990). *L'analyse des données en sociologie*. (Data analysis in sociology). Paris: Puf.

Cibois, P. (1991). *L'analyse factorielle*. (Factor analysis.) Paris: Puf.

Cibois, P. (1992). *Tri-deux, version 2* [computer program]. Paris: UFR sciences socials Paris V.

Cibois, P. (1993). Le PEM, pourcentage de l'écart maximum: un indice de liaison entre modalités d'un tableau de contingence (The PEM, the percentage of the maximum difference between modalities in a contingency table). *Bulletin de Méthodologie Sociologigue, 40*, 43–63.

Clark, T. N., and Lipset, S.M. (1991). Are social classes dying? *International Sociology, 6*, 397–410.

Debizet, J. (1990). La scolarité après 16 ans. *Données Sociales*. Paris: Ministère de l'Economie, des Finances et du Budget. INSEE, 330–335.

Dubet, F. (1991). *Les lycéens* (The high school students). Paris: Seuil.

Education in Finland 1994. (1994). *Education, 1994, 3*, 27–40.

Gottfredson, L. (1981). Circumscription and compromise: A developmental theory of occupational aspiration. *Journal of Counseling Psychology, 28*, 545–579.

Guichard, J. (1993). *L'Ecole et les représentations d'avenir des adolescents* (School and the future representations of adolescents). Paris: Puf.

Guichard, J. (1994, June). *Social and cultural experiences of adolescents and the categorization of occupations*. Paper presented at the Eighth Biennial Meeting of the International Society for the Study of Behavioural Development, Amsterdam, the Netherlands.

Guichard, J., Devos, P., Bernard, H., Chevalier, G., Devaux, M., Faure, A., Jellab, M., and Vanesse, V. (1994). Habitus culturel et représentation des professions (Cultural habitus and representations of occupations). *L'orientation scolaire et professionnelle, 23*, 379–464.

Häyrynen, Y.-P. (1970). *The flow of new students to different university fields*. Helsinki: Suomalainen Tiedeakatemia.

Heran, F. (1987). La seconde nature de l'habitus. Tradition philosophique et sens commun dans le langage sociologique (The second nature of habitus. Philosophical tradition and common sense in the sociological language.) *Revue francaise de sociologie, 28*, 385–416.

Husen, T., and Tuijnman, A. (eds.), (1992). *Schooling in modern European society: A report of the Academia Europa.* Oxford: Pergamon.

Huteau, M. (1985). *Le system educatif Francais* (The system of education in France). Paris: Research Centre, INETOP.

Motola, M. (1994). The impact of socio-cultural factors on vocational behavior. A cross national comparison of French and Finnish students. Unpublished licentiate thesis. The Department of Psychology, University of Joensuu, Finland.

Nurmi, J.-E. (1991). How do adolescents see their future? A review of the development of future orientation and planning. *Developmental Review, 11*, 1–59.

Nurmi, J.-E., Poole, M.-E., and Seginer, R. (1995). Track and transition: A comparison of adolescent future-oriented goals, explorations and commitments in Australia, Israel and Finland. *International Journal of Psychology, 30*, 355–375.

OECD (Organization for Economic Cooperation and Development) (1985). *Education at a glance: OECD indicators.* Paris: OECD.

Osipow, H.S. (1983). *Theories of career development.* Englewood Cliffs, NJ: Prentice-Hall.

Sinisalo, P. (1993). Conceptions of vocational interests: from personality constructs to representations. In H. Perho, H. Räty, and P. Sinisalo (eds.), *Crossroads between mind, society and culture.* Joensuu, Finland: Joensuu University Press.

Statistics Finland (1991). *Education in Finland.* Helsinki: Education and Research.

Wach, M. (1992). Projets et représentations des études et des professions des élèves de troisième et de terminale en 1992 (Future plans and educational and professional representations of the third and the final year pupils in 1992). *L'Orientation scolaire et professionnelle, 21*, 297–339.

Chapter Four
Dutch and Swedish Adolescents' Understanding of Peace and War

Ilse Hakvoort, Solveig Hägglund, and Louis Oppenheimer

Introduction

During the past century, philosophers, historians, social scientists, and politicians, among others, have expressed their concern about our apparent inability to develop a world of peace (Russell, 1916). Building a world in which people can live in peaceful coexistence requires, according to Evans (1993), international and intranational efforts to meet needs "for security and order, for a reasonable standard of living, and for recognition of identity and worth" (p. 39). The issue is not as much to resolve particular conflicts or disputes as to create "the conditions that will ensure that problems needing such attention won't occur, or recur, at all" (p. 40). According to Grossi (1994), to attain this goal it will be necessary to "rethink peace, to put peace into practice and to ensure its respect," which "has become a pledge for human intelligence and a challenge for men at the dawn of the 21st century" (p. 412). Because attitudes toward peace and war are based on knowledge and beliefs that are co-constructed by sociocultural structures (Oppenheimer, 1995, 1996), rethinking peace "presupposes a logically prior investigation of the structure of systems of knowledge and belief" (Chomsky, 1972, pp. 43–44) in different sociocultural settings. In addition, beliefs about peace and war are related to the understanding of the relationship between the "I" and the "We"; that is, the true value of peace and coexistence can be understood only following a process of decentering (Piaget, 1980).

The research described in this chapter is a first step in "rethinking peace" by obtaining insights into the way adolescents in two different countries or sociocultural settings (i.e., the Netherlands and Sweden) perceive peace, war, and strategies to attain peace. Adolescence is the developmental period in which children become part of social institutions and become affected by the values, norms, and attitudes set by these institutions. We assume that this interactive process in particular will shape individuals' perspectives on society (i.e., on the sociocultural structure) and the human condition. Consequently, we consider the way adolescents from different cultures perceive peace, war, and strategies to attain peace as indices for changes that may occur or are required in institutional values, norms, and attitudes.

The purpose of this chapter is to report empirical results from a comparative study of adolescents' conceptions of peace, war, and strategies to attain peace. The comparisons focus on variations according to nationality (i.e., Dutch and Swedish adolescents) and gender.

Previous Research

Efforts in studying children's and adolescents' knowledge about and attitudes toward international issues such as peace and war have generated various lines of research. In part these lines have been determined by historical changes in international political conditions that affected the amount of research as well as its focus. Though many studies within the field of peace research have been documented, earlier studies that focus on a developmental approach and offer empirical data on adolescents' understanding of peace and war are limited.

Peace-research studies with children can often be clustered around the outburst of armed conflicts or increasing international tensions. For instance, a series of studies focused on the effects of these conflicts on personal and mental development of children (e.g., Kahnert, Pitt, and Taipale, 1983; Leavitt and Fox, 1993; Punamäki, 1987; Toner, 1994). Similarly, the presence and growth of nuclear arsenals led to studies in which the threat of a nuclear war on the psychological development of children and adolescents as examined (see Boyd et al., 1994). Besides the study of the direct implications of conflicts, research was directed also to young people's attitudes toward war in general and to specific wars in particular (Tolley, 1973). In addition, attitudes toward enemies, nationalism, and politics were studied (cf. Muller-Brettel, 1993).

In these different research approaches, it was assumed that children understand concepts such as peace, war, enemy, violence, nation, nationality, and so on. The realization that such an understanding is subject to developmental changes led in the 1960s to a growing interest in the examination of developmental courses for these conceptions. During that period and later, numerous studies examining the development of concepts like "nation" and "international relations" emerged (e.g., Barrett and Short, 1992; Jahoda, 1964; Piaget and Weil, 1951; Targ, 1970), while the developmental patterns for children's conceptions of peace and war were studied also. In the following section these studies on the development of adolescents' conceptualizations of peace and war are discussed in greater detail.

To grasp the relevance of the earlier studies, it should be noted that the meaning or definition of the concept of peace has been a topic of discussion for several decades (Galtung, 1964, 1969; Brock-Utne, 1989). The discussion about how the concept of peace should be interpreted was initiated by Galtung (1964), who proposed a distinction between a negative and a positive dimension of peace. *Negative peace* was defined by the absence of physical and direct violence between groups or nations; *positive peace,* by cooperation patterns aiming at the integration of or collaboration between groups or nations. That is, whereas negative peace was characterized by "state" descriptions, positive peace was defined as more "process-oriented," which required the understanding of dynamic processes (Chandler and Boutilier, 1992). After some years of discussion, Galtung (1969) redefined the concept of positive peace to include "what it is not," that is, the absence of indirect or structural violence.

The differentiation between negative and positive peace has been adopted by other researchers (Brock-Utne, 1989), though the discussion about the exact definition of negative peace and positive peace, in particular, continued. Brock-Utne specified the dimensions of organized and unorganized and direct and indirect violence in greater detail for negative peace and positive peace. That is, organized violence was observed at the macro level (i.e., the collective or society), while unorganized violence was shown by individuals on the micro level. Consequently, according to Brock-Utne, negative peace should be defined as either the absence of unorganized violence (e.g., crime), organized violence (i.e., usually war), or both. The second dimension involving indirect violence, in particular, concerned violence that negatively affects the quality of life. Consequently, positive peace should also include references to conditions that will permit longevity and optimal life conditions. The concept of *war* was defined as "organized, collective, personal violence, usually between states but possible within one nation-state—so-called domestic wars" (Brock-Utne, 1989, p. 43); consequently, negative peace included the negation of these aspects of war also.

Since Cooper's (1965) exploratory study of the development of the concept of war, two waves of research on children's understanding of peace and war can be observed. In both waves special attention was paid to developmental changes in children's understanding of peace and war, and the age limit extended to include adolescence. Though limited in number, only studies that involved adolescents are presented in the following review.

The First Wave
The Concept of Peace

In an exploratory study, Cooper (1965) studied conceptions of war with English and Japanese children and adolescents (age range: five to sixteen years). In this study, a Piagetian cognitive-developmental perspective was adopted. It was assumed that the understanding of the reciprocity of relationships among events was necessary for adolescents to comprehend relationships between actions, causes, and effects of peace and war. The adolescents were requested to give written associations to the words "peace" and "war." Peace defined by "inactive and personal considerations of quiet and silence" (Cooper, 1965, p. 5) was found to be the most important image of peace with English adolescents. That is, "peace of mind" was most frequently associated with peace; occasionally "boredom" and peace being "uninteresting" were mentioned. Associations referring to international efforts to attain peace, such as respite of war by diplomacy and reconciliation, were mentioned infrequently. Contrary to the English adolescents, the Japanese adolescents associated peace frequently with international relationships. No clear relationship was present between the understanding of the reciprocity of events and the development of conceptions of peace.

In the studies by Haavelsrud (1970) and Rosell (1968) a slightly revised and translated version of Cooper's questionnaire was used. In both studies, the developmental courses for conceptions about peace and war were thought to be affected by socialization processes rather than cognitive maturity. These authors emphasized the role of social and political environments (i.e., the sociocultural structure) in the formation of conceptions of peace and war. According to Rosell (1968), fourteen-year-old Swedish adolescents perceived peace predominantly as the negation of war. While Rosell assumed that fourteen-year-olds would be able to perceive peace more as a process toward cooperation and integration, no positive relation with age could be demonstrated for these conceptions. Swedish adolescents were well acquainted with concrete aspects of peace (e.g., joy, happiness, passivity, and respite of war). The conceptions of peace of adolescents from West Berlin (mean ages: fifteen and seventeen years), however, showed an age-related increase in references to coexistence, relationships among people, nations, and parties (Haavelsrud, 1970).

The Concept of War

With regard to the development of the concept of war, Cooper (1965) reported that English adolescents emphasized consequences of war, as well as war activities such as fighting, killing, and dying, more than concrete objects of war (e.g., guns and planes) and subjects in wars (e.g., soldiers and armies). The adolescents' growing concern about consequences of war and war activities corresponded with an increase in negative emotional responses (e.g., "war leads to pain and suffering"). The Japanese adolescents mentioned more concrete objects of war until the age of fourteen. They appeared to be less concerned than their English peers with the consequences of war and war activities such as fighting, killing, and dying.

Rosell (1968) and Haavelsrud (1970) replicated Cooper's (1965) findings with Swedish and West Berlin adolescents, respectively. Swedish fourteen-year-olds associated war predominantly with consequences, while associations with war activities correlated negatively with age. The older adolescents from West Berlin were concerned with negative consequences of war on people; war was frequently evaluated negatively. Contradictory to the findings of Cooper (1965) and Rosell (1968), Haavelsrud reported that approximately 20 percent of the fifteen- and seventeen-year-old adolescents still associated war with concrete objects like weapons. Female adolescents mentioned such concrete objects less and war activities (e.g., fighting, killing, and dying) more frequently than boys. In Rosell's (1968) study, the Swedish adolescents were asked to define war to a friend. In contrast to the free association procedure, this question demonstrated consequences of war to correlate negatively with age, while the issue of conflict (i.e., interpersonal and between nations) showed a strong age-related increase in the definitions. The latter finding suggested that different assessment procedures (i.e., questions) appealed to different aspects of the concept of war.

In summary, the studies from the first wave were, foremost, exploratory. Despite the failure to embed these studies in consistent theoretical frameworks, they offered indications for age-related changes in conceptions of peace and war and a dependency of these conceptions upon the employed assessment procedure (i.e., type of question), gender, and culture.

The Second Wave

The Concept of Peace

After an interval of approximately two decades, a second wave of studies dealing with adolescents' conceptions of peace was observed (e.g., Covell, Rose-Krasnor, and Fletcher, 1994; Hakvoort and Oppenheimer, 1993; Hall, 1993; McCreary Juhasz and Palmer, 1991; Spielmann, 1986).

In the studies by Spielmann (1986) and McCreary Juhasz and Palmer (1991), a greater emphasis on peace rather than war was present. To study the development of attitudes toward peace, Spielmann (1986) asked adolescents (ages thirteen to fourteen and seventeen to eighteen years) to write an essay titled "Thoughts about Peace" prior to and following the visit of Anwar Sadat (president of Egypt) to Israel. The essays of the thirteen- and fourteen-year olds, obtained prior to Sadat's visit, were optimistic and utopian. Peace was associated with the fulfillment of many kinds of wishes (i.e., personal as well as social and national wishes). The expected changes in social climate as a consequence of peace, such as the absence of fear and anxiety, were thought to result in changes in everyday activities. Themes referring to social activities like parties and festivals, as well as the freedom to travel and security, were mentioned frequently in the essays. Of interest was the low frequency of issues such as open borders, diplomatic relationships, and commercial and economic cooperation. This utopian view changed to a more realistic approach after Sadat's visit. The essays became more attuned to the pessimism of adult society: The adolescents became aware of the price that had to be paid for peace.

The seventeen- and eighteen-year-old adolescents demonstrated a reverse shift. While prior to Sadat's visit the essays from these adolescents expressed a pessimistic view by pointing out problems and obstacles that could prevent the implementation of peace, after Sadat's visit the essays from this age group were more optimistic and an increase in hope for peace was observed. No clear indications for differences between Jewish and Arab adolescents were reported by Spielmann (1986).

In an attempt to obtain composite patterns in conceptions of peace, McCreary Juhasz and Palmer (1991) asked thirteen- and fourteen-year-old adolescents from Sydney (Australia), Toronto (Canada), and Chicago (United States) to complete the "Peace in the Family Questionnaire." Several of the questions in this questionnaire were almost identical to those used in the studies from the first wave (the questions dealing with associations and definitions, in particular). Three clusters of responses were observed in the associations with and definitions of peace. Similar to the findings of

Cooper (1965), Rosell (1968), and Spielmann (1986), McCreary Juhasz and Palmer (1991) reported "a wide range of positive feelings" from which the composite pattern emerged of "inner joy and happiness in a calm and tranquil atmosphere" (p. 851). A second pattern involved social connotations of peace (i.e., relationships characterized by caring and sharing, understanding, cooperation, and harmony). This pattern closely resembled the responses observed with adolescents from West Berlin (Haavelsrud, 1970). The third cluster of responses referred to the "elimination of peace-threatening attitudes and behaviors prefaced by no (e.g., no fighting, no violence, no war, no hatred)" (p. 852). Questions dealing with what changes could make life more peaceful for the adolescents resulted in responses dealing with the elimination of conflict-producing behaviors (e.g., fighting) and social consciousness such as a concern for the homeless, animals, environmental abuse, and the quality of life. Processes toward peace involved reaching compromises and cooperation. When asked how world peace could be achieved, changes in attitudes by improvements in interpersonal relationships and skills were predominant responses (e.g., improving interactions between members of a family, families, societies, and nations, as well as understanding of and respect for racial and religious differences). No differences in conceptions of peace between the adolescents from the three countries were mentioned by McCreary Juhasz and Palmer.

More recent studies (Covell, Rose-Krasnor, and Fletcher, 1994; Hakvoort and Oppenheimer, 1993; Hall, 1993) were partly based on studies from the first wave (e.g., Cooper, 1965; Haavelsrud, 1970; Rosell, 1968). In their study of Dutch children's and adolescents' (age range seven to seventeen years) conceptions of peace, war, and strategies to attain peace, Hakvoort and Oppenheimer (1993) adopted a social-cognitive developmental approach (Selman, 1980). In this approach it was assumed that the ability of role taking is necessary for the development of conceptions of peace relating to conflict resolution, collaboration, coexistence, and cooperation. That is, to be able to discuss peace or strategies to attain peace in any of the former terms, the understanding of the mutual or reciprocal relationship between points of view of different individuals and nations was assumed to be a developmental prerequisite. Conceptions of peace and war were assessed by verbal associations as was the case in earlier studies (e.g., Cooper, 1965). Strategies to attain peace were measured by newly developed questions involving interpersonal and international relationships. All measures were presented individually to the adolescents as interviews. According to Hakvoort and Oppenheimer (1993),

Dutch adolescents associated peace primarily with negative peace (i.e., the absence of war and war activities) or a state of quietness. A few adolescents associated peace with more abstract concepts such as the violation of human attitudes and universal rights. The latter type of conception was more evident in the adolescents' responses when asked about strategies to attain peace from their own personal perspectives.

The assumption that the understanding of the mutual or reciprocal relationship between points of view of different individuals and nations (i.e., mutual role taking) is required for the formulation of more abstract, norm-related reasoning about strategies to attain peace was confirmed. In addition, the findings of this study demonstrated that different referential settings (e.g., thinking about peace and strategies to attain peace from different societal positions) resulted in differences between the actual and potential understanding of peace.

In agreement with Hakvoort and Oppenheimer's (1993) findings, Covell, Rose-Krasnor, and Fletcher (1994) reported that abstract conceptions of peace were most frequently (35.1 percent) observed with the older Canadian adolescents (grades eight to ten and eleven to thirteen). In general, however, peace was described in concrete and general terms by all adolescents. This is a finding that, according to Covell, Rose-Krasnor, and Fletcher, "may reflect a complexity and ambiguity in the concept itself" (p. 732). In agreement with theories dealing with concept development, it was thought that the infrequent occurrence of instances of peace resulted in too few "peace exemplars" to stimulate the development of abstract conceptions of peace. It is, however, also possible that the obtained findings were the result of the pen-and-paper procedure used by Covell, Rose-Krasnor, and Fletcher. The authors reported that almost all adolescents gave only one response. Consequently, it could be argued that this procedure may have prompted stereotypical conceptions of peace rather than the potential levels of understanding that can be obtained by a verbal procedure.

To examine whether the results of earlier studies could be replicated with 354 Australian adolescents (mean ages 11.6, 13.6, and 15.6 years), Hall (1993) used a written questionnaire consisting of a mixture of open-ended and multiple-choice questions. In their conceptualizations of peace, Australian adolescents emphasized primarily reconciliation (i.e., international and positive contributions to peace). Social harmony as a characteristic of peace was observed from the age of nine, while respite from hostilities, quietness, and solitude decreased with age. Hall reported girls to express a more complete concept of peace than boys. That is, girls included social harmony as well as reconciliation in their conceptions of peace.

The Concept of War

The results from the studies in the second wave replicated those from the first wave. For instance, Hall (1993) reported that Australian adolescents mentioned predominantly concrete aspects of war and warfare such as military hardware with a recognition of the causes and consequences of war. According to Hall, war was conceptualized by an undifferentiated range of interpersonal, intergroup, and international conflicts.

Dutch adolescents associated war primarily with war activities, weapons, and soldiers (Hakvoort and Oppenheimer, 1993). While for these concrete aspects no gender differences were observed, girls and boys differed in their discussion of war when friends were involved. Girls more than boys discussed war in terms of quarrels among friends and in relation to their immediate environments. Boys perceived war more frequently to be unrelated with their immediate environments and referred to distant nations, armies, and soldiers.

According to Covell, Rose-Krasnor, and Fletcher (1994), Canadian adolescents evidenced a general and abstract level of understanding for war, while concrete aspects disappeared as the adolescents were older. War was frequently defined as a conflict between nations (i.e., the general level) and an expression of incompatible goals (i.e., the abstract level).

In summary, the studies from the second wave were also primarily exploratory since no consistent theoretical frameworks were present. In most cases, the indications found earlier for age-related changes in conceptions of peace and war and the dependency of these conceptions upon the employed assessment procedure (i.e., type of question), gender, and culture were replicated.

Though the Piagetian cognitive-developmental theory was the major theoretical framework used to study developing conceptions of peace and war, theoretical models referring to political socialization (Haavelsrud, 1970; Rosell, 1968) and concept development (Covell, Rose-Krasnor, and Fletcher, 1994) were also used. In a few cases only, however, the analyses and interpretations of the findings were in sufficient detail to permit the study of predicted relationships between developmental patterns for conceptions of peace and war and the development of cognitive or social-cognitive abilities (i.e., the role-taking ability; Hakvoort and Oppenheimer, 1993).

The research discussed previously demonstrated that peace is a complex concept and that the assessment of its development is sensitive to the measures employed. In most studies, a pen-and-paper (i.e., written) procedure was followed to assess conceptions of peace and war. Because such procedures did not permit any prompting, responses may have reflected mere socially desirable or stereotypical conceptions. The few studies in which a verbal interview procedure was used suggest that higher levels of understanding of peace and war were assessed.

Finally, though in most studies adolescents from different nations were involved, and in some studies from more than one country (McCreary Juhasz and Palmer, 1991) or from different sociocultural settings within one country (Spielmann, 1986), no systematic comparisons between adolescents from different countries or sociocultural settings were made. Given the importance of cross-cultural comparisons with regard to issues such as peace and war, the absence of such comparisons was surprising.

The Comparative Approach

The empirical studies previously discussed showed that peace and peace-related concepts are complex and multidimensional. The few cross-cultural comparisons indicated that adolescents' knowledge about and attitudes toward manifestations of peace and war did not develop in a sociocultural and historical vacuum; this knowledge reflected attitudes present in sociocultural settings with their own unique histories (Oppenheimer, 1995, 1996). These two assumptions are important motives for the comparative approach in the present study. If it is anticipated that cultural factors affect variation in psychological behavior, cross-cultural research approaches may contribute to our understanding in at least three ways. First, it will enable us to test whether empirical findings from one cultural setting are also valid in another cultural setting. Second, a cross-cultural approach allows the exploration of "other cultures in order to discover psychological variations that are not present in one's own limited cultural experience" (Berry et al., 1994, p. 3). A third motive relates to the purpose to "generate a more nearly universal psychology . . . that will be valid for a broader range of cultures" (Berry et al., 1994, p. 3). These three motives for doing cross-cultural comparisons are perceived as different steps in addressing the question of universal and socioculturally related aspects of the conceptualization of peace. Because there is not (as yet) a "grand" theory of the development of adolescents' understanding of peace and peace-related concepts, theoretically generated studies in the traditional sense have to be complemented by explorative approaches.

In the present study it was assumed that the Netherlands and Sweden represent two different sociocultural contexts for socialization and development. Both countries are similar because they belong to northwestern Europe, share democratic political systems, and have almost identical standards of social and economic development involving education, health care, child care, and social welfare. It is also assumed that adolescents in both countries face similar prospects for future education and employment and that they share identical experiences with regard to information in the mass media (i.e., news about world events, fashion, and music).

However, sociocultural dissimilarities between the two countries are also anticipated. For instance, one obvious difference is the historical fact that the Netherlands was involved in the Second World War while Sweden was not. Dutch adolescents are raised within a context of collective memories and symbols relating to the war (e.g., war cemeteries, parents and grandparents telling about the war, annual memory services for the fallen, and liberty and peace celebrations), while Swedish adolescents rarely, if ever, experience these kinds of cultural manifestations of memories of peace and war. Another difference with potential significance for family patterning and child rearing involves the impact of religion and religious values; that is, the Netherlands represents a mixed Catholic and Protestant tradition and Sweden a Protestant tradition only. Differences such as these are assumed to influence the conditions for understanding peace and war in the two countries.

Gender as a Special Case of Culture

Traditionally, gender has been referred to as a cause of differentiation without further consideration of the mechanisms underlying the differentiation processes. The recent increase in empirical research and theoretical conceptualizations within the feminist tradition (Brock-Utne, 1989; Gilligan, 1982; Harding, 1991; Haste and Baddely, 1991) and increasing emphasis on cultural-contextual factors in developmental processes (Bronfenbrenner, 1979; Cole, 1992; Elder, Modell, and Parke, 1993) have created the foundations for a different view on gender and variations in developmental outcomes. Instead of regarding gender as an independent individual variable, gender is now looked upon as a social construction and gender cultures are perceived as specific contexts for development (Hägglund, 1996).

Differences between male and female conceptions of peace and peace-related issues have been reported in several studies (Haavelsrud, 1970; Hakvoort and Oppenheimer, 1993; Hall, 1993). Various findings indicated a more personal-caring core element in girls' conceptions and a more technical-justice core element among boys. In anthropological studies, gender differences in social personality have repeatedly been reported: males are more "self assertive, achievement-oriented and dominant, and females more socially responsive, passive and submissive" (Berry et al., 1994, p. 25). According to a sociocultural paradigm of development, gender differences like these are interpreted as influenced by existing gender subcultures and their interrelation in a given societal system.

In research dealing with peace and war, little attention has been paid to the extremely high correlation between males and acts of violence (Brock-Utne, 1989). This is noteworthy because in education in general and in programs for peace education in particular, the educational goals frequently stress nonviolent values, cooperational competence, and human concern (Bjerstedt, 1993; Calleja, 1994). Because there is ample evidence that females develop sociomoral concepts that are better attuned to these issues than males, the influence of gender subcultures in the processes of developing conceptions of peace and war should be included in the analyses of empirical observations. One of the purposes of the research reported in this chapter is to focus on such analyses.

Purpose of the Comparative Study

The major purpose of the Dutch-Swedish comparative study is to describe and analyze patterns in the development of conceptions of peace, war, and strategies to attain peace among adolescents from both countries in order to examine universal and (sub)culture-specific characteristics in these developments.

The guiding hypothesis of this study involved the assumption that conceptions of peace and war, as well as strategies to attain peace are part of and reflect adolescents' development of social knowledge. In agreement with findings of qualitative changes in the development of social abilities (e.g., role taking; cf. Oppenheimer, 1978; Selman, 1980), qualitative changes are also expected in the development of conceptions of peace, war, and strategies to attain peace. Because variations, which may be attributed to cultural and subcultural influences, are expected in the type and content of conceptions, gender is included as a variable in the analyses in the comparative Dutch-Swedish study.

The qualitative changes in adolescents' conceptions are assumed to parallel the development of the ability of mutual role-taking, which develops between the ages of ten and thirteen (Selman, 1980). According to Selman, young children are not able to understand that their own point of view (i.e., perceptions, thoughts, and emotions) differs often from those of other children. Following the realization that different persons possess different points of view, adolescents come to understand that interpersonal relationships are reciprocal—that is, that points of view affect one another and are co-constructed in social interactions. When adolescents develop this understanding, they are able to place themselves in a third-person position (i.e., to step out of a two-person interaction) and view and understand the interaction from the third-person perspective. This ability defines mutual role-taking. Eventually in adolescence, they realize that there is no complete understanding of the social environment and that some social conventions, norms, and rules involve compromises (Hakvoort and Oppenheimer, 1993). The developing understanding that points of view differ and the ability to infer and comprehend the points of view of other people are thought to prevent the occurrence of misconceptions about other people and personal prejudices, and are thought to be necessary for a peaceful collaboration between nations (Piaget, 1989).

With respect to conceptions of peace, it is assumed that peace will be perceived initially as the negation of war (i.e., negative peace). In the course of development and in particular during adolescence, peace will become perceived also as a process toward integration or bilateral cooperation (i.e., positive peace; Galtung, 1964). In addition, it is expected that older adolescents will be able to define peace also in terms of abstract, norm-related concepts rather than concrete, materially related ones.

Method: Participants
The participants were 161 Dutch (n = 76) and Swedish adolescents (*n* = 85). The adolescents of each nationality were divided into two age groups with mean ages 13.10 years (19 females and 19 males) and 15.10 years (21 females and 17 males) for the Dutch adolescents and 13.9 years (22 females and 19 males) and 15.10 years (24 females and 20 males) for the Swedish adolescents. The adolescents were selected from schools situated in middle-class urban neighborhoods in the Netherlands and Sweden and were all of Dutch or Swedish nationality, respectively.

Materials and Procedure

To assess the development of the understanding of peace, war, and strategies to attain peace, all adolescents were individually interviewed at school using identical semistructured interview procedures in both countries. All the interviews were taped and transcribed. This interview procedure was developed and tested in a previous study (Hakvoort, 1989; Hakvoort and Oppenheimer, 1993). The interview and the coding procedure for the responses were discussed in detail prior to the comparative study to solve any differences in wording and interpretation that could prevent a comparison of the findings.

To allow the complexity of the concepts of peace and war to be reflected in the responses, different types of questions, thought to appeal to different aspects of these concepts, were included in the semi-structured interview:

1. The adolescents were requested to offer associations with the word "peace."

2. Following these free associations, the adolescents were asked to define "peace" to a class mate (i.e., peer) and to a five-year-old child. The purpose of these definitions was to probe other aspects of the peace concept than were obtained by free association.

3. Adolescents' conceptions of strategies to attain peace were assessed. The adolescents were required to formulate such strategies from different (social) positions—from an unspecified position, from the position of boss of their own country (i.e., a national position), from the position of boss of the world, and from the position of leader of a country in war (i.e., international positions).

4. To assess adolescents' conceptions of war, they were requested to express their associations with war and to define war to a classmate (i.e., peer) as well as to a five-year-old child.

Prompting techniques were used during the interviews to assess adolescents' potential understanding of the concepts. All participants were assured before the interview that there were no right or wrong answers. Prior to the interview, information was collected with respect to age, date, grade, gender, number of siblings, and the professions of both parents (i.e., information about socioeconomic status, SES). The total assessment procedure took approximately forty-five minutes.

Coding

The adolescents' responses to the different questions of the semistructured interview procedure were systematically transformed and aggregated into nominal categories. To achieve this, each response was reduced to its component themes. These thematic components, or units, were then assigned to and coded in different categories. Thematic components, specified and detailed descriptions of relevant content characteristics within a nominal category, were recorded in a coding manual to result in an unambiguous procedure. For the categorization of thematic components in the responses to the questions about the concept of peace (i.e., free associations and definitions of peace), eight major categories were used (see Table 4.1). Earlier empirical findings (Hakvoort and Oppenheimer, 1993) and theoretical considerations formed the guiding principle in the creation of the nominal categories. One of the general coding principles, used in the construction of these eight nominal categories, distinguished between thematic components based on concrete and material contents and components based on abstract and norm-related contents. In addition, the categorization system permitted a distinction between expressions

Table 4.1 The Eight Major Response Categories for Peace

Category 0	Missing	No conception of peace or not a straightforward answer.
Category 1	War-related	Think about war, war activities.
Category 2a*	Religion	Responses based on religion.
2b	Material-related Nature/pollution	Giving presents to people; building houses; taking care of nature; preventing destruction.
Category 3i	Positive emotions at an individual level	Being amiable, friends.
3g	Positive emotions at a global level	Conferences between leaders of different nations; a good economy is important; when countries go into business they become dependent.
Category 4i	Negation of war at an individual level	Absence of quarrels; absence of quarrel activities.
4g	Negation of war at a global level	Absence of war, war activities, and hostility; quietness, stillness.
Category 5a	Disarmament	Abolition or reduction of (nuclear) weapons.
5b	Sharing	Supporting suffering people.
Category 6	Human attitudes	Respect between and acceptance of people; no discrimination; tolerance.
Category 7	Universal rights	Liberty; freedom of speech and press; right to demonstrate; taking care of democracy; having fair elections.

* Distinct types of responses within a particular category are referred to by *a* and *b* (e.g., Categories 2a and 2b). Responses at the individual or global level are referred to by *i* and *g*, respectively (e.g., Categories 3i and 3g).

for positive and negative peace. Finally, a distinction was made between thematic components at an individual level (i.e., references to the immediate, interpersonal environment) and at a more global level (i.e., references to intranational and international relationships).

For the categorization of the responses to the questions about strategies to attain peace, an identical coding scheme was used (i.e., the same eight major, nominal categories, see Table 4.1). However, an additional nominal category (5b) was constructed to include "sharing." Ideas about "sharing" appeared only in the strategies to attain peace, for instance, when the importance was mentioned of "sharing goods with poor people, taking care of third world countries," and so on.

For the responses to the questions about war, the thematic components were assigned into and coded by means of ten major nominal categories (see Table 4.2).

With regard to the use of the different sets of nominal categories, two general categorization rules should be described explicitly. First, to prevent

Table 4.2 The Ten Major Response Categories for War

Category 0	Missing	No conception of war or not a straightforward answer.
Category 1	Peace-related	The absence of peace.
Category 2	Weapons/soldiers	The army, bombs, machine guns, Germans, Hitler, pistols, rifles, tanks, warship, nuclear weapons, enemy.
Category 3	Quarrel, conflict	Conflicts between peers.
Category 4	War activities	Shoot, kill, destroy, violence, fight.
Category 5	Human aspects of war	No kindness, no trust, egoism of people.
Category 6a*	Negative consequences of war	People dying, houses destroyed, poor people, a lot of blood, no food, misery.
6b	Positive consequences of war	People will protest; afterwards there will be peace.
Category 7	Negative emotions	Being afraid, crying, pitiful, a lot of pain, fright, fury.
Category 8a	Nonmutual conflict	A conflict between national leaders or nations, without referring to mutuality,
8b	Mutual conflict	Mutual character of fights is emphasized.
Category 9	Qualitative evaluation of war	Innocent people are punished or killed; they try to kill people to see justice done; they are angry because others attack their country.

*Distinct types of responses within a particular category are referred to by *a* and *b*.

verbal abilities from biasing the assessment of conceptual developmental levels, every category could be coded only once. When the obtained frequency tables for the nominal categories were transformed into data files for analyses, the use of a particular category obtained a score of 1; when the category was not used, a score of 0 was given. By this procedure, the assumption of independence of the categories was met. A second categorization rule allowed the identification of more than one thematic unit in the responses. However, an exception was made by the inclusion of a so-called exclusive category 0 (i.e., missing data). When a response was assigned to this category (i.e., category 0), it was not possible to identify any other theme and, in addition, to code any other category.

Interrater-reliability coefficients were computed between two or more raters for both data sets in the Netherlands as well as Sweden. For this purpose, parts of the interview protocols were read and coded by native speakers in each country. For the Dutch data, interrater-reliability coefficients between 0.80 and 0.97 were found. For the Swedish data, interrater-reliability coefficients ranged from 0.80 to 0.85.

The main focus of the thematic analyses dealt with variations and similarities in the distribution of the thematic components. For the sake of clarity, these variations were studied with respect to the dimensions involving concrete versus abstract conceptions, negative versus positive peace, and individual versus global orientations in the understanding of peace. These dimensions permitted a clustering of the categories into three distinct groups. The first group of categories represented a concrete level of reasoning involving concrete-negative-individual, concrete-negative-global, concrete-positive-individual, and concrete-positive-global reasoning. The second group of categories represented a transfer from concrete to abstract reasoning and involved negative-global (e.g., disarmament) and positive-global (e.g., sharing) reasoning. The third group of categories dealt with an abstract level of reasoning in terms of human attitudes and human rights. The presentation of the responses to the questions about peace and strategies to attain peace follows the order of these three dimensions.

The categories dealing with adolescents' associations and definitions concerning war represented a concrete versus abstract dimension. To this dimension, categories were added that included value-oriented responses and emotional attitudes toward war. Hence, three groups of categories or category clusters could be formed. The first group of categories represented a concrete level of reasoning (i.e., war-related objects, war-related activities, and conflicts at an individual level). The second group involved an abstract level of reasoning (i.e., nonmutual international conflicts and mutual international conflicts). Finally, the third group of categories represented responses with an evaluative, emotional orientation such as human aspects of war, negative consequences of war, and negative emotional attitudes toward war.

Results

To examine the influence of nationality, age, and gender on adolescents' conceptions of peace and war (i.e., the interaction with different content categories) hierarchical loglinear analyses were used (Wickens, 1989). Hierarchical loglinear analysis aims at finding the best model to describe the obtained data (i.e., describing the independence and/or interactions between the variables).[1]

The Concept of Peace and Strategies to Attain Peace: Concrete Level of Reasoning

Concrete-Negative-Individual Orientation (Nominal Category 4i)

A large proportion (75 percent) of the adolescents demonstrated a concrete-negative-individual orientation (i.e., category 4i) in at least one of the seven responses to the questions dealing with peace (associations, definitions, and strategies). The most general themes in this category were "you should not fight or quarrel with friends at school" and "you should not be angry with your boyfriend."

Although a majority of adolescents did use this category, the data showed a variation in the frequency of this category over the different questions. The concrete-negative-individual orientation in the responses was most frequently used in the responses to questions in which the subjects were encouraged to associate with peace (26 percent), had to define the concept of peace to a peer (34 percent), in particular to a five-year-old (57 percent), and when asked to formulate strategies to attain peace from an unspecified position (24 percent). When strategies had to be formulated from any of the specified positions (i.e., a national leader, a world leader, or a leader of a country in war) very few themes of this nature were evident.

The statistical testing of independence of the variation in relation to country (C), age (A), and gender (G), demonstrated a systematic variation in the explanations of the concept of peace to a five-year-old. Dutch females and Swedish males were more inclined to use this category than the other participants ([CAG][CG4i], $G^2 = 4.12$, $df = 4$, $p > 0.05$). For strategies to attain peace from an unspecified position, a similar pattern was found. This category was more frequently used by Dutch females and Swedish males ([CAG][CG4i], $G^2 = 1.66$, $df = 4$, $p > 0.05$).

Concrete-Negative-Global Orientation (Nominal Category 4g)

This orientation was most frequently found in the responses. Almost all adolescents mentioned the absence or negation of war or war activities in at least one of their responses to questions about peace and strategies to attain peace.

Like with the category previously discussed, the tendency to use the concrete-negative-global orientation varied across the questions. The highest frequency for this orientation was observed for the question pertaining to the formulation of strategies from the specified position as a leader of a country in war (96 percent). The lowest frequency was evident when the adolescents were requested to explain peace to a five-year-old (42 percent).

The analyses of variations in the use of this category revealed systematic interactions between gender and country. Males more often than females referred to the absence of war and war activities when defining peace to a friend ([CAG][G4g], $G^2 = 8.43$, $df = 6$, $p > 0.05$). Furthermore, when explaining peace to a five-year-old, the statistical analyses indicated a dominance of males' responses in this category. There was also a systematic interaction with country ([CAG][C4g][G4g], $G^2 = 6.04$, $df = 5$, $p > 0.05$): Dutch adolescents more frequently used this category than Swedish adolescents. A similar contribution of country and gender was found in the responses to the question of how to make peace from an unspecified position ([CAG][C4g][G4g], $G^2 = 3.93$, $df = 5$, $p > 0.05$). Male and Dutch adolescents more frequently mentioned strategies such as "to stop war and war activities" than females and Swedish adolescents. However, when the same question was asked from the position of being the leader of their own country, the analyses revealed only that the Swedish adolescents used this category more than the Dutch adolescents ([CAG][C4g], $G^2 = 4.03$, $df = 6$, $p > 0.05$).

Concrete-Positive-Individual Orientation (Nominal Category 3i)

The thematic components characterizing this orientation included peace to mean being friends, being nice, playing together, and so on. In total, 86 percent of the adolescents used this thematic component at least once in the responses.

This category was observed more often in responses to questions requiring adolescents to associate to and to define peace than in questions requiring them to formulate strategies to attain peace. "Being friends" did not seem to be regarded as a very effective strategy to attain peace, particularly not from the position of being a national or international leader.

Various significant interactions between age, country, gender, and variations in the distribution of this category could be demonstrated. Female adolescents and younger adolescents used this category more often when free associations were requested ([CAG][G3i][A3i], G^2 = 8.68, df = 5, p > 0.05). Females also used positive emotions more frequently when asked to define peace to a five-year-old ([CAG][G3i], G^2 = 3.88, df = 6, p > 0.05). Also, when required to formulate strategies to attain peace from an unspecified position, female adolescents more frequently than male adolescents offered strategies involving making friends, being nice to each other, and feeling happy ([CAG][G3i][C3i], G^2 = 6.19, df = 5, p > 0.05). For the latter question, Swedish adolescents considered this strategy more often appropriate than Dutch adolescents.

Concrete-Positive-Global Orientation (Nominal Category 3g)
Compared to the use of the concept of negative peace on a global level by almost all adolescents, the concept of positive peace on a global level was used considerably less. Only 58 percent of the adolescents mentioned in their responses characteristics of positive peace (i.e., showing a concrete positive orientation on a global level), such as international meetings and conferences, economical and commercial relations, a united Europe, and exchange of trade. The use of this category was most frequently observed in three of the questions requiring adolescents to formulate strategies to attain peace.

The statistical analyses indicated that the Swedish adolescents used the concept of positive peace from a global perspective more often than Dutch adolescents when formulating strategies to attain peace from an unspecified position (proportion 25.5 percent; [CAG][C3g], G^2 = 3.13, df = 6, p > 0.05). When required to formulate strategies to attain peace from the position of leader of the world, female adolescents as well as the older adolescents used this category more frequently (i.e., proportion 20.5 percent; [CAG][A3g][G3g], G^2 = 8.48, df = Ê5, p > 0.05). While this category was also evident when asked to formulate strategies from the position of leader of a country (proportion 32.9 percent), no comprehensible model could be fitted to the empirical data.

From Concrete to Abstract Levels of Reasoning
Negative-Global Orientation in Responses to Questions about Peace and Strategies to Attain Peace (Nominal Category 5a: Disarmament)
Comparatively few responses involving this category were observed. Disarmament was mentioned by 37 percent of the adolescents in one of their

responses and was most frequently observed in the responses to the question concerning strategies to attain peace from the position of a world leader (26 percent). In the associations with peace, as well as in the definitions of peace, the theme of disarmament was hardly mentioned.

The statistical analyses revealed country to interact with the occurrence of this theme ([CAG][CA5a], $G^2 = 2.28$, $df = 4$, $p > 0.05$). The Dutch adolescents mentioned disarmament as a strategy to attain peace more frequently than the Swedish adolescents. Although the overall use of this category is low, the difference between Dutch and Swedish adolescents is of interest.

Positive-Global Orientation in Responses to Strategies to Attain Peace (Nominal Category 5b: Sharing)
The category "sharing" included references to different kinds of support of suffering people around the world such as helping; sending money, clothes and medicine; taking care of the wounded, and so on. In total, 51 percent of the adolescents used this category in at least one of their responses.

Little variation in the use of "sharing" across the questions dealing with the formulation of strategies was present. For each of the four questions dealing with strategies approximately 20 percent of the adolescents used this category. The statistical analyses indicated that Swedish adolescents used this category more than Dutch adolescents in their responses to the question to formulate strategies to attain peace from an unspecified position ([CG][C5b], $G^2 = 2.23$, $df = 2$, $p > 0.05$; in this model, age was collapsed because too many of the expected frequencies in the cells were too low). When responding from the position as leader of their own country, female adolescents referred more frequently to sharing, supporting, and helping as a strategy than male adolescents ([CAG][G5b], $G^2 = 9.90$, $df = 6$, $p > 0.05$). An identical gender difference was found for the responses to the question from the position of a leader of a country in war ([CAG][G5b], $G^2 = 8.74$, $df = 6$, $p > 0.05$). The females from the youngest age group, in particular, used this category more often. The analyses of the responses from the position of a leader of the world indicated a complex interaction pattern between country, age, and gender. This finding was, however, not strong enough to be interpreted unequivocally.

The Concept of Peace and Strategies to Attain Peace: Abstract Level of Reasoning
The thematic components considered to represent an abstract level of reasoning and coded as such involve primarily ideas and views that corresponded

to a positive definition of the concept of peace. In these categories respect for other people, tolerance, democratic values, and equality were the frequent themes that were emphasized by the adolescents.

Orientation toward Human Attitudes (Nominal Category 6)
This category was observed with 60 percent of the adolescents. The most frequent use of this category was evident for the responses to the strategy questions and in particular when in the position of a world leader.

The statistical analyses indicated that more male than female adolescents referred to this category when explaining peace to a classmate ([CAG][G6], $G^2 = 3.05$, $df = 6$, $p > 0.05$). When asked how peace can be achieved from an unspecified position, from the position of leader of a country as well as from the position of leader of the world, Dutch adolescents used this category more frequently than Swedish adolescents ($G^2 = 6.46$ [$df = 6$], $G^2 = 2.96$ [$df = 2$], and $G^2 = 4.02$, [$df = 4$], respectively, with $p > 0.05$). There was also an indication for an increase in the tendency to use this category as the Dutch adolescents were older. With the Swedish adolescents a decrease with age in the use of this response category was observed.

Orientation toward Human Rights (Universal Rights; Nominal Category 7)
In this category, the thematic components referring to democracy, justice, freedom, and the right to demonstrate were coded. Approximately 47 percent of the adolescents used this category at least once in their responses to the questions.

The highest frequency for the use of this category was observed in the responses to the questions of how to attain peace from the position of leader of a country and leader of the world. A significant effect for country was evident in the question involving the position of leader of a country only. Though in the resulting model, age was collapsed because too many of the expected frequencies in the cells were too low, it was the Dutch adolescents again who used this category more frequently than the Swedish adolescents ([CG][C7], $G^2 = 4.12$, $df = 2$, $p > 0.05$).

The Concept of War
In this section, the questions with respect to the concept of war (i.e., the questions requiring the adolescents to associate to war, to define war to a peer and to a five-year-old child) will be discussed. As was noted previously, the nominal categories were designed according to levels of reasoning (concrete versus abstract) and evaluative-emotional contents.

Concrete Level of Reasoning

War-related objects (e.g., weapons, soldiers, and bombs), war-related activities (e.g., shooting, killing, and fighting), and conflicts at an individual level (e.g., quarrels) were mentioned frequently at least once in the responses to any of the questions dealing with war. The proportions for these themes were 57 percent, 84 percent, and 59 percent, respectively.

Though the statistical analyses revealed interactions between themes involving war-related objects and activities, age, country, and gender, these interactions were too complex to permit a straightforward interpretation. Conflicts at an individual level were referred to most frequently in the responses to the question requiring the adolescents to explain war to a five-year-old child. No significant interactions with age, country, or gender were found.

Abstract Level of Reasoning

Two categories were defined to represent an abstract level of reasoning. Both categories referred to conflicts at an international, macro level. The first category involved thematic components in which reference was made to war as a conflict between two nations without any mention of the mutuality of the conflict. The second category involved components in which the mutuality of international conflicts was indicated. Relatively few adolescents (40 percent) offered themes in which no mention was made of the mutuality of international conflicts. Thematic components in which war was perceived as a conflict between nations were most frequent when the adolescents were asked to explain war to a peer. Responses referring to the mutuality of international conflicts occurred even less (31 percent). The most frequent use of this category was observed also when the subjects explained war to a peer. No significant interactions with age, country, or gender were found.

Evaluative, Emotional Orientation

The final categories discussed in this chapter deal with thematic components in which evaluative and emotional aspects of war were mentioned. The data revealed that human aspects related to war were hardly mentioned. Thematic components in which negative consequences of war were expressed such as destroyed buildings, dead friends, graveyards, no food, and so on were offered by 65 percent of the adolescents at least once in their responses to any of the questions. Negative consequences were mentioned in particular in the associations to war (65 percent) and barely

(16 percent) in the definitions of war to a classmate (Question 6b) and to a five-year-old child (Question 6c: 8 percent). More female than male adolescents associated war with negative consequences. In addition, 43 percent of the adolescents expressed negative emotional attitudes toward war at least once in their responses (e.g., being afraid, pitiful, crying, and so on). This category was most frequently used by female adolescents in the associations to war.

Discussion

The main focus of the present study was to examine adolescents' conceptions of peace, war, and strategies to attain peace and to study the contributions of gender and nationality (i.e., country or culture) in variations of thematic components. The findings demonstrated amply that peace and war are complex and multifaceted concepts and are situated in a three-dimensional space. The axes of this space consist of the dimensions concrete versus abstract reasoning (i.e., reflecting increasing cognitive abilities), negative versus positive conceptualization (i.e., reflecting a progressing understanding of dynamic processes; cf. Chandler and Boutilier, 1992), and individual versus general or global perception (i.e., reflecting increasing social cognitive abilities). In addition, variations in reasoning about peace and war were observed that related to cultural factors such as nationality (i.e., country) and gender. No clear age-related variations in reasoning about peace and war could be demonstrated in this study. The latter finding is not surprising if it is noted that major changes in conceptions of peace and war are observed during earlier ages (e.g., between the ages of nine and twelve; Hakvoort, 1996). The findings for the age groups studied suggest that from the age of thirteen a (temporal) stabilization in the development of conceptions of peace and war is present.

In particular in Dutch and Swedish adolescents' associations with and definitions of peace concrete reasoning was evident. In this reasoning, however, different dimensions of the concept of peace could be distinguished. These dimensions are similar to distinctions made in discussions about the concept of peace in earlier research (Brock-Utne, 1989; Galtung, 1964, 1969); that is, the distinction between negative and positive peace, as well as between individual and global perspectives. The adolescents' ability to relate peace to the absence of organized, direct violence (i.e., situations characterized by the absence or negation of war and war activities) corresponds with earlier findings (e.g., Hakvoort and Oppenheimer, 1993; Hall, 1993; Rosell, 1968). In addition, adolescents perceived peace to involve social relationships and positive feelings between people. In short, all adolescents in the present study conceptualized peace and strategies to attain peace on a concrete level of reasoning.

Abstract conceptions of peace appeared primarily in adolescents' formulations of strategies to attain peace. The present study does not warrant the conclusion, however, that concrete levels of reasoning are replaced by more abstract levels of reasoning as the adolescents are older. Rather, adolescents' understanding of peace, and strategies to attain peace in particular, appears to become extended or elaborated. Instead of a radical change, adolescents' conceptions of peace showed a progressive inclusion of abstract, norm-related ideas about peace. That is, references were made to the absence of indirect, structural violence (e.g., discrimination and dictatorships), or the presence of equality, respect, and tolerance among people, groups, and nations, as well as universal, human rights and democratic systems. In other words, adolescents seem to understand the complexity of the concept of peace and use a set of different dimensions in their responses in which concrete as well as abstract features of the concept of peace are combined. Which dimension was emphasized in the conceptions of peace depended upon the focus of the question. That is, different types of conceptions of peace were obtained by the request to define peace and the request to formulate strategies to attain peace. The latter request resulted in different conceptions again depending on the position from which strategies had to be formulated (i.e., from the position of leader of the world or from the position of leader of a country). For example, when requested to formulate strategies from the position of a national or international leader, conceptions of peace were characterized by global rather than individual perspectives.

Variations in the responses that could be related to the nationality of the adolescents were most clearly evident in conceptions about strategies to attain peace. However, with definitions of peace, nationality-related differences were also evident. Dutch adolescents more frequently than their Swedish peers defined peace in terms of negative peace (i.e., the negation of war and war activities). When strategies to attain peace had to be formulated from the position of a leader, however, the opposite nationality-related difference was observed. Swedish adolescents more frequently than their Dutch peers conceptualized peace by the absence or negation of war and war activities. Differences between the Dutch and the Swedish adolescents in the strategies formulated to attain peace occurred also in the references to positive, global strategies (e.g., positive international relations, global meetings and conferences, and trade exchanges), disarmament, and sharing (e.g., sending clothes, food, and medicines to countries in war, helping and taking care of people). With the exception of the position of leader of a country in war, Dutch adolescents as compared to Swedish adolescents more often used abstract, norm-related values like equality, nondiscrimination, and democratic values as important strategies for building and keeping peace. In addition, with strategies formulated from the position of world leader, Dutch adolescents also referred more often to disarmament than Swedish adolescents. When the position was unspecified, Swedish adolescents referred more frequently than their Dutch peers to positive global strategies and sharing as a strategy to attain peace.

These nationality-related differences suggest different orientations toward strategies to attain peace. To attain and keep peace, Dutch adolescents emphasized structural, societal prerequisites for peace that are present in their own country (i.e., the Netherlands). Their conceptions of peace, as expressed in this study, appeared to be dominated by the idea that foremost, peace must be taken care of in one's own society; that is, peace does not necessarily imply a state of nonwar. Consequently, nonoppressive societal structures, liberty, and democracy were regarded necessary to maintain peace. Perceptions of peace by Swedish adolescents differed in two respects from those of their Dutch peers. When discussing general strategies, Swedish adolescents focused more on a global orientation by referring to international collaboration and sending help to other countries. In addition, to attain peace from the position of a national leader, "stopping all war activities" was considered the most relevant strategy by Swedish adolescents.

If these exploratory findings for the differences between Swedish and Dutch adolescents' orientations toward peace are summarized, it could be argued that Swedish adolescents demonstrate an orientation emphasizing "peace attainment," while Dutch adolescents show an orientation that focuses on "peace keeping."

From a cross-cultural perspective it is of importance to examine whether sociocultural and sociohistorical differences between the Netherlands and Sweden can function as explanations for the summarized differences between Dutch and Swedish adolescents in their orientation toward peace. Earlier in this paper, we assumed that nations or societies develop their own social institutions (e.g., socialization and education) based on sociohistorical processes that are often unique for each nation or society. Based on this assumption, it can be argued speculatively that the emphasis on the creation and maintenance of social structures necessary to prevent violence and war and the positive evaluation of such structures is present more saliently in a society in which war and threats of war have been recent reality (i.e., in the Netherlands) than in a society in which war and war activities, for centuries, have been taking place elsewhere in the world. In addition, it can be speculated that prioritizing activities to stop any war "out there" is more logical in a society, like the Swedish, that has experienced peace as a more or less normal situation for many centuries. The differences may also be related to political and cultural variations such as educational practice and child-rearing patterns. Additional research is definitely needed to test these assumptions.

In short, the findings in the present study do not yet permit unequivocal conclusions with respect to whether and how cultural factors influence nationality-related differences in adolescents' view of peace and strategies to keep and attain peace, in particular. The findings demonstrate, however, important and complex variations in the underlying rationales for the understanding of peace and strategies to attain peace that are likely to coincide with sociohistorical differences between the Dutch and Swedish societies.

When gender differences are examined in greater detail, the inclusion in the responses of positive emotions at an individual level appeared to be particularly sensitive for gender. Females' more frequent use of personal, individual, and social associations and definitions was reported already in earlier research (Hakvoort and Oppenheimer, 1993). Of interest, however, is that this gender difference decreased substantially when females had to respond from a perspective that was not their own (e.g., in the present study, these other perspectives were operationalized by the positions of national leader, world leader, and leader of a country at war). This finding suggests that gender differences in the verbalization of the understanding of the concept of peace and strategies to attain peace are a consequence of the wording of questions and the nature of tasks.

A frequent gender difference reported in the literature concerns the observation that females are more concerned with other human beings and social relations than males and that males are more concerned with social rules and justice than females (cf. Harding, 1991). While in the present study, such differences in gender-related concerns were small, their direction was always in correspondence with the earlier findings. The concrete-positive and individual category (e.g., being friends) was more frequently used by female than male adolescents in the definitions of peace, as well as in the formulation of general strategies to attain peace. When strategies to attain peace had to be formulated from the position of a leader, the responses suggested a gender difference in the conception of leadership. According to the female adolescents, leaders should use strategies involving, for example, sending clothes and money and taking care of and helping people (i.e., sharing) to attain peace. A world leader should, again according to the female adolescents, be concerned with more concrete-positive and global strategies to attain peace (e.g., organizing international meetings and conferences, economical and commercial relations, and so on). While male adolescents did not exclude such "female conceptions" from their responses, they mentioned such conceptions less. When a contrast is made between both gender groups, the female adolescents in this study confirmed earlier findings that demonstrated females' greater emphasis on positive social actions as effective strategies to attain peace.

In agreement with earlier studies, the associations to and definitions of war were dominated by concrete aspects of the war, like war-related objects (e.g., weapons, soldiers, and bombs), war-related activities (e.g., shooting, killing, and fighting), and conflicts at an individual level (e.g., quarrels). Only a few adolescents associated war with abstract concepts like nonmutual and mutual international conflicts. Conceptions of war as a nonmutual or mutual conflict between nations, though infrequent, were primarily observed in explanations of war to a peer. An evaluative, emotional orientation, including negative consequences of war and negative emotional attitudes toward war, was observed in the association responses in particular. More female than male adolescents associated war with negative consequences and negative emotions.

The present study is clearly a first step in the examination of culture- and gender-related differences in the way children and adolescents perceive and understand the world they live in. The limits set by the scope of this chapter required us to make a selection of the variables that could be presented and discussed. Nevertheless, the findings suggest that the Netherlands and Sweden—two societies thought to be part of Western culture—represent two different sociocultural settings resulting in differences in adolescents' conceptions of peace and war. These findings have direct implications for peace-education curricula and peace educators.

At the end of the nineteenth century, peace educators expressed their concern about how to educate children so that they would be able to deal with conflicts and would be prepared for a global society (Bjerstedt, 1993). Since the Second World War and the formation of the United Nations, in particular, education has been considered as one of the major instruments to promote peace. For instance, a UNESCO recommendation in 1974 emphasized the role of education in fostering international understanding and "in promoting cooperation and solidarity across national boundaries and strengthening awareness of and commitment to basic rights and liberties" (Thelin, 1991, p. 9). At present, educators wish to do more than offer a learning climate in which children learn to develop a critical and meaningful understanding and interpretation of the world. In a rapidly changing world, in which a multitude of information channels permit international dialogue, the exchange of experience with respect to the practice of peace education and its outcomes is perceived as a necessary task (see Bjerstedt, 1993). Research concerning peace-education curricula have been based occasionally on developmental theory and design (e.g., in evaluations of educational programs on cooperation and conflict solution). However, these examples are rare (Hägglund, 1996).

The main focus in this chapter has been on the concept of peace, a focus that has been directed probably by the realization that Western culture is in general a bellicose culture (Bjerstedt, 1993) in which attitudes toward war are (not yet) valued negatively (Oppenheimer, 1995, 1996). Developing conceptions of peace should be our main concern, in particular when considering means to foster such conceptions in the course of peace-building activities. In any attempts to promote such peace-building activities (e.g., peace education), observed differences in sociocultural settings should be taken into account. For instance, peace-education curricula should be adapted to differences in orientation toward peace (e.g., an orientation of "peace attainment" with the Swedish adolescents and an orientation of "peace keeping" with the Dutch adolescents), as well as differences in the understanding of peace and war between female and male adolescents.

Notes

1. The hierarchical loglinear analyses were carried out in the following steps. First, it was necessary to define a "hypothetical" model that could be tested against the empirical data. Because the numbers of participants belonging to the independent variables country (C), age (A), and gender (G) were a priori selected (see the Participants section) and the interactions between these "predictors" (i.e., C x A x G, henceforth [CAG]) were not of any particular interest for the analyses, the interaction was automatically included in every tested model.

Next, the model of independence between the variables and its predictors was tested. For example, for the responses to free associations, the model of independence for category 3i was [CAG] [3i]. The computed likelihood for the model of independence resulted in a ratio Chi-square $G^2 = 23.86$ ($df = 7$. $p < 0.01$). A significant ratio-Chi-square indicated that this model did not fit the empirical data (i.e., G^2 is relatively large in relation to the degrees of freedom). To achieve an improvement of fit, interactions of category 3i with one of the predictors C, A, and G were systematically added to the model (i.e., [CAG][C3i], [CAG][A3i], and [CAG][G3i]). Not one of these models fit (i.e., all *p* values were smaller than 0.05). Of the added interactions, however, the interaction with age indicated the best improvement of the fit. Consequently, the analysis could be continued with the model [CAG][A3i] as point of departure, while the interactions with the other two predictors were systematically added again (i.e., [CAG][A3i][C3i] and [CAG][A3i][G3i]). The latter model, including interactions between category 3i and age and between category 3i and gender, resulted in a model that fit the data. To be sure the best description of the data was found, models with higher order interactions were tested also. Because no significant improvements of the fit were found, the simpler model (i.e., with less interactions) was selected to describe the data best. In the presentation of the results, only the simplest models are presented. In the text, only the proportion of participants who used a particular theme in their responses to a question are presented. In the analyses themselves, the proportions of users as well as nonusers of a particular theme or thematic unit were included.

References

Barrett, M., and Short, J. (1992). Images of European people in a group of 5–11-year-old English schoolchildren. *British Journal of Developmental Psychology, 10,* 339–363.

Berry, J. W., Poortinga, Y. H., Segall, M. H., and Dasen, P. R. (1994). *Cross-cultural psychology. Research and applications.* Cambridge, UK: Cambridge University Press.

Bjerstedt, Å., ed. (1993). *Peace education: Global perspectives.* Stockholm: Almqvist and Wiksell International.

Boyd, B. J., Wallinga, C., Skeen, P., and Paguio, L. P. (1994). Children's and adolescents' response to the prospect of nuclear war: A review. *International Journal of Behavioral Development, 17,* 697–715.

Brock-Utne, B. (1989). *Feminist perspectives on peace and peace education.* New York: Pergamon Press.

Bronfenbrenner, U. (1979). *The ecology of human development: Experiences by nature and design.* Cambridge, MA: Harvard University Press.

Calleja, J. (1994). *Alternative trends to peace-building: A collection of critical essays.* Malta: Mireva Publications.

Chandler, M. J., and Boutilier, R. G. (1992). The development of dynamic system reasoning. *Human Development, 35,* 121–137.

Chomsky, N. (1972). *Problems of knowledge and freedom.* London: Fontana.

Cole, M. (1992). Context, modularity, and the cultural constitution of development. In L. T. Winegar and J. Valsiner (1992), *Children's development within social context. Vol. 2. Research and methodology* (pp. 5–32). Hillsdale, NJ: Erlbaum.

Cooper, P. (1965). The development of the concept of war. *Journal of Peace Research, 2,* 1–17.

Covell, K., Rose-Krasnor, L., and Fletcher, K. (1994). Age differences in understanding peace, war, and conflict resolution. *International Journal of Behavioral Development, 17,* 717–737.

Elder, G. H., Modell, J., and Parke, R. D., eds. (1993). *Children in time and place. Developmental and historical insights.* Cambridge, UK: Cambridge University Press.

Evans, G. (1993). *Cooperating for peace: The global agenda for the 1990s and beyond.* St. Leonards, Australia: Allen and Unwin.

Galtung, J. (1964). Editorial. *Journal of Peace Research, 1,* 1–4.

Galtung, J. (1969). Violence, peace and peace research. *Journal of Peace Research, 6,* 167–191.

Gilligan, C. (1982). *In a different voice.* Cambridge, UK: Cambridge University Press.

Grossi, V. (1994). *Le pacifisme européen 1889–1914* (European pacifism 1889–1924). Bruxelles: Bruylant.

Haavelsrud, M. (1970). View on war and peace among students in West Berlin public schools. *Journal of Peace Research, 7,* 99–120.

Hägglund, S. (1996). Developing concepts of peace and war: Aspects of gender and culture. *Peabody Journal of Education, 71,* 29–41.

Hakvoort, I. (1989). *Children and adolescents about peace.* Master's thesis. Universiteit van Amsterdam, Department of Developmental Psychology.

Hakvoort, I. (1996). *Conceptualizations of peace and war from childhood through adolescence:*

A *social-cognitive developmental approach.* Doctoral dissertation. Universiteit van Amsterdam, Department of Developmental Psychology.

Hakvoort, I., and Oppenheimer, L. (1993). Children's and adolescents' conceptions of peace, war, and strategies to attain peace: A Dutch case study. *Journal of Peace Research, 30,* 65–77.

Hall, R. (1993). How children think and feel about war and peace: An Australian study. *Journal of Peace Research, 30,* 181–196.

Harding, S. (1991). *Whose science? Whose knowledge?: Thinking from women's lives.* Milton Keynes, UK: Open University Press.

Haste, H., and Baddely, J. (1991). Moral theory and culture: The case of gender. In W. M. Kurtines and J. L. Gewirtz, eds., *Handbook of moral behaviour and development. Vol 1: Theory* (pp. 223–249). Hillsdale, NJ: Erlbaum.

Jahoda, G. (1964). Children's concepts of nationality: A critical study of Piaget's stages. *Child Development, 35,* 1081–1092.

Kahnert, M., Pitt, D., and Taipale, I., eds., (1983). *Children and war.* Proceedings Siuntio Baths. Geneva, Switzerland: GIPRI.

Leavitt, L. A., and Fox, N. A. (1993). *The psychological effects of war and violence on children.* Hillsdale, NJ: Erlbaum.

McCreary Juhasz, A., and Palmer, L. L. (1991). Adolescents' perspective of ways of thinking and believing that promote peace. *Adolescence, 26,* 849–855.

Muller-Brettel, M. (1993). *Bibliography on peace research and peaceful international relations: The contributions of psychology 1900–1991.* München: K.G. Saur Verlag.

Oppenheimer, L. (1978). *Social cognitive development: A theoretical and empirical elaboration.* Doctoral dissertation. University of Nijmegen, Centrale Reprografie.

Oppenheimer, L. (1995). Peace, but what about social constraints? *Peace and Conflict: Journal of Peace Psychology, 1,* 383–397.

Oppenheimer, L. (1996). War as an institution, but what about peace? Developmental perspectives. *International Journal of Behavioral Development, 19,* 201–218.

Piaget, J. (1980). *To understand is to invent: The future of education.* Harmondsworth, UK: Penguin Books.

Piaget, J. (1989). Is an education for peace possible? *The Genetic Epistemologist, 17,* 5–9. (Original publication 1934.)

Piaget, J., and Weil, A. M. (1951). The development in children of the idea of the homeland and of relations with other countries. *International Social Science Bulletin, 3,* 561–578.

Punamäki, R.-L. (1987). *Childhood under conflict: The attitudes and emotional life of Israeli and Palestinian children.* Research Report no. 32. Tampere Peace Research Institute, Finland.

Rosell, L. (1968). Children's view of war and peace. *Journal of Peace Research, 5,* 268–276.

Russell, B. (1916). *Principles of social reconstruction.* London: George Allen and Unwin.

Selman, R. L. (1980). *The growth of interpersonal understanding: Developmental and clinical analyses.* New York: Academic Press.

Spielmann, M. (1986). If peace comes . . . future expectations of Israeli children and youth. *Journal of Peace Research, 28,* 231–235.

Targ, H. (1970). Children's developing orientations to international politics. *Journal of Peace Research, 7,* 79–97.

Thelin, B. (1991). *Peace education: A tentative introduction.* Stockholm: Swedish National Board of Education. Reports R 91:11.

Tolley, H., Jr. (1973). *Children and war: Political socialisation to international conflict.* New York: Teachers College Press.

Toner, I. J. (1994). Children and political violence: An introduction. *International Journal of Behavioral Development, 17,* 593–594.

Wickens, T. D. (1989). *Multiway contingency tables analysis for the social sciences.* Hillsdale, NJ: Erlbaum.

Part Two

Social Change and Political Conflicts

Part Two

Social Change and Political Conflicts

Chapter Five
The Gains and Losses of Bulgarian Youths during the Transition from Socialism to Democracy
A Longitudinal Study

Luba Botcheva

Introduction

There is now widespread agreement among researchers that ontogenetic development varies substantially in changing historical conditions and that the latter, interacting with age-graded and nonnormative influences can promote or suppress individual development (Baltes, 1983; Brent, 1978; Dannefer, 1984; Featherman and Lerner, 1985; Magnusson, 1990; Nesselroade and von Eye, 1985; Riegel, 1976). Studies have shown that young people frequently show marked differences in the effects of historical events (Elder, 1974, 1979, 1991). These studies have compelled researchers to investigate the resources, values, and expectations that people bring to new situations, and what the impact of these is on the resulting life course.

Bulgaria is one of the eastern/central European countries in transition from a totalitarian system to a democratic one. Since early 1990, the country has embarked on a course of democratization and economic liberalization, and it has adopted a policy designed to create a free-market economy. The dynamic social and political changes of the past few years have had a major impact on Bulgaria's youth. On the one hand, the transition to democracy increases the opportunities of young people in education, traveling, leisure, acquisition of new social roles, and competitiveness with other generations. On the other hand, young people (among other social groups) suffer from reduced living standards and feel the negative effects of the structural reforms in the economy and society. The rebuilding of almost all social institutions complicates the processes of identity formation and value orientation, and it affects personal decisions about central aspects of life.

This chapter will focus on the impact of social transformations on adolescent development during Bulgaria's shift from socialism to democracy. First, I will briefly discuss the political transformations that took place during early 1990s in Bulgaria. Second, I will describe the theoretical framework guiding the research program. Third, I will discuss the empirical results of this longitudinal study, which was started before the democratic changes and has continued through them. This study was conducted in unique and nonreplicable conditions, and despite its methodological limitations it can tell us a lot about the short-term effects of social changes. Few social scientists have the opportunity to analyze a natural experiment because baseline data are rarely collected in advance of social upheaval. This study, which began for different purposes, produced a valuable data set that can be readily analyzed for the effects of the fall of the socialist system.

Political Transformations in Bulgaria

Bulgaria was part of the Eastern bloc under the strong domination of the Soviet Union. During the Communist period the country underwent a transition from an agrarian-industrial to an industrial-agrarian model. However, economic development under forty-five years of socialism was, with few exceptions, regressive in nature.

Bulgaria had the most egalitarian model of social policy of all the socialist countries. This meant that citizens were guaranteed jobs, free health care, and free public education. After the collapse of socialism in 1989 this social policy could no longer be maintained, and the result was disappointment and an increased sense of insecurity.

Since early 1990, the country has changed course dramatically. In November 1989, President T. Zhivkov, who had been in power since 1954, was ousted; the first anti-Communist coalition was established, and in June 1990 the first free multiparty parliamentary elections were held. The former Communist Party won a small majority in the Parliament. In 1991 a second election was held, which UDF—a coalition of anti-Communist parties and organizations—won. This government was in power until the end of 1991, when an expert government came into power. In 1994 a third election was held, and the Socialist Party (previous Communist Party) won the elections. During these four years, various reforms to ensure the respect for human rights and liberties were made. But the frequent change of governments created a sense of instability and vague future prospects. Young people participated very actively in the ousting of the old regime, especially in the period 1990–1991, when they participated in several demonstrations and strikes, which led to changes in the government.

In economics, a series of laws encouraging the development of private business and property were voted in, although structural reforms in the economy and privatization are quite slow, negatively affecting living standards and increasing unemployment. The main reforms in the cultural field were related to the de-ideologizing of science, education, and the arts. The social paradigm shifted from collectivism to individualism.

The general trends of social change taking place in Bulgaria can be described as a transition from a society of constraint toward a society of choice, from uniformity toward pluralism, from predominantly collectivist to individualistic culture.

Theoretical Framework

Our research is based on several theoretical frameworks, such as Elder's studies of lives and historical changes (1991), Bronfenbrenner's ecology of human development (1979), and the concept of development as joint occurrence of gains and losses (Baltes and Baltes, 1990).

Developmental Environments

Using Bronfenbrenner's ecology of human development (1979) we can sketch out four levels of the developmental environment of young people that are being transformed during the transition from totalitarian socialism to democracy in Bulgaria: macrolevel (changes at the national level), exolevel (changes in the settings in which the developing person does not participate actively), mesolevel (changes in the immediate settings and their interrelations), and microlevel (changes in activities, roles, and personal relations).

The *macrosystem* refers to consistencies in the form and order of the lower-order system that exist within a given culture or subculture (Bronfenbrenner, 1979). During socialism the main characteristics of the macrosystem were related to the control of the state over the lives and actions of citizens and the lack of freedom and personal choice. The essence of social changes at this level of environment concerns the transition from a totalitarian to democratic society, the shift from a society of social constraint and restriction to a society of personal choice and individualism.

Social changes in the *exo-environment* refer to the changes in economic, cultural and political institutions. The effect of the changes in these institutions is not direct, as young people do not participate in them actively. They affect individuals' lives through the regulations and requirements they impose on the intermediate settings of the developing person (such as work, family, peers, community, school). For example, the development of the labor market affects the life of the individual through changes in living standards, changes in family economics and possible interruption in professional careers of parents, and new opportunities for work for young people.

Changes in the *meso-environment* of young people concern the transformations in their social settings (education, peers, community, work, family) and the interactions between them. They are related to changes in opportunity structures and to the behavioral demands, expectations, and responsibilities of young people. For example, in a situation of increased unemployment affecting both parents and young adults, a new kind of expectation or behavioral demand on adolescents might arise—the expectation that they will take on economic responsibility for the family, start work early rather than continuing their educations, and so on.

Changes at the *micro-environmental* level reflect the macro- and mesolevels, and in periods of drastic transformations they are crucial. The main changes at this level concern establishment of new patterns of roles, activities, and personal relationships within a social setting. For example, the economic adjustments of families lead to changes in the distribution of activities in family economics and to shifts in personal relationships—either to more support or to disruption (Elder, 1974).

These sets of changes affect individual development. However, we do not consider individual development as a monolithic process of progression and growth, but as a joint occurrence of gains and losses both within and across domains (Baltes and Baltes, 1990).

Gains and Losses

The gains and losses in individual development during social transformations can be analyzed in three ways: (1) as a result of changing opportunities for and restrictions on development, created by social institutions and settings; (2) as a result of the changing balance between human resources and available developmental options; and (3) as an expression of the multidirectionality of human development.

First, during global social transformation leading to changes in all institutions, a restructuring of the available pathways for development emerges. These transformations will benefit in the long run all segments of society, but in the short term they adversely affect young people by creating unstable and vague conditions of life.

The big gain for individual development during the transition to democracy is related to the increase of opportunities for personal choices within social institutions, and to the increase of the fields relevant for youth identification and value orientation. But at the same time the lack of clear rules and standards for realization of these choices and the instability during rapid transformations complicates the accomplishment of various developmental tasks. This leads to the loss of a sense of security in youth's future prospects, a factor negatively affecting their well-being.

Second, the gains and losses in individual development during social transformations depend not only on the varying conditions in social institutions, but also on the balance between an individual's resources and developmental options in a specific situation. According to the fit between available resources for development and the opportunities and restrictions of the environment, we can outline different types of "gainers" and "losers" during social transformations, such as advantaged and disadvantaged age cohorts, youths with higher and lower levels of psychosocial maturity, or groups living in various communities, regions, and settings, in which social transformations have different effects.

The third aspect for the analysis of gains and losses in individual development is related to the view of development as a multidirectional process. This means that the direction of changes in psychological functions varies within and across domains (Baltes and Baltes, 1990). The positive changes in one function can lead to negative changes in another.

Youth Behavioral Style, Social Identification, Value Estimations, and Well-Being

Studies of personality and politics (Greenstein, 1987; Sniderman, 1975) have shown that political systems impose specific behavioral demands and values on individuals. They create patterns of traits, beliefs, and attitudes that determine styles of behavior, patterns that are adaptive under the specific conditions of life within a society. The well-adjusted personality in a given social system usually identifies with the predominant culture, shares its values, and subsequently has a behavioral style that is adequate and adaptive to this system. Thus, despite different theoretical approaches, most studies agree that the well-adjusted personality in a democratic society is open-minded, independent, and respectful of the individual rights and values of other people (Inkeles, 1961; Sniderman, 1975). In totalitarian and authoritarian societies the state exercises firm control over the life of the individual. Independence and freedom of choice are not valued, and that is why the predominant adaptive behavior style is less active and independent than in democratic societies (Curtis, 1979).

The transition from socialism to democracy affects the conditions for personal choice in various social institutions, which in turn determine the way young people behave, feel, evaluate, and identify themselves in social reality. The emergence of new prevailing behavioral styles and personality patterns is a long process. It is related to the establishment of stable and fairly clear rules and regularities in the society. During a rapid transformation we can expect only a shift, a tendency toward a more active and independent style of behavior and way of thinking.

Behavioral style is not a single action or behavior, but a combination of behaviors that express a certain orientation and predominant motivation in a given domain of life. Following Ajzen and Fishbein (1980), the assumption was made that most social behaviors are rational and that they are based on the information that people have about their social reality. So it was expected that a change in the conditions of life and changes in the predominant value system of a socialist society would increase the probability that its members will start to exhibit more active and independent behavior.

Social identification is a characteristic of psychosocial functioning that expresses the way people define themselves in social reality—the way they answer the question "Who am I in social life?" It is based on social comparison with other people, the place one has in the social system, and one's concrete experience of different forms of activity. It was expected that the changes in these aspects of life during social transformations will affect the way people see themselves as active or passive in various social domains.

Another important characteristic of social relevance for the individual is his value system, the internalized social standards for behavior (Ball-Rokeach, 1984). Values are related to the question of what is good, what is desirable, what ought to be done (Scheibe, 1970). During social transformations, existing values in a society are reevaluated. This is a long process, and quick changes in a value hierarchy cannot be expected. Rather, it was assumed that there would be a reevaluation of existing values, and most probably of values that are related to the shift from social restriction and control to freedom of choice.

The last but not least important characteristic of psychosocial functioning that reflects social changes is well being; the way people feel about their self-identifications. It is determined both by one's social identification as an active or a passive person and by one's overall evaluation of social reality. How good (or how bad) is it to be socially active and independent of (or passive and dependent on) the social constraints of life?

Hypotheses

1. The shift from a society associated with social constraint and collectivism toward a society of individualism and choice will affect the way young people act, feel, evaluate and identify themselves in social life. More specifically, social transformations will affect those aspects of identifications, behavior, well-being, and value estimations that describe youngsters as either active, independent, and able to influence the social life around them, or passive and dependent on the social constraints around them.

2. The way identifications, values, behavioral style, and well-being change during social transformations will vary both within and between social domains (economics, culture, politics). This variability will be due both to the irregularity of social changes in these domains and to the differing sensitivity of psychological variables to these changes.

From Socialism to Democracy: A Longitudinal Study in Smolyan, Bulgaria

Participants and Procedure

Our study was started in April 1989, before the democratic changes took place in Bulgaria. The same people were studied every year in the period 1989–1992. The initial sample included 217 adolescents and young adults aged between sixteen and thirty years (116 Christian, 101 Muslim; 120 female, 97 male). In sex, religion, educational level, and socioeconomic background, the sample was representative of the young population of Smolyan, a little mountain town that is a regional center in south Bulgaria. It is interesting for its mixture of Bulgarian Christians and Bulgarian Muslims (*pomatci*) in the population.

Every year between 70 and 100 adolescents from the initial sample participated in the study (Table 5.1). The most likely reason for attrition involves the life transitions that took place during the period of the study. Most of the young people in the sample finished school, married or started work, and moved to other places. Because of the poor information system

Table 5.1 Number of Participants Annually by Gender and Age

Year	Age		Male,	Female,	Total
	Mean	SD	N	N	
1989	21.5	4.8	97	120	217
1990	20.3	4.7	32	40	72
1991	21.0	5.4	38	37	75
1992	21.1	5.2	51	62	113

in Bulgaria, it then became quite difficult to locate them. In the analysis all participants giving a response in a particular year were used. The statistics for successive years were therefore based on somewhat different subsets of the 158 participants who responded at least once after the first year. Because those who participated in the study and those who did not might give systematically different responses, we compared them by means of one-way ANOVA. For not even one variable were there significant differences at the 0.05 level. Accordingly, the data from the several respondent groups that permit comparison of a particular pair of adjacent years were combined in further analyses."

The data were collected once per year between 1989 and 1992. Participants were asked to complete a questionnaire we had developed, which was based on Ajzen and Fishbein's (1980) measurement techniques. Questionnaires were administered by well-trained interviewers, who explained to participants that all information they gave would remain anonymous, and that their identities would not be used in reporting the study.

Measurements
On the basis of the theoretical considerations discussed above and a pilot study, we developed several measures. They measured the extent to which the respondents were active, independent, and influencing their social environment, or the extent to which they were passive and dependent on the social constraints around them. Because these characteristics can be domain-specific, we explored them in three domains: economics, culture, and politics.

Behavioral Style
Behavioral style was measured by three pairs of situations, revealing the behavior in the economic, cultural, and political domains of two imaginary persons: one passive and dependent on social constraints; the other, active, independent, and influencing the conditions of life. The two models could be provisionally (conventionally) considered to be a citizen of a socialist society (person 1) and a citizen of a democratic society (person 2). The names of the persons, Didi and Gogo, are gender-neutral nicknames in Bulgaria. For example, in order to assess the predominant behavioral style in economic life, we constructed the following descriptions.

Person 1
Didi has few opportunities to choose his place of work. He works where he has been assigned and develops only those abilities and skills that are required by

his bosses. The amount of money he earns does not depend on him. His salary is quite stable. With the money he earns he cannot buy the things that he needs, either because he does not have the money to buy them, or because he cannot find these items in the shops and must seek out special ways to acquire them. Usually Didi spends his holidays at the places proposed by the trade unions. He invests his money mainly to improve his housing. He does not seek opportunities for additional work (private or state), because he does not believe that this will improve his status; rather, he believes that additional work is a source of more hassles.

Person 2
Let us think about Gogo. Gogo can choose his place of work. He works at the places where he can apply the best of his abilities and skills. He develops those personal qualities that allow him to increase permanently the quality of his work and the amount of his salary. The money he earns guarantees that he can buy all the items he needs and likes. Gogo can spend his holidays where he wants. He can invest his money in additional enterprises. He regularly seeks opportunities for additional work (private or state).

After reading each behavioral description, young people rated the extent to which they behaved like those imaginary people on a seven-point scale ranging from 3 (extremely false) to −3 (extremely true) for person 1 and −3 (extremely false) to 3 (extremely true) for person 2. Adding the scores obtained by the two situations was a suitable way of combining the two responses into a single score, which could range from −6 to +6. Combined scores were calculated for the three domains investigated (economic, cultural, political). A positive score indicates that young people behave mostly like person 2, the active independent person who can influence the conditions of life ("citizen of democratic society"); a negative score indicates that the "socialist," passive type of behavior predominates in this particular domain.

Social Identification
Youth social identification was measured by nine pairs of adjectives (three pairs for each domain). The adjectives describe an active independent or a passive person. The list of characteristics was composed on the basis of a content analysis of the interviews conducted in the pilot study. We asked young people to list the adjectives would they use to describe an active or a passive person in various domains of social life. The pairs of adjectives

used in the main study for social identification in economic life were *poor-rich*, *unsatisfied-satisfied*, and *nonenterprising-enterprising;* in cultural life they were *uneducated-educated, uncultured-cultured, unsophisticated-sophisticated;* and in political life they were *unprotected by law-protected by law; oppressed-free; dependent-independent.* Participants rated themselves on a seven-point scale ranging from –3 to +3. The scores for every group of three items were averaged to create a single score, indicating how an individual identifies socially in a given domain of economic, cultural, or political life. The Cronbach alpha reliabilities for these subscales were 0.51, 0.69, and 0.75, respectively.

Value Estimations

Young people were asked to evaluate each of the characteristics used for their self-identification on a seven-point scale, as follows: "According to me, to be enterprising is:" ("Bad" = –3; "Good" = +3). The scores for the estimations of the characteristics of the passive person were reversed. By summing up the scores for every pair of characteristics (e.g., enterprising-nonenterprising) a combined score was obtained, showing the extent to which the characteristics of the socially active person are positively evaluated and those of the passive one are negatively evaluated. A large sum of the two scores means that the characteristics of "activity" (enterprising) are considered as more positive and the characteristics of "passivity" (nonenterprising) are thought to be more negative. Then the scores for every three pairs of characteristics within a given domain were averaged to create a single score, identifying the range of bad/good evaluations of social passivity and activity within each domain. The Cronbach alpha reliabilities for these subscales were 0.61, 0.54, and 0.57 respectively.

Well-Being

We were interested not only in how young people identify themselves within different social domains, but also in how they feel about these identifications. Participants can identify themselves from our theoretical perspective negatively, as socially passive (for instance, they might describe themselves in economics as nonenterprising) and they can feel badly about this identification because according to them to be nonenterprising is bad. On the other hand, a person can have the same negative identification but can feel good about it because he believes that to be nonenterprising is good. In order to capture this subjective feeling about one's identification, we calculated a well-being score. It was calculated as a product of the corresponding self-identification and value estimation scores. In each domain, the score for the identification of the individual with proposed pairs of adjectives (e.g., nonenterprising-enterprising) was multiplied by the score on the relevant value estimation scale. The bipolar scale treats the statement that one defines himself as enterprising and feels good about it as equivalent to the statement of a person who defines himself as nonenterprising but feels good about it. For each domain—economics, culture, and politics—a combined well-being score was generated by averaging the products of the multiplication of the corresponding identification and value estimation scores within a given domain.

Statistical Procedure

Change in a given variable between two consecutive years was captured by subtracting a score in the earlier year from the corresponding score in the later year; thus a positive number indicates an increase in the score with the elapse of time after the earlier year. The amount of change was tested by means of a t-test.

Statistical significance of the within-subject change of those who participated in both years is treated by means of the paired t-test. The between-subject change for the participants who participated in one year, but not in the other, was tested by two-sample t-test. With few exceptions the paired differences and the two-sample differences were closely similar and were pooled by weighting them inversely with the squares of their estimated errors (Moses, 1986).

A positive difference in the investigated variables means that young people in a subsequent year function more actively and independently in various domains of social life.

Results

Table 5.2 Mean Changes in Behavioral Style, Social Identification, Value Estimations, and Well-Being between 1989 and 1990

1989 vs. 1990	Mean Difference	SE(d)
	Behavioral Style	
Economics	0.00	0.34
Culture	−0.51	0.29
Politics	0.68	0.36

(continued)

Table 5.2 *(continued)*

1989 vs. 1990	Mean Difference	SE(d)
	Social Identification	
Economics	–0.31*	0.12
Culture	–0.10	0.10
Politics	–0.47*	0.17
	Value Estimations	
Economics	0.69*	0.24
Culture	–0.06	0.10
Politics	0.21	0.12
	Well-Being	
Economics	–0.39	0.24
Culture	–0.18	0.20
Politics	–0.78*	0.33

*$p<0.05$. Positive numbers = mean increase; negative numbers = mean decrease.

Changes between 1989 and 1990
Social Identification
Significant changes are observed in Table 5.2 in the way young people identify themselves in economic and political life. During 1989–1990 youths started to identify themselves as less independent and influencing their social environment. In economic life young people identified themselves as less rich, enterprising, and economically satisfied; in political life, they identify themselves as less protected by law, less free and independent.

Value Estimations
In 1990, young people estimated the characteristics of an economically active person more positively and those of the passive one as worse than in 1989. Thus, the respondents started to evaluate being nonenterprising, poor, and unsatisfied more negatively and being enterprising, rich, and satisfied more positively.

Well-Being
The change was found in the way young people felt about their identifications in political life: in 1990 young people not only identified themselves as less able to influence political life but also felt worse about it.

Table 5.3 Mean Changes in Behavioral Style, Social Identification, Value Estimations, and Well-Being between 1990 and 1991; for (1) Persons Responding in Both Years, (2) the Combined Mean Change Estimate

1990 vs. 1991	Matched Mean Difference	SE	Combined Mean Difference	SE
	Behavioral Style			
Economics	0.00	0.50	0.06	0.40
Culture	0.65	0.44	–0.55	0.36
Politics	–0.53	0.40	–0.24	0.33
	Social Identification			
Economics	–0.19	0.17	–0.11	0.14
Culture	–0.31	0.17	–0.01	0.12
Politics	–0.13	0.28	0.09	0.21
	Value Estimations			
Economics	0.19	0.34	0.46*	0.23
Culture	–0.16	0.14	0.02	0.10
Politics	–0.13	0.28	–0.11	0.08
	Well-Being			
Economics	–0.47	0.28	–0.44	0.24
Culture	–0.56	0.30	–0.05	0.23
Politics	–0.25	0.664	–0.39	0.44

*$p<0.05$. Positive numbers = mean increase; negative numbers = mean decrease.

Changes between 1990 and 1991

Table 5.3 shows that in the period 1990–1991 essentially no significant changes occurred. The only significant change was that young people in 1991 started to evaluate more positively the characteristics of an economically active person (such as enterprising, rich, satisfied), and more negatively the characteristics of the passive one (i.e., nonenterprising, poor, unsatisfied). This also means that their good/bad estimations of social activity/passivity had diverged over time.

Changes between 1991–1992

Behavioral Style

As seen in Table 5.4, in 1992 young people reported a behavioral style in cultural domain closer to the active person (the citizen of a democratic society) than to the passive one (socialist personality) compared with 1991: they reported that they could apply more new technologies in their work, they

Table 5.4 Mean Changes in Behavioral Style, Social Identification, Value
Estimations, and Well-Being between 1991 and 1992, for (1) Persons
Responding in Both Years, (2) the Combined Mean Change Estimate

1991 vs. 1992	Matched Mean Difference	SE	Combined Mean Difference	SE
Behavioral Style				
Economics	0.07	0.18	0.08	0.12
Culture	0.65***	0.16	0.64*	0.15
Politics	−0.71***	0.15	−0.71*	0.14
Social Identification				
Economics	−0.63***	0.17	−0.77***	0.14
Culture	−1.13***	0.11	−1.13***	0.11
Politics	−0.98***	0.21	−0.88*	0.18
Value Estimations				
Economics	−0.43	0.30	−0.80*	0.18
Culture	−0.32*	0.13	−0.23	0.11
Politics	0.13	0.22	−0.18*	0.07
Well-Being				
Economics	−0.54	0.33	−0.82*	0.27
Culture	−2.18***	0.23	−2.34*	0.19
Politics	−1.98***	0.41	−1.18*	0.34

*$p<0.05$, ***$p<0.001$. Positive numbers = mean increase; negative numbers = mean decrease

could be better informed about national and world events by various resources, and they could choose among many cultural events. In the political
field however, the behavioral style shifted during 1991–1992 toward the
passive: youths reported that they were less active in elections and did not
participate actively in decision making in various organizations.

Social Identification
Young people identified themselves in 1992 in all domains as less active,
independent, and able to influence the social environment around them
than in 1991. Young people identified themselves in economics as less
rich, enterprising, and satisfied; in culture as less educated, cultured, and
sophisticated; and in politics as more dependent, oppressed and, insecure.

Value Estimations
During 1991–1992 the respondents started to evaluate more positively

such characteristics as nonenterprising, poor, and unsatisfied, and more negatively such characteristics as enterprising, rich, and satisfied in the domain of cultural life.

Well-Being

In 1992, young people not only identified themselves as less able to influence the social environment around them than in 1991, but felt worse about their identifications in political and cultural life than the previous year.

Discussion

Summary

During 1989–1992, several social transformations took place that might be related to the observed changes in the variables investigated.

The first year of our study, 1989–1990, included the last eight months of the old regime and the beginning of the social transformations in Bulgaria, such as the ousting of President T. Zhivkov, who had been in power since 1954, and establishment of the first anti-Communist coalition.

The results showed that, during this time, the participants in the study started to identify themselves as less independent and less able to influence their social environment, especially in economic and political life. They felt worse about their self-identifications. Young people started to value more the characteristics of socially active person and less those of the passive one.

In the second period of our study, 1990–1991, the first multiparty free elections were held. The law for restitution of land was voted in, and the new constitution was adopted. During such period, however, no significant changes in adolescent thinking were found.

During the third year of our study, 1991–1992, most radical changes in social institutions took place. Legislative and municipal elections were held. The first non-Communist government came into power. The principal laws allowing the development of private business and property were voted in. The Convention for Human Rights was ratified. Interestingly, the findings also showed that most of the studied variables changed significantly in this period. The participants identified themselves in all domains of social life as less active and independent, and they felt worse about it. Although the adolescents reported an increase in active behavioral style in cultural life, in political life a tendency toward a passive style was observed.

Macrosocial Transformations and Psychosocial Development

The aim of the study was to link macrosocial transformations with individual psychosocial changes during the transition from socialism to democracy. During this transition, young people reported a more active behavioral style and became more sensitive in their value estimations of activity and passivity, but at the same time they identified themselves as less able to influence their social environment, and they felt worse about it. These results reflect the short-term effects of social changes and can give a general framework for future investigations of the interaction of developing individuals and changing economic, cultural, and political institutions. They can be considered as a first step for studying this issue, and most of our interpretations may be considered as hypotheses for future research.

Multidirectional Changes: Gains and Losses

The present study showed first that the most significant changes were found in the last period of the study (1991–1992), the least between 1990 and 1991. These results might be interpreted in several ways. First, they could be a direct reflection of the amount of change on the social level. The most radical changes in social institutions took place in the last period of our study. Second, the results could reveal the time-lag effects of the preparation for transition to a new experience (Bronfenbrenner, 1979). The periods before 1991 could have been a latency period for the development of adolescent thinking. It may be that some changes in adolescent thinking initiated during this period were realized later on.

Some of the changes found in this study seemed to be domain-specific. The most changes were found in the economic domain. A possible reason might be that this is the domain that most directly influences everyday experience in terms of living standards, conditions of employment, and so on. It may well be that these experiences then affect psychosocial variables, such as identification, values, and well-being.

The results also showed that the variables under study have different sensitivities to social changes. As a whole, the most sensitive variables are youths' social identification and well-being. Behavioral style shows less change over time. Note too that some variables seemed to change in different directions during the social transformation.

The most consistent result concerns young people's social identification and well-being: adolescents tended to define themselves as less independent and less able to influence their social environment, and they felt worse about it. This finding could be a reflection of several processes.

First, it is well known (Elder, 1979) that short-term radical changes, provoking a readjustment of people's lives to new principles, increase anxiety and emotional stress and negatively affect well-being. Second, it is possible that the transition from a stable and monolithic society toward a diverse one broadens one's outlook and self-awareness about social passivity and activity. This might lead to relatively more precise social identifications over time. It is also possible that people living in a uniform society have few opportunities to compare differing patterns of choices and social activity. That is why they tend to give more global and higher estimations of the characteristics concerning social activity. It is also possible that when there is an increase in new opportunities, young people think that their earlier skills and knowledge become inadequate, and this is reflected in a decrease in their self-regard. It may be that more detailed analyses of self-efficacy beliefs, locus of control, and engagement style are needed to understand their development.

Third, some preliminary data from our studies show that the decrease in self-identification scores and well-being is related to youths' unrealistic expectations about the outcomes of socialist-type behavior. The poor fit between behavioral expectation and real outcomes of this type of behavior in new conditions is a possible source of young people's dissatisfaction and worse feelings over time. The higher expectations for democratic changes, combined with everyday experience of the high social cost of reforms, might lead young people to envision themselves as less able to influence their social environment. In order to understand the processes underlying identity development in conditions of rapid social change, we should more closely examine the individual's reasoning about self-identifications and other aspects of ego development, such as moral principles, interpersonal style, conscious concerns, and cognitive complexity (Hauser, Powers, and Noam, 1991).

Young people's behavioral style showed little change over time. Moreover, the changes in this variable are domain-specific. As a whole, young people tended to report more active behavior during the time observed. Only in the last period did a slight decrease in the predominant active political behavioral style appear. A possible interpretation of this result is that the political activities we studied, such as party participation and defense of human rights, will diminish as the democratic conditions improve. Perhaps the establishment of democratic institutions will provoke other types of activities related to indirect political involvement.

It is worth mentioning that the findings described above are quite consistent for the whole sample. No significant effects of age and religious background were found. This allows us to interpret the results as representing general tendencies of development of youth social identification, behavioral style, and value estimations under conditions of rapid social change. The nonsignificant age effects suggest that the revealed tendencies are due mainly to the changing social context, not to the maturation of the adolescents.

Finally, a couple of methodological limitations of the study should be mentioned. First, the sample does not permit cohort comparisons, which could help to analyze the interplay of sociohistoric and age-graded influences. Some of the questions about the social determination of the changes in variables could not be answered because it is difficult to relate the measurements of objective status of individuals in a socialist system with those in an emerging democratic society. Also, the use of self-reported measures does not allow us to reveal the tendencies in behavioral changes over the time of study.

Despite these limitations, the study presented here can give us a general framework for future investigations of the interaction of developing individuals and changing economic, cultural, and political institutions. It suggests that the changes in social institutions during the transition to democracy had contradictory effects on youth development. The big gain is the increase in the options of choices for social identification and value orientation. But at the same time the lack of clear social rules and instability negatively affected the well-being of the respondents. These findings invite further longitudinal investigations to determine the varying patterns of youth development in conditions of social change. For example, it would be interesting to examine the groups of different types of " gainers" and "losers," which may vary among different regions (urban, rural); communities (Muslim, Christian); and socioeconomic groups. We also expect to find individual differences in the way young people cope with social changes, which will depend on the psychological resources they bring to the new situations (Elder, 1991). The existing level of psychosocial maturation may mediate the effects of social changes. Those who have already achieved higher levels of social maturation might be expected to experience less negative effects. Even within disadvantaged groups there may be some individuals who will cope better than others. These hypotheses will be tested in our ongoing study with a representative sample, including different age cohorts, defined by the main life transitions and special socioeconomic context.

Notes

This study was supported in part by the Ministry of Education of Bulgaria and by a grant from Sapio Foundation to Luba Botcheva. The contribution of Yassen Zlatkov to the theoretical model of the empirical study is acknowledged. The paper was partly written while the author was a Fellow at the Center for Advanced Study in Behavioral Sciences. I am grateful for the financial support provided by the Johann Jacobs Foundation. I thank Professor Lincoln Moses for his valuable consultations in statistical analysis and helpful comments on earlier versions of the paper. I am grateful to Kathleen Much for her editorial assistance.

References

Ajzen, I., and Fishbein, M. (1980). *Understanding attitudes and predicting social behavior.* Englewood Cliffs, NJ: Prentice Hall.

Ball-Rokeach, S. (1984). *The great American values.* New York: Free Press.

Baltes, P. B. (1983). Life-span developmental psychology: Observations on history and theory revisited. In R.M. Lerner (ed.), *Developmental psychology: Historical and philosophical perspectives* (pp. 79–111). Hillsdale, NJ: Erlbaum.

Baltes, P. B. (1987). Theoretical propositions of life-span developmental psychology: On the dynamics between growth and decline. *Developmental Psychology, 23,* 611–626.

Baltes, P. B., and Baltes, M. M. (1990). Psychological perspectives on successful aging: The model of successful optimization with compensation. In P. B. Baltes and M.M. Baltes (eds.), *Successful aging: Perspectives from the behavioral sciences* (pp. 1–34). New York: Cambridge University Press.

Brent, S. B. (1978). Individual specialization, collective adaptation, and rate of environmental change. *Human Development, 21,* 21–23.

Bronfenbrenner, U. (1979). *The ecology of human development: Experiments by nature and design.* Cambridge: Harvard University Press.

Clausen, J. S. (1991). Adolescent competence and the shaping of the life course. *American Journal of Sociology, 4,* 805–843.

Curtis, M. (1979). *Totalitarianism.* New Brunswick, NJ: Transaction Books.

Dannefer, D. (1984). Adult development and social theory: A paradigmatic reappraisal. *American Sociological Review, 49,* 100–116.

Dornbusch S. M., Petersen, A. C., and Hetherington, E. M. (1991) Projecting the future of research on adolescence. *Journal of Research on Adolescence. 1,* 7–17.

Elder, G. H., Jr. (1974). *Children of the great depression: Social change in life experience.* Chicago: University of Chicago Press.

Elder, G. H., Jr. (1979). Historical change in life patterns and personality. In P. B. Baltes and O.G. Brim, Jr. (eds.), *Life-span development and behavior (Vol. 2)* (pp. 118–175). New York: Academic Press.

Elder, G. H., Jr. (1991). Lives in social change. In Walter R. Heinz (ed.), *Theoretical advances in life course research (Status passages and the life course, Vol. 1)* (pp. 58–86). Wenheim: Deutscher Studien Verlag.

Featherman, D. L.,and Lerner, R. M. (1985). Ontogenesis and sociogenesis: Problematics for theory and research about development and socialization across the life span. *American Sociological Review, 50,* 659–676.

Greenstein F. (1987). *Personality and politics: Problems of evidence, inference, and conceptualization.* Princeton, NJ: Princeton University Press.

Hauser, S. T., Powers, S., and Noam, G. (1991) *Adolescents and their families: Paths of ego development.* New York: Free Press.

Inkeles, A. (1961). National character and modern political systems. In F. L. K. Hsu (ed). *Psychological anthropology: Approaches to culture and personality* (pp. 178–197). Homewood, IL: Dorsey Press.

Lerner, R. M. (1991). Continuities and changes in the scientific study of adolescence, *Journal of Research on Adolescence, 1,* 1–5.

128   Luba Botcheva

Magnusson, D. (1990). Personality development from an interactional perspective. In L. Pervin (ed.), *Handbook of Personality* (pp.193–222). New York: Guilford Press.

Moses, L. (1986). *Think and explain with statistics.* Reading, MA: Addison-Wesley.

Nesselroade, J. R., and von Eye, A., eds. (1985). *Developmental and social change: Explanatory analysis.* New York: Academic Press.

Petrovski, A. V. (1984). *Voprosi istorii i teorii psihologii* (Topics of history and theory of psychology). Moscow: Pedagogika.

Riegel, K. F. (1976). The dialectics of human development. *American Psychologist, 31,* 689–700.

Scheibe, K. (1970). *Beliefs and values.* New York: Holt, Rinehart and Winston.

Sniderman, P. (1975). *Personality and democratic politics.* Berkeley: University of California Press.

Waterman, A. (1992). Identity as an aspect of optimal psychological functioning. In G. R. Adams and T. Gullotta (eds.), *Adolescents' identity formation* (pp. 50–73). Newbury Park, CA: Sage Publications.

Chapter Six
Timing of First Romantic Involvement
Commonalities and Differences in the Former Germanies

Rainer K. Silbereisen and Beate Schwarz

Introduction

In this chapter, we deal with influences that shape developmental time-tables during adolescence, broadly seen as the second decade of life. More specifically, we are interested in the prediction of individual differences in the timing of transitions to autonomy in adolescents' interpersonal behaviors, particularly first relations with the opposite gender. We investigated the potential precursors of such differences by focusing on childhood adversities and experiences with parents and peers. German unification provided the opportunity to conduct the study in a parallel fashion with samples from both former East and West Germany. This enabled us to analyze commonalities and differences between young people from two different political backgrounds.

One way to understand differences in the contexts affecting adolescent development in the former Germanies is to recognize the pervasive influence of the government and other societal mass institutions in the lives of the young in East Germany, and the corresponding freedom from such interferences and control for those growing up in West Germany. In East Germany the entire life course was more institutionalized and individual decisions concerning one's life path were much less prevalent (Behnken and Zinnecker, 1992). This was particularly true for domains of development which have an immediate impact on society, such as vocational development. In contrast, such institutional control was largely absent in West Germany, and parental support behaviors were likely to be a more important factor (Dettenborn, Boehnke, and Horstmann, 1994).

Variations in the Timing of Psychosocial Transitions

Adolescence is characterized by a multitude of transitions to the new roles, privileges, and obligations of adulthood. The actual timing of particular psychosocial transitions during adolescence reflects societal norms and cultural beliefs (Feldman and Rosenthal, 1994). The age at which young people begin to show behavioral autonomy rather than following parents' advice is known to depend on the families' position in regard to belief systems, such as collectivism or individualism. If the domain of behavior refers to an issue such as self-enhancement through the pursuit of personal goals, families and societies with more individualistic beliefs would regard movement in this direction as being appropriate at an earlier age than families and societies with a more collectivist orientation. Adoption of equally complex responsibilities for members of the family, however, would be expected to occur earlier in groups with collectivist beliefs, than in those with individualistic beliefs (Triandis, 1990).

It is unlikely that the former Germanies differed greatly in beliefs concerning the transitions occurring at a more personal level, such as the age of first romantic experience, the core of the present chapter. Other transitions which are typical of adolescence, however, were presumably more affected by institutions which differed between the two countries.

A case in point concerns the "social clocks" represented by schools and the related institutions of postsecondary education. In earlier research, Silbereisen, Vondracek, and Berg (1997) investigated the timing of adolescents' first vocational plans. As might be expected, given the differences in the length of schooling and the system of occupational guidance, samples raised in former East and West Germany differed from each other. Adolescents from East Germany reported making such plans considerably earlier than those from West Germany. In addition, the predictors of individual differences showed certain features which were specific to country. For example, the role of achievement-related experiences within one's family was regarded as being of less importance in East Germany than in West Germany. This was interpreted as resulting from the higher level of institutionalization of career decisions in the East, demanded by the ideological belief that societal necessities come before individual self-determination.

In the present study, we are not concerned with transitions which are closely related to institutional timetables. Rather, we concentrate on a number of transitions that belong to the personal realm of intimacy and love. For instance, there are no norms in the usual sense of the term which dictate when one "should" fall in love for the first time. Although most adolescents have this experience within a relatively narrow timewindow (soon after entering the second decade of life), failure to have a first romantic relationship during this time does not result in normative sanctions by others.

As mentioned earlier, the similarity of the cultural background between the two Germanies meant that it was not reasonable to expect great differences in timetables for autonomy in interpersonal relations, particularly those with the other gender. Despite this, observations on life before unification emphasize the usefulness of studying possible commonalities in detail. For instance, young people used to marry considerably earlier in East Germany than in West Germany (Nauck, 1993). This was due in part to the advantage of receiving state-subsidized housing once marriage had taken place. One could imagine that one consequence of the earlier timing of marriage would be a more rapid movement towards romantic involvement in adolescence.

The Role of Adversities for the Timing of Transitions

However, irrespective of whether East and West Germany differ in the timetables of psychosocial transitions, the predictors of individual differences could also be the same or different in different political regions. In line with our earlier studies (Silbereisen, Schwarz, and Rinker, 1995), the focus in this chapter is on childhood adversities. When we refer to adversities we mean events that challenged individuals' adaptive capacities to a degree that usually required more than a routine response and often had lasting effects. Many adversities, such as parental divorce or serious illness, are known to put children's healthy development at risk. They can have negative effects on development by overtaxing parents' resources and capabilities to provide adequate support and supervision for their offspring (Elder, Caspi, and Van Nguyen, 1986). With respect to East Germany, however, it seems reasonable to assume that people's position was better due to the extended system of public child care (Nauck, 1993). One might therefore expect adversities there to have had less impact than in the West.

Other immediate consequences of adversities may reinforce their negative impact. It is likely, for instance, that experience of early adversities leads children to take over adultlike responsibilities sooner, in place of the help that, under better circumstances, would have been provided by the parents (Weiss, 1979). Again, one could argue that adolescents raised in former East Germany were likely to be better prepared for such roles as both parents were generally in employment. This meant that the young had to take over family responsibilities at an earlier age (Bertram, 1992).

Although the idea that the effects of adversities in East Germany were less pronounced sounds plausible, there are also arguments for the opposite prediction. The better support provided by day care and youth centers, while particularly relevant for single parents or families in jeopardy, may also be a source of risks. Such settings provide numerous opportunities for affiliation with peer groups, a condition which is often regarded as increasing individuals' proneness to problem behavior (Patterson, DeBaryshe, and Ramsey, 1989). Similarly, pursuing adultlike responsibilities earlier in adolescence may provide more freedom than is appropriate and could distract from school.

The linkage between early adversities and the later timing of psychosocial transitions is presumably best described as a cumulative and interactive process, that involves coping with earlier responsibilities and experiencing greater freedom than agemates do. The hypothesized effect on earlier timetables may be further reinforced by the fact that the situation at home could lack the emotional closeness that other adolescents enjoy.

Corroborating such a hypothetical scenario requires empirical evidence. The contribution of the present study can rely on retrospective reports on early adversities, pubertal timing, leisure behaviors, and parental support behaviors during childhood. Variables relating to the number of responsibilities and the amount of leeway with peers, however, were only available for the period of the study. Consequently, dependent on the adolescents' actual age, the transitions had either already taken place or were still to come. Only in the latter case were we able to interpret individual differences in responsibilities and leeway as precursors of differences in the timing of transitions.

Hypotheses

Where childhood experiences are concerned, higher levels of parental support behaviors in the domains of culture and education were predicted to correspond to later timing of psychosocial transitions. It was reasoned that joint involvement of parents and children in areas such as music, or active parental involvement in adolescents' homework, are likely to distract children from unsupervised activities and company outside the home, thus reducing the chance of early motivation for intimate relations.

Females are known to begin romantic relationships earlier than males (Steinberg, 1993). In spite of this well-established finding, it is also known that with regard to many other behaviors, in both males and females, high preference for female-typed behavior is expected to correspond to later timing, whereas high preference for male-typed behavior is expected to correspond to earlier timing. This is because female-typed behaviors indicate a more traditional and less aggressive behavioral style than male-typed behaviors.

Data gathered on a number of other leisure behaviors enabled us to characterize individual differences in the major foci of such activities. In brief, activities that provide opportunities for peer contacts were predicted to correspond to earlier transition, whereas activities that concentrate on self-improvement were expected to correspond to later transition.

Finally, the perceived timing of puberty relative to agemates was predicted to be associated with adolescents' timetables. More specifically, individuals who report earlier maturation were expected to demonstrate the features of interpersonal autonomy referred to earlier, and vice versa. This hypothesis was based on a rather extensive body of research that showed a relationship between early maturation and more advanced involvement with the opposite gender (Stattin and Magnusson, 1990; Silbereisen and Kracke, 1993). The timing of such behaviors, however, was not investigated in previous research.

In formulating these expectations, we have not yet distinguished between the samples from East and West Germany, apart from making reference to the potentially differential role of adversities for the two groups. The study remains explorative in this regard, although one could imagine how differences in opportunities for certain leisure activities might play a significant role in shaping their experience.

The remainder of this chapter is organized into four parts. First, we describe the samples and the variables concerning adversities and childhood experiences, comparing the two parts of Germany. Secondly, the analyses and results on the prediction of individual timing differences in select psychosocial transitions are reported. Romantic involvement, the target domain, is indicated by three markers, namely, the timing of first love, steady friendship, and sexual experiences. In order to assess whether the predictors we found are specific for romance, the variable of alcohol use was added for comparison. This is a behavior that gains importance, roughly parallel in time to growing romantic involvement, but certainly due in part to different antecedents. Next, experiences and activities pursued during adolescence are added to the prediction of timing differences in East and West Germany. Finally, the results are discussed against the backdrop of adolescent life-worlds in the two former Germanies.

A Survey on Youth in the Germanies

The data presented in this chapter represent a cohort of young people in mid-adolescence, aged 13 to 19 years (M = 16.5 years, SD = 2.1). This age period was chosen because its beginning marks the transition to secondary schooling in many federal states. Its ending marks the transition to postsecondary education for college-bound youth.

Samples

Stratified, nonrandom samples of German adolescents who lived with their families were drawn from both parts of the country. Strata were chosen to be representative in terms of community size, level of schooling, and gender. In order to compensate for differences in the population size and size of age cohorts, participants from former East Germany and the share of younger age-groups were overrepresented. Without this we would not have had sufficient sample size for subgroup comparisons.

The data were gathered in the summer of 1991, one year after German unification, accomplished as part of the Shell Youth '92 Study (Jugendwerk der Deutschen Shell, 1992) which covered an age range between thirteen and twenty-nine years. The samples of thirteen- to nineteen-year-olds included in the present study comprised 1,683 adolescents (588 East Germany, 1095 West Germany).

Measures

The adolescents were interviewed in a face-to-face situation at their homes by trained interview staff from an experienced survey institute. The interview covered more topics than are dealt with in this chapter (duration sixty to ninety minutes).

Timing of Psychosocial Transitions

The adolescents reported whether and, if so, at what age (in full years) they had first experienced (1) falling in love, (2) going steady with a romantic friend, (3) having a sexual experience, and (4) consuming alcohol "seriously" (i.e., more than sipping from somebody's glass). Three of the four issues referred to the development of advanced intimate relationships with the other gender. Drinking experience was added to the list for reasons of comparison.

The wording concerning the psychosocial transitions had to follow the model of earlier Shell studies (Jugendwerk der Deutschen Shell, 1981; 1985). Mainly in order to avoid problems of acceptance by the respondents, but also in reminiscence of comparable material in earlier German research, it was not specified (and thus left open to adolescents' beliefs) what "first sexual experience" should mean in particular. It is important to note, however, that in those earlier studies, as well as in comparative studies in Hungary, the timing of first sexual experience was always more than one year later than the timing of first falling in love. Presumably it is fair to say that for most respondents the wording meant heterosexual activities from heavy petting to intercourse. Concerning the consumption of alcohol, we also had to follow the wording chosen in earlier investigations under the Shell format. Judged from qualitative pretests it is clear that "serious" means consumption resulting in substance-related mood changes, including (but not exclusively indexing) drunkenness.

Our view on the likely interpretation of the items by the adolescents is supported by previous experience and the fact that the sample studied is, as the German population, rather homogeneous in terms of ethnic origns and cultural orientation. Certainly, the interpretation of the items could be different in other cultural contexts.

Psychosocial Adversities
Based on lists of relevant events discussed in previous research (e.g., Rutter, 1979), the adolescents were asked whether a number of salient life events had occurred before the age of nine. The events encompassed relocation to a different town, loss of a parent due to divorce or death, serious illness in the family, parental unemployment, unskilled occupation of a parent, and school problems of the child.

Examination of the frequency distribution of the occurrence of these events revealed that adolescents who reported two or more events comprised about 10 percent in each part of the country. These adolescents formed the high adversity group; all others were assigned to the low adversity group.

Experiences and Activities below Thirteen Years of Age
Adolescents were asked how frequently they had participated in a number of experiences and activities between the ages of three and twelve years (1 = never to 4 = very frequently). For *gender-typed role playing activities,* scores on female role-plays (4 items; e.g., playing house) and male role-plays (4 items; e.g., playing cops and robbers) were obtained. Information on four other scales on *leisure activities* was also gathered. Each comprised four items. The topics referred to cultural activities (e.g., attending

a museum), consumer-role behaviors (e.g., strolling in the mall), creative activities (e.g., dressing up), and technical activities (e.g., playing with construction kits). The internal consistencies (Cronbach's alphas) of these variables ranged between 0.61 and 0.87.

Parental Support Behaviors below Thirteen Years of Age
Adolescents were given a number of statements and asked to rate on 4-point scales (4 = applies fully) the degree to which they represented their own experiences between the ages of six and twelve years. Guided by Steinberg and colleagues (1992) and based on the results of exploratory factor analyses, the following variables relating to parental support behaviors were defined. Internal consistencies were between 0.66 and 0.75. *Cultural encouragement* assessed whether the family was conducive to joint cultural activities (5 items; e.g., In my family we often played music together). *Expectations to succeed* referred to parents' perceived belief in their child's ability to succeed (4 items; e.g., When I was younger, my parents had high expectations for me). *School involvement* encompassed parental supervision of school achievement (4 items; e.g., My parents asked me regularly how I did in school).

Control Variables
In addition, gender (2 = female, 1 = male), educational level (3 = college-bound track, 2 = medium track, 1 = low track), and perceived maturational timing were assessed. The latter information was gathered using a similar approach to that of Dubas, Graber, and Petersen (1991). Adolescents were asked, "When I was between eleven and twelve years of age, compared to my agemates I developed: earlier, neither earlier nor later, later." The respondents were not requested to focus on any specific aspect of pubertal changes that may have occurred. For the analyses, the three response categories were dummy-coded into variables indicating fast or slow maturation (relative to the neutral response).

Results
Predicting the Timing of Transitions
Tests of our hypotheses regarding the timing of first romantic involvement required the application of a specific approach, known as the proportional hazard model, or Cox regression (Cox, 1972).[1] The Cox regressions were carried out separately for the samples from former East and West Germany. The variables were included in the following stepwise

fashion: (1) gender and educational level, (2) level of adversities, (3) child-hood play experiences, (4) parental support behaviors during adolescence, (5) perceived pubertal timing. Below, only the risk ratios for the final step in the analyses are reported. This is because the variables included later in the hierarchy did not exhaust the effect of variables included earlier in the hierarchy. In other words, the effects of the various domains of variables were unique.

The results for the timing of the four exemplary psychosocial transitions among the adolescents from West Germany are shown in Table 6.1. As revealed by significant risk ratios larger than 1, at any given age females were more likely to have entertained a steady friendship or have experienced first sexual contacts. In other words, they underwent these transitions earlier than males.

Looking first at commonalities across the four topics of transitions, adversity is a prime example. Belonging to the high adversity group corresponded significantly to earlier timing of first love, steady relationship

Table 6.1 Predicting the Timing of Transitions among Adolescents from Former West Germany: Childhood Variables

Predictors	Fall in Love	Steady Friendship	Sexual Experience	Alcohol Use
		Transitions		
Female	1.08	1.21**	1.24**	0.91
Education	1.03	1.01	1.03	1.03
Adversity	1.21**	1.16*	1.13	1.25***
Female Play	1.03	0.97	0.98	0.99
Male Play	1.15*	1.17*	1.30***	1.19**
Cultural Activities	0.99	0.77**	0.95	0.93
Consumer Roles	1.06	1.07	0.95	1.04
Creative Activities	1.23**	1.16*	1.12	1.10
Technical Activities	0.85*	0.97	1.00	0.98
Cultural Engagement	0.76	1.02	0.76	0.46**
School Involvement	1.04	0.96	0.91	0.91
Expectation Success	1.24	1.03	1.20	1.85*
Fast Maturation	1.11*	1.13*	1.20**	1.05
Slow Maturation	0.95	0.92	0.91	0.94
Chi-Square	59.86	46.34	43.84	63.48
p	< 0.001	< 0.001	< 0.001	< 0.001
% censored	26	43	54	45

*$p < 0.05$; ** $p < 0.01$; *** $p < 0.001$.

with girlfriend/boyfriend, and first experiences with alcohol. Although not significant, the direction of effects was the same for first sexual experiences. Interestingly enough, the timing of first love did not reveal a gender effect.

Among the childhood play activities, male-typed activities stand out. In all of the four transitions analyzed, adolescents who reported higher levels of such activities in the past underwent the transitions in adolescence considerably earlier. Other effects of play behavior concentrated on the juxtaposition of creative compared to technical play activities in predicting the timing of first romance. Whereas creative behaviors corresponded to an earlier timing of adolescents' first love and steady friendship, technical activities were inversely related to first love.

Where parental support behaviors are concerned, cultural encouragement and expectations to succeed need to be considered. Except for the timing of going steady with a girlfriend or boyfriend, adolescents who reported more cultural encouragement tended to undergo the transition later. However, this effect was significant for alcohol consumption only, indicating that higher levels of engagement in joint cultural activities within the family predicted a later timing of first contacts with alcohol use. In contrast, particularly for alcohol, high expectations to succeed were associated with earlier rather than later experiences with alcohol. Apparently, this kind of parental behavior has negative overtones.

Finally, adolescents who reported having matured faster than agemates also reported an earlier timing of first romantic love, steady relationship with a girlfriend or boyfriend, and first sexual experiences. In contrast, late maturers did not differ from the majority of young people where such experiences were concerned.

In all, six of the fourteen variables considered did not show any significant effect. Interestingly enough, school involvement and educational level belonged to this group. Thus, the timetables were pretty much the same across educational challenges and parental involvement in school affairs.

The results on the sample from former East Germany are shown in Table 6.2. At a glance it is clear that fewer effects were significant (but note that the sample size was smaller compared to the West). We shall now focus on the differences and commonalities relative to the adolescents from former West Germany.

Concerning the sociodemographic variables, gender and adversities showed similar results to those reported for the West. East German

Table 6.2 Predicting the Timing of Transitions among Adolescents from Former East Germany: Childhood Variables

Predictors	Fall in Love	Transitions Steady Friendship	Sexual Experience	Alcohol Use
Female	1.24*	1.26*	1.05	0.94
Education	0.99	0.88	0.96	0.92
Adversity	1.21*	1.23*	1.22+	0.92
Female Play	0.95	0.96	1.09	1.14
Male Play	1.07	1.16+	1.11	1.10
Cultural Activities	0.90	0.89	0.79+	1.03
Consumer Roles	1.40***	1.35***	1.27**	1.15+
Creative Activities	1.10	1.06	1.09	0.86
Technical Activities	1.03	0.99	0.98	0.93
Cultural Engagement	1.06	0.84	0.88	0.73
School Involvement	1.07	1.12	0.91	0.76**
Expectation Success	0.96	1.24+	1.14	1.18
Fast Maturation	1.06	1.23**	1.16*	1.09
Slow Maturation	0.92	0.97	0.86+	0.96
Chi-Square	48.45	55.03	32.90	27.66
p	< 0.001	< 0.001	< 0.01	< 0.05
% censored	20	35	49	38

$+ p < 0.10$; $* p < 0.05$; $** p < 0.01$; $*** p < 0.001$.

females, however, were earlier than males in the timing of first romantic love and a steady intimate relationship, but not sexual experience, in comparison with the West. Furthermore, although the high-adversity adolescents, like their agemates from West Germany, showed an earlier involvement with the other sex, there was no significant difference with regard to the timing of first alcohol experiences.

Further differences between the political regions referred to play behaviors during childhood. In contrast to West Germany, neither male-typed behaviors, nor creative or technical activities, differed in predicted timing of transitions. Rather, the pursuit of play activities which introduce media use and consumer roles corresponded to earlier transitions. The latter variable was totally irrelevant in West Germany.

With parental support behaviors, only school involvement was important for East German students. Adolescents whose parents reportedly showed more involvement in school-related tasks had their first experiences with alcohol later than their agemates. Finally, first sexual experiences (and being involved in a steady relationship) were likely to take place earlier among fast maturers and later among slow maturers.

In passing we should add that according to the results of ANOVAs, only the leisure activities revealed mean differences between the parts of the country. Whereas adolescents from East Germany reported significantly higher levels of cultural and technical activities, their levels in consumer-related and creative activities were lower.

In sum, although commonalities between the samples occurred, some differences were also found. In particular, the pattern of reported childhood play activities seemed to be rather different between the samples. Whereas in West Germany earlier timetables corresponded to higher levels of male-typed behaviors in childhood, in East Germany it was activities that apparently prepared for future consumer roles that made a difference.

The Role of Concurrent Experiences

Thus far, we have not addressed the effects of concurrent experiences and relations with parents and peers reported by the adolescents. Since the assessments of adolescent experiences refer to the period during which the study was conducted, the temporal relation to the transitions is complex. In some cases, the transition had already taken place; in other cases assessments and transitions happened more or less at the same time; in still others the transitions had yet to take place. Nevertheless, we found it interesting to see whether the same or different relations would apply to the samples from former East and West Germany. Before reporting the results, the variables used in addition to those utilized in the earlier analyses need to be described.

Parental monitoring as evidenced by sharing information with their mothers, was gauged by asking adolescents whether they discussed at home (1 = never, 4 = always) "Where you spend your time after school" and "What's going on in your life." The correlation between the items was 0.47 ($p < 0.001$). Adolescents were further asked whether they offered their parent(s) *emotional support* (three items; e.g., help with a personal problem). This variable was added because we thought that higher levels would indicate a more mature stage of development. The internal consistency was 0.69 (Cronbach's alpha).

Problematic peer affiliations were gathered by asking adolescents who belonged to a clique of friends whether members in general approve if one "gets really smashed" and "skips school" (Kaplan, 1980). The response

Table 6.3 Predicting the Timing of Transitions among Adolescents from Former West Germany: Concurrent Variables

| | Transitions | | | |
| | Fall in Love | Steady Friendship | Sexual Experience | Alcohol Use |
Predictors				
Monitoring	0.88*	0.81***	0.78***	0.84**
Support	1.12*	1.13	1.03	0.99
Problem Peers	1.02	1.04	1.08*	1.16***
Peer Activities	1.82***	1.89***	2.02***	1.40**
Cultural Activities	0.86	0.91	0.83	0.81+
Chi-Square	59.86	60.40	58.98	48.79
p	<0.001	<0.001	<0.001	<0.001

Note: Other variables in the equations (see Table 6.1) not shown.
+ $p < 0.10$; * $p < 0.05$; ** $p < 0.01$; *** $p < 0.001$.

scale ranged from 1 (strictly against it) to 4 (don't care about it). The correlation between items was 0.55 ($p < 0.001$). The score was set to 0 for adolescents who did not belong to a clique. Finally, the adolescents gave information on the frequency (4 = often) with which they engaged in *cultural self-improvement activities* (nine items; e.g., to read books) and *peer activities* (ten items; e.g., to do things with friends). The internal consistencies were 0.66 and 0.76, respectively.

We were interested in the role of adolescents' concurrent experiences above and beyond the variables studied in the earlier sections of this chapter. Consequently, the analyses were conducted stepwise. First, all the variables analyzed thus far were introduced; second, the new variables were added, thus indicating effects exclusive of the other variables.

The risk ratios for concurrent experiences reported by the sample from the *West* are shown in Table 6.3. For the sake of brevity, the risk ratios for the other variables (demographics, adversities, experiences and behavior before age thirteen; see Table 6.1) are not repeated.

As revealed by the figures, the frequency with which adolescents pursued self-improvement activities did not make a difference. Likewise, with the exception of the timing of first romantic relations, the emotional support for parents was not relevant. In contrast, risk factors for earlier psychosocial transitions were more frequent leisure activities with peer friends and less frequent exchange of information with mothers. For alcohol initiation and first sexual experiences, contacts with deviant peers were important.

Table 6.4 Predicting the Timing of Transitions among Adolescents from Former East Germany: Concurrent Variables

	Transitions			
Predictors	Fall in Love	Steady Friendship	Sexual Experience	Alcohol Use
Monitoring	0.87+	0.86+	0.76**	0.76**
Support	1.01	0.95	1.02	1.11
Problem Peers	0.99	1.02	1.08	1.13**
Peer Activities	1.34*	1.86***	2.02***	1.09
Cultural Activities	1.08	1.03	0.77	0.94
Chi-Square	11.48	27.66	36.08	22.48
p	<0.05	<0.001	<0.001	<0.001

Note: Other variables in the equations (see Table 6.2) not shown.
+ $p < 0.10$; * $p < 0.05$; ** $p < 0.01$; *** $p < 0.001$.

The results found for adolescents from East Germany are shown in Table 6.4, again omitting the other variables in the equation (see Table 6.2). The pattern was highly similar to that reported for the West German sample. The major risk factor for earlier timing in the interpersonal domain was more frequent peer contacts. For alcohol, however, peer contacts had no importance at all. Thus, normative peer activities seem to be less involved in alcohol initiation than is the case with the West German sample.

Discussion

German adolescents from both parts of the country, aged thirteen to nineteen years, were asked to report whether and, if so, at what age they had experienced their first romance, steady friendship with a girlfriend or boyfriend, and sexual contact. The results showed that those who reported having faced adversities during childhood made the various transitions earlier than their agemates. Fast maturers were also earlier with regard to romantic involvement.

Effects of experiences and activities before the age of thirteen revealed differences between the two parts of the country. Whereas more frequent creative play behaviors corresponded to earlier transitions in West Germany, it was behaviors introducing media use and consumer roles which did so in East Germany. Additional analyses included activities that took place at the time of assessment during adolescence, that is, at age thirteen or older. Among them, levels of monitoring and higher levels of peer-oriented leisure activities corresponded to earlier transitions.

For comparison purposes, the age of initiation into alcohol use was also included in the analyses. The pattern of risk factors differed from that for romantic involvement, and also showed more differences between the two countries. Contact with problematic peers during adolescence was a risk factor in both parts of the country, while adversities during childhood and other variables played a role in West Germany only.

Before we proceed, some caveats need to be mentioned. All data discussed in this paper were gathered from adolescents, and were, in part, retrospective in nature. It is obvious that the results may have been flawed by memory biases and by the fact that predictor variables and reports on transition ages were provided by the same participants. The latter can result in an exaggeration of relations among variables. Having admitted this, it is also fair to say that this is not the only study with such problems. In addition, self-reports on the kind of adversities we used seem to be rather reliable because no judgment or evaluations are required beyond the simple statement that a particular adversity has taken place (Brewin, Andrews, and Gottlieb, 1993). Finally, due to the format of the various Shell studies with which we had to comply, a more explicit and detailed assessment of sexual experiences (and alcohol consumption) was not possible. While the possibility of a range of interpretations by the adolescents is acknowledged, this would only affect our results if one would need to admit reliable differences in this regard between the samples or subgroups (by education or adversity, for instance). The latter, however, is actually quite unlikely. Moreover, as Meschke and Silbereisen (1996) recently reported, the median transition ages of "first sexual experiences" in this sample are close to independent statistical data on the timing of first intercourse.

Let us now concentrate on some of the salient findings. Despite some differences between East and West Germany, adolescents who had faced a higher number of adversities tended to fall in love earlier, entertain a steady relationship with a boyfriend or girlfriend earlier, and have sexual experiences at a younger age-level than agemates. This result is in line with a number of related analyses concerning other psychosocial transitions reported elsewhere. Silbereisen, Schwarz, and Rinker (1995), for instance, obtained particularly strong effects of early adversities on such transitions, which are, in comparison to romantic involvement, characterized by strong normative, institutional underpinnings, such as the timing of first vocational plans. Adolescents faced with adversities develop vocational plans earlier, presumably because they perceive more constraints and fewer opportunities, mitigated by lower school success and other consequences of difficulties during childhood (Silbereisen, Vondracek, and Berg, 1997).

Our present results on the association between adversities and the timing of transitions to more grown-up behaviors also fit well into research on more severe experiences of adversities. Reporting studies of street children, Aptekar (1994) described a number of strategies used by families, particularly mothers, aimed at coping with extreme poverty (known to be the main reason for living on the streets). In such families boys are raised to be independent as soon as possible so that they can contribute to their families' well-being. Many of these children's problems are directly related to this fact. For example, aggression from the community, which is a common occurrence, actually results from the children's apparent disrespect for traditional adult authority and common timetables for autonomy. Although this research addresses conditions a far cry from the adversities we studied, it nevertheless demonstrates continuity in the consequences of adversities on the timing of growing up.

In addition to adversities, we assessed the role of experiences and activities that took place before the age of thirteen. The frequency of male-type activities corresponded to earlier transitions to intimate relationships. Note that this was an effect above and beyond gender differences that pointed to earlier transitions in favor of females. Although this pattern was significant in West Germany only, the results for the East German sample pointed in the same direction. In our view, more frequent male-type play behaviors suggest higher levels of activity and risk-taking. In other words, male and female adolescents with more proactive behavioral preferences are likely to approach developmental tasks, such as the development of intimate relations, earlier than agemates.

Another commonality between East and West Germanies concerns the role of differences in perceived maturational tempo. Those who developed faster than agemates established romantic relations and had sexual experiences earlier than others. This result is in line with research that shows that seeing oneself as having developed faster than others is indeed an antecedent, rather than a consequence, of advanced relations with the other gender (Silbereisen and Kracke, 1993).

One particularly interesting difference emerged between subjects from former East and West Germany. Childhood activities that prepared for consumer roles were relevant in East Germany, but not the creative and other playful activities which were observed in West Germany. Although we have no independent evidence, one possible way to understand this result for East German adolescents is in terms of the opportunity structures that were available before the political unification of Germany. Department stores that invite window shopping, for instance, did not exist outside large cities. Likewise, a Walkman, or even simple portable cassette players, represented very expensive consumer goods.

Reporting higher frequencies of such playful activities can be seen as indicating that the respective adolescents belonged to better-off families, perhaps families who maintained contacts to relatives and friends in the more prosperous West. The result, while hinting at a lack of measurement equivalence (note, however, that the means did not differ between the samples) also is telling for the situation within former East Germany. The relation between such childhood activities and adolescent transitions could be mediated by peer popularity, rooted in the opportunities for pleasurable activities that adolescents from these privileged families could offer their peers.

Concerning the experiences and activities shown during adolescence (actually at the age the assessments were conducted for the particular subject), the predominant impression is one of pronounced similarity between the two sociopolitical regions. Parental monitoring was associated with later transitions to romantic involvement; and earlier engagement in peer activities. These results are in line with the often reported fact that heterosexual relationships evolve from within unsupervised free-time activities with peers (Steinberg, 1993). Actually, we should add that this pattern is typical for individualistically oriented European and North American cultures. In this regard, however, the two Germanys are certainly alike.

Overall, then, commonalities prevailed concerning the correlates of individual differences in the timing of psychosocial transitions. One may wonder whether this would be true for other psychosocial transitions as well. Fortunately enough we can refer to further analyses. According to Silbereisen (in press), it looks as if commonalities do indeed prevail with regard to psychosocial transitions which, like romantic involvement, do not follow "clocks" driven by norms and expectations of social institutions. The timing of first vocational plans, or of first involvement in politics, however (certainly influenced by institutions such as schools, employers or political parties), revealed interesting differences in the pattern of antecedents. In a nutshell, the basic feature was that the activities and experiences that mirrored individual differences on an activity-versus-passivity dimension played a role in the timing of transitions in West Germany, whereas the same conditions were much less important in East Germany.

Returning to romantic involvement, further research should analyze the role of individual adversities, such as divorce, in more detail. Another major research issue should be the cross-validation of the present results by prospective data. Finally, we may ask whether, and when, the differences regarding the role of agency in the timing of some psychosocial transitions will disappear as the process of German unification progresses and becomes an everyday reality.

The recent unification of Germany has provided a unique social experiment for the study of the interaction between changing environments and developing individuals. The particular challenge for research is the fact that people share the same language and culture in spite of having grown up in dramatically different sociopolitical cirumstances.

Notes

The studies reported in this chapter were conducted during the first author's tenure at Pennsylvania State University. We are grateful for the support received from the German Research Council (Si 296/14–1,2,3; Principal Investigator: Rainer K. Silbereisen). Special thanks go to the colleagues of our research consortium at the University of Siegen (Principal Investigator: Jürgen Zinnecker) and the University of Bamberg (Principal Investigator: Laszlo Vaskovics). We also thank Burkhard Rinker for his collaboration in preparing the data for analysis, and Verona Christmas for her work with the manuscript.

1. This statistical procedure is a member of a family of methods called survival analysis (Willet and Singer, 1991). In contrast to the case of analyzing incremental change in an outcome variable, where one would apply regression analysis, the aim of the procedure was to predict the timing of an event that marks the shift from one state to another, namely, the shift to romance. The statistical treatment of such "event data" represents a specific problem related to the fact that, depending on the length of the period of observation, there are always cases for which the event has not yet occurred by the time the data collection has ended. Treating such "right censored" cases as missing data would lead to seriously biased estimates of the event timing. In other words, the timing of initial romantic involvement would be biased downward because the dropped cases represent those with later timing. Survival analysis techniques provide a means for handling such data without bias and without any loss of information. A description of the algorithms of these estimation techniques is beyond the scope of this paper, but a well-written technical introduction is given by Yamaguchi (1991).

In general terms, the Cox regression depicts the probability of the event occurring to a particular person during a time interval, given that the event has not occurred up to that point. Cox regression helps to estimate the effect of continuous or categorical predictors on the hazard function. For instance, we may ask whether higher levels of creative leisure activities in childhood are associated with changes in the hazard function concerning the timing of the first steady friendship. One convenient way of expressing such effects of predictors is indicating the change in the likelihood of the event occurring associated with a one-unit change in the predictor (for an exact definition see Yamaguchi, 1991). A coefficient of 1.5 for the variable "creative leisure," for instance, would indicate that the likelihood of having experienced a steady friendship is 50 percent (or 1.5 times) more likely at any given age for adolescents who entertained a level of creative leisure one unit higher than others. These coefficients are termed here as risk ratios. The analyses throughout this chapter were conducted with the COXREG routine in SPSS for Windows (SPSS, 1993).

References

Aptekar, L. (1994). Street children in the developing world: A review of their condition. *Cross-cultural Research, 28*(3), 195–224.

Behnken, I., and Zinnecker, J. (1992). Lebenslaufereignisse, Statuspassagen und biografische Muster in Kindheit und Jugend (Patterns of life-course transitions in childhood and adolescence). In Jugendwerk der Deutschen Shell (ed.), *Jugend '92, Vol. 2, Im Spiegel der Wissenschaften* (pp. 127–143). Opladen: Leske and Budrich.

Bertram, H., ed. (1992). *Die Familie in den neuen Bundesländern* (The family in the new federal states of Germany). Opladen, Germany: Leske and Budrich.

Brewin, A. F., Andrews, W. M., and Gottlieb, I. H. (1993). Psychopathology and early experiences: A reappraisal of retrospective reports. *Psychological Bulletin, 113*, 82–89.

Cox, D. R. (1972). Regression models and life tables. *Journal of the Royal Statistical Society, 34*, 187–202.

Dettenborn, H., Boehnke, K., and Horstmann, K. (1994). Value preferences in the United Germany: Teachers and students from East and West compared. In A. M. Bouvy, F. J. R. van de Vijver, P. Boski, and P. Schmitz (eds.), *Journeys into cross-cultural psychology* (pp. 268–277). Amsterdam: Swetz and Zeitlinger.

Dubas, J. S., Graber, J. A., and Petersen, A. C. (1991). A longitudinal investigation of adolescents' changing perceptions of pubertal timing. *Developmental Psychology, 27*, 580–586.

Elder, G. H., Jr., Caspi, A., and Van Nguyen, T. (1986). Resourceful and vulnerable children: Family influences in hard times. In R. K. Silbereisen, K. Eyferth, and G. Rudinger (eds.), *Development as action in context: Problem behavior and normal youth development* (pp. 167–186). Berlin: Springer.

Feldman, S. S., and Rosenthal, D. A. (1994). Culture makes a difference . . . or does it? A comparison of adolescents in Hong Kong, Australia, and the United States. In R. K. Silbereisen and E. Todt (eds.), *Adolescence in context: The interplay of family, school, peers, and work in adjustment* (pp. 99–124). New York: Springer.

Feldman, S. S., Rosenthal, D. A., Mont-Reynaud, R., Leung, K., and Lau, S. (1991). Ain't misbehavin': Adolescent values and family environments as correlates of misconduct in Australia, Hong Kong, and the United States. *Journal of Research on Adolescence, 1*, 109–134.

Jugendwerk der Deutschen Shell (ed.) (1981). *Jugend '81* (Youth '81). Hamburg: Jugendwerk der Deutschen Shell.

Jugendwerk der Deutschen Shell (ed.) (1985). *Jugendliche und Erwachsene '85* (Adolescents and adults '85). Opladen, Germany: Leske and Budrich.

Jugendwerk der Deutschen Shell (ed.) (1992). *Jugend 1992* (Adolescence and Youth 1992). Opladen, Germany: Leske and Budrich.

Kaplan, H. B. (1980). *Deviant behavior in defense of self.* New York: Academic Press.

Meschke, L. L., and Silbereisen, R. K. (1996, March). *The influence of puberty, family processes, and leisure activities on the timing of first sexual experience.* Paper presented at the Biennial Meeting of the Society for Research on Adolescence, Boston, MA.

Nauck, B. (1993). Strukturelle Differenzierung der Lebensbedingungen von Kindern in West- und Ostdeutschland (Differential social structures in the life of East and West German children). In M. Markefka and B. Nauck (eds.), *Handbuch der Kindheitsforschung.* Neuwied, Germany: Luchterhand.

Patterson, G. R., DeBaryshe, B. D., and Ramsey, E. (1989). A developmental perspective on antisocial behavior. *American Psychologist, 44*, 329–335.

Rutter, M. (1979). Protective factors in children's responses to stress and disadvantage. In M. W. Kent and J. E. Rolf (eds.), *Primary prevention of psychopathology. Vol. 3, Social competence in children.* Hanover, NH: University Press of New England.

Silbereisen, R. K. (in press). Early adversities and psychosocial development in adolescence: A comparison of the former Germanys. In R. K. Silbereisen and A. von Eye, *Growing up in times of social change.* Berlin: De Gruyter.

Silbereisen, R. K., and Kracke, B. (1993). Variation in maturational timing and adjustment in adolescence. In S. Jackson and H. Rodriguez-Tomé (eds.), *Adolescence and its social worlds* (pp. 67–94). East Sussex, NJ: Erlbaum.

Silbereisen, R. K., Schwarz, B., and Rinker, B. (1995). The timing of psychosocial transitions in adolescence: Commonalities and differences in unified Germany. In J. Youniss (ed.), *After the Wall: Family adaptation in East and West Germany* (New Directions in Child Development). San Francisco: Jossey-Bass.

Silbereisen, R. K., Vondracek, F. W., and Berg, L. A. (1997). Differential timing of initial vocational choice: The influence of early childhood family relocation and parental support behaviors in two cultures. *Journal of Vocational Behavior, 50*, 41–59.

SPSS. (1993). Cox regression. *In SPSS for Windows™*. *Advanced statistics—Release 6.0.* (pp. 275–348). Chicago: SPSS, Inc.

Stattin, H., and Magnusson, D. (1990). *Pubertal maturation in female development.* Hillsdale, NJ: Erlbaum.

Steinberg, L. (1993). *Adolescence.* New York: McGraw-Hill.

Steinberg, L., Lamborn, S. D., Dornbusch, S. D., and Darling, N. (1992). Impact of parenting practices on adolescent achievement: Authoritative parenting, school involvement, and encouragement to succeed. *Child Development, 63*, 1266–1281.

Triandis, H. C. (1990). Cross-cultural studies of individualism and collectivism. *Nebraska Symposium on Motivation, 37*, 41–133.

Weiss, R. S. (1979). Growing up a little faster: The experience of growing up in a single-parent household. *Journal of Social Issues, 35*, 97–111.

Willet, J. B., and Singer, J. D. (1991). How long did it take? Using survival analysis in educational and psychological research. In L. M. Collins and J. L. Horn (eds.), *Best methods for the analysis of change: Recent advances, unanswered questions, future directions* (pp. 310–327). Washington, DC: American Psychological Association.

Yamaguchi, K. (1991). *Event-history analysis.* Newbury Park, CA: Sage.

Chapter Seven
Adolescents, Families, and German Unification
The Impact of Social Change on Antiforeigner and Antidemocratic Attitudes

Bärbel Kracke, Maren Oepke, Elke Wild, and Peter Noack

Introduction

The influx of migrating people or asylum seekers who left their home countries for economic or political reasons is a topic which by the end of the twentieth century is of relevance to almost every industrialized country (e.g., Treibel, 1990). As a consequence, forming attitudes toward incoming people, often perceived as "foreigners," and the resulting more complex society, has become a task to be faced by today's adolescents. How adolescents approach this task depends on the complex interplay of a variety of social and personal factors such as the individual interpretation of the changes as threat or challenge. The purpose of our chapter is to examine the causes for maladaptive responses among German adolescents to the challenges of a multicultural society. More specifically, we want to address the impact of several aspects of social change and family influences on antiforeigner and national-authoritarian, also referred to as "right-extremist," attitudes. We will start by giving a short overview about current theoretical conceptualizations of the emergence of right-extremist attitudes before presenting our own empirical study.

Today no comprehensive theory about the reasons for the emergence of adolescents' right extremism exists. In particular, empirical data on the development of antiforeigner attitudes and the readiness to resort to violence are lacking (Fend, 1994). The majority of the theoretical approaches addressing these phenomena are not empirically tested. Many empirical studies are rather epidemiological in nature, determining the quantitative potential of right extremism but neglecting reasons for its emergence. Fend (1994) characterizes the empirical research on right extremism as a "step-child" of youth research.

Current theories focus mainly on single influencing factors. They either refer to processes on the macrolevel, namely societal change (e.g., Heitmeyer, 1988), or focus on influences on the microlevel, especially of the family (e.g., C. Hopf, 1992, 1993; W. Hopf, 1991), the school (W. Hopf, 1991; Schubarth and Melzer, 1993), and the peer group (Hennig, 1982; Wasmund, 1982), or else emphasize the importance of personality characteristics of antidemocratic adolescents (Adorno, et al., 1966; C. Hopf, 1992).

The most influential theory in Germany explaining adolescents' rightist orientations was proposed by Heitmeyer (1988), who claimed that these orientations are a reaction to the individualization processes characteristic of modern societies. According to this line of thought, the modernization of industrial production, with its consequences such as the isolation and mobility of families, leads to an increasing individualization which, in turn, causes the breaking up of traditional pathways into adult life. Together with the lack of role models and insecure economic circumstances, this is assumed to contribute to adolescents' feelings of confusion, leading them to search for orientation in rightist ideologies that seem to provide security by offering community and direction in the complex world. Heitmeyer originally assumed rightist orientations to prevail mainly among the "losers" of modernization, such as unemployed adolescents with low levels of education who are not integrated into social networks. Heitmeyer's own empirical findings, however, did not support this assumption. Those adolescents with the most extreme rightist orientations, for instance, turned out not to show low self-esteem as an indicator of a state of confusion. On the contrary, they had rather high self-esteem, were optimistic about their personal futures and felt highly integrated into their peergroup. This finding, as well as research of others, initiated a shift in the current debate. For example, an interview study by Bommes and Scherr (1992) showed that positive future perspectives could well go along with rightist attitudes among adolescent apprentices. Feelings of insecurity and experiences of deprivation were, thus, regarded as of only limited explanatory value for adolescents' right extremism.

Later on, the general moral climate in society, which seemed to promote an open discourse about justified inequality between Germans and foreigners (either asylum seekers or so-called "guest-workers"), came into focus as another important source of rightist orientations. In this discourse, sometimes referred to as "Wohlstandschauvinism" (Wealth Chauvinism), differences between the poor and wealthy are explained with reference to individual or collective abilities and achievements. Wealth is strictly defined as legitimate merit. Additionally, social-Darwinistic ideas, such as the suppression of weaker individuals as part of the nature of human beings and therefore characteristic of societies, are typical of this line of thought. These argumentations serve to justify inequality (Bommes and Scherr, 1992) and are also—at least implicitly—supported by politicians and the media. The public debate regarding asylum seekers in Germany, in particular, was an arena for these claims.

W. Hopf (1994) criticized the recent approaches accounting for adolescents' right extremism mainly in terms of Wohlstandschauvinism because they lack theoretical explanations and empirical data on why privileged adolescents should tend to show more extremist attitudes than deprived adolescents. His analyses of a large data set of East and West German adolescents showed more support for the deprivation hypothesis, which claims that mainly adolescents who experience a cumulation of social problems such as economic, educational, and socioemotional deficits show rightist attitudes. W. Hopf (1994) found that in particular adolescents from lower-status families (assessed by parents' job position, and educational and vocational qualifications), who were in lower school tracks and had little social support when in trouble showed higher authoritarian orientations and higher levels of antiforeigner attitudes. Nevertheless, he also found a substantial minority of East and West German adolescents who came from high-status homes and showed high levels of antiforeigner attitudes. Like W. Hopf, who reports more frequent instances of rightist attitudes among adolescents with lower education, Willems (1993) shows that among rightist offenders, adolescents from lower educational tracks are overrepresented.

In sum, the theoretical approaches to explain right extremism in adolescents referring to macrolevel factors point out two sources of influence: (1) experiences of deprivation, particularly in the educational domain, and (2) a more general moral climate in society that justifies violence or unfairness against people of foreign origin.

Family Influences

Starting with the studies on the authoritarian character conducted by Adorno and his colleagues (1966), another tradition of theories about the development of adolescents' rightist attitudes focuses on the family as the most important agent of socialization. The family influence, however, has been conceptualized in different ways. While the study of Adorno and his colleagues mainly addressed the general educational and emotional climate in the family, other studies considered also parents' political attitudes (e.g., Fend, 1994; Bengston and Troll, 1978, Kracke, et al., 1993) and parental behaviors related to politics (e.g., Krampen, 1991).

Concerning the family climate, results show that families of rightist adolescents are generally more authoritarian. Highly restrictive and coercive parental behaviors as well as low emotional support and frequent conflicts seem to characterize families of right extremist adolescent offenders (W. Hopf, 1991). In the same vein, Klein-Allermann, and colleagues (1995) reported that family conflict predicted adolescents' readiness to show violence, while antidemocratic attitudes were predicted by variables not related to the family climate. Still, it seems to be necessary to distinguish adolescents who actually commit antiforeigner offenses and those who show rightist attitudes without using physical violence. Children from homes where violence is a major means of communication seem to be especially prone to show violence themselves, whereas rightist attitudes may also be shown by adolescents from less violent families. Still, the latter families also seem to be characterized by certain aspects of restrictiveness. Fend (1991, 1994) and Hofer and colleagues (1994), for instance, showed that adolescents with rightist orientations are more likely to have parents who prefer conservative educational goals such as conformity to authorities, punctuality, and discipline. In contrast, liberal adolescents seem to have parents who encourage independence in thought and action as well as behavioral and emotional autonomy (Mussen, 1984). Furthermore, a warm and accepting family climate seems to go along with more tolerant political attitudes as reported by Noack and colleagues (1995).

Beyond the indirect effect of the more general family climate on adolescents' political attitudes, more direct effects of, for instance, parents as political models could also be assumed. Fend (1991, 1994) reported a high concordance between adolescents' and parents' antiforeigner attitudes. Krampen's (1991) research showed that fathers' encouraging children to concern themselves with politics is predictive of adolescents' political knowledge, everyday political activities, and their self-concepts of political abilities. In search of family characteristics predicting an intergenerational transmission of political values, Khoshrung-Sefat and colleagues (1983) concluded from their review of research on political socialization in the family that a democratic parenting style and low levels of punishment as well as an active political climate in the family all raise the likelihood of intergenerational similarity in political values. Similar findings were reported for East German families before German unification (Keiser, 1991) and for East and West German families after the reunion (Kracke et al., 1993). The latter studies of German adolescents did not particularly stress democratic parental behaviors but rather emotionally positive and connected relationships. Likewise, Oswald and Stuendel (1990) identified these variables as relevant predictors both of the transmission of political values and of a high frequency of communication between family members. The positive influence of frequent conversations on the intergenerational transmission of political values was also reported by Fend (1991). These mechanisms promoting the transmission of values seem to be characteristic of both authoritarian and democratic families. Summarizing the results of his study, Fend (1994) concluded that rightist attitudes are not projections of a negative self-concept or a reflection of lower social integration into the peer group. Rather, his findings point particularly to the influence of political socialization processes in the family.

School and Peer Influences

Experiences in other important socialization contexts for adolescents besides the family, namely the school and the peer group, have also been found to be related to adolescents' antidemocratic attitudes and behaviors. First, the specific school track adolescents attend seems to provide a specific social climate more or less favoring aggressiveness and political intolerance. The majority of studies (Fend, 1994; W. Hopf, 1994; Noack and Kracke (1995) reported higher antiforeigner and national-authoritarian attitudes in adolescents from lower school tracks. Reasons for this relationship between level of schooling and lower political tolerance are discussed as having two aspects: (1) the confoundation of school track and lower social status which, in turn, is associated with lower political tolerance, and (2) the specific pragmatic way of thinking which is favored in lower educational tracks (in higher tracks more differentiated ways of thinking are promoted) (W. Hopf, 1994). Beside the impact of school track, school failure also seems to be related with adolescents' right-extremist attitudes (Schubarth and Melzer, 1993; Klein-Allermann et al., 1995)

Secondly, values and attitudes of the peer group can become important guidelines for adolescents' political orientations (Hennig, 1982; Wasmund, 1982), especially in middle adolescence when peer pressure and conformity to the peer group are most influential (Brown, Clasen, and Eicher, 1986). Krampen (1991), for instance, found that friends' concerns with political issues were predictive for adolescents' political knowledge, everyday political activities, and their self-concept of political abilities. Furthermore, 90 percent of rightist offenses are conducted in groups (Willems, 1993).

Summarizing the various findings on important influences on adolescents' rightist orientations presented so far, Khoshrung-Sefat and colleagues'

(1983, p. 55) definition of political socialization might be a useful integrator. According to the authors, political socialization is a complex, lifelong learning process influenced directly and indirectly by a multitude of socialization agents that may operate simultaneously, interact, overlap, and accumulate. At the same time, reciprocal influences of children on adult socialization agents or peers could occur. Therefore, more complex approaches than focusing on only one aspect of social context are needed to explain political orientations in adolescents. The lifelong learning process points especially to the relevance of the family, in addition to societal changes that may impact adolescents only indirectly.

Our empirical work so far has examined adolescents' antidemocratic attitudes in East and West Germany after unification and related social factors. Particularly, the impact of social change, family processes, and school-related problems were studied as predictors of the readiness to use violence and express antiforeigner and antidemocratic attitudes. In contrast to previous research, which assumed that social change should impact adolescents' rightist attitudes without directly assessing the influence of change, we measured adolescents' perception of social change. The development of the instrument is described by Noack and colleagues (1995) in greater detail.

The Empirical Study

The purpose of the present chapter is to examine the impact of the interplay between social change and parental political attitudes on adolescents' political orientations. More specifically, we wanted to investigate (1) whether specific aspects of social change would influence adolescents' antiforeigner and antidemocratic attitudes, and (2) whether the impact of social change on adolescents' attitudes is mediated by their parents' political attitudes. To examine these questions cross-sectional and longitudinal analyses were carried out. Because of Germany's forty-year history of separation into two countries with rather different political and educational systems and the currently differing paces of social change in East and West Germany, one question in our analyses always is whether the assumed processes are the same in East and West German families.

Sample

The data analyzed in the present study stem from a four-year longitudinal investigation conducted in two German cities of similar industrial backgrounds with about 300,000 (Mannheim, West Germany) and

500,000 (Leipzig, East Germany) inhabitants. The assessments started in Fall 1992 with a total sample of 503 adolescents (51.5 percent female) who were about 15.2 years old. A total of 351 mothers and 303 fathers also participated in the study. The data were assessed by questionnaires addressing various aspects of individual and familial development as well as the families' economic situation and perceptions of societal changes. The questionnaires were completed at home. Data from 285 families are available including adolescents' and both parents' responses at the first measurement point and responses of 180 families at the second measurement one year later. The sample sizes of the present study vary from 201 to 227 families due to missing data in the respective cross-sectional analyses at the first measurement point. In the longitudinal analyses, sample sizes vary between 103 and 112 families. In each analysis, East and West German families are almost equally represented, whereas girls are slightly overrepresented (58.1 percent).

Measures
Social Change
Two aspects of social change were addressed. On the family level, changes in purchasing power were assessed to capture experiences of economic deprivation. Mothers and fathers were asked individually to indicate whether it had become easier or more difficult to spend money on various goods as compared to five years ago. They judged ten items (e.g., clothes, hosting guests, rent, child care) on five-point-scales (1 = much easier, 3 = the same, 5 = much more difficult).

Factor analyses conducted separately for both parents in the two parts of the country yielded two highly reliable scales for East German families. The first factor (Purchasing Power I) included expenses on consumer goods such as clothes, travel, car, grocery, or hosting guests; the second factor (Purchasing Power II) included expenses for more basic family needs such as rent or child care. Although for West German families a one-factor solution would have been also adequate to indicate whether families can make ends meet regardless of which expenditures are concerned, for the sake of comparability two scales were analyzed in both samples. The internal consistencies were high in both samples (Purchasing Power I Cronbach alphas, East: mothers 0.86, fathers 0.86; West: mothers 0.91, fathers 0.95; Purchasing Power II Cronbach alphas, East: mothers 0.77, fathers 0.78; West: mothers 0.76, fathers 0.83). For the present analyses fathers' and mothers' responses, which were highly correlated, were combined.

The second aspect of social change addressed in our research refers to individual experiences of change of macrocontextual conditions. As described by Noack and colleagues (1995), we developed a new instrument comprised of twenty-six items forming six scales to assess individual perceptions of change in different aspects of life in society. Each item was presented as a descriptive statement (e.g., "People help each other") and had to be rated by each family member regarding (a) change or stability during the last five years (1 = much less today, 3 = the same; 5 = much more today), (b) the present situation (from 1 = does not apply, to 4 = fully applies), and (c) the individual evaluation of the present situation (from 1 = very bad, to 4 = very good).

In the present analyses, we refer to adolescents' and parents' responses to only one scale—Uncertainty—reflecting anomie (e.g., "Everything is so uncertain that anything may happen"). This scale consists of six items and has acceptable internal consistencies in all subsamples (Cronbach alphas from 0.68 to 0.79).

Rightist Attitudes

Two aspects of rightist attitudes were analyzed: Adolescents' and parents' Antiforeigner Attitudes were comprised of four items: slogans to reflect ethnic competition (e.g., "There are too many foreign students in German schools" or "Foreigners are taking away our jobs"). Respondents rated from 1 = does not apply, to 4 = fully applies. The internal consistencies of this rather short scale were high, with Cronbach alphas ranging from 0.70 to 0.83.

The National-authoritarian Attitudes scale was comprised of eight statements addressing the superiority of the Germans over other nations (e.g., "Germans have some virtues like diligence, faithfulness, and sense of duty other people do not have"), sympathy for national socialism (e.g., "National socialism was originally a good idea but was realized badly"), and the demand for authoritarian actions (e.g., "Whoever does not want to conform to our society has to be forced to do so"). Cronbach alphas ranged from 0.51 to 0.72.

Results

Perceptions of Social Change and Rightist Attitudes as a Function of Area of Living, School Track, and Adolescent Gender

Before we look at the relationships between experiences of social change and rightist attitudes, we first examine whether there are mean differences in social change and rightist attitudes between East and West Germany, lower and higher school tracks, and adolescent gender. Table 7.1 shows the results of multifactorial analyses of variance with all aspects of social change as dependent variables. First of all, no differences between adolescent boys and girls in the perception of social change were found. School track was important with respect to changes in the family budget. Independent of residency, adolescents in the lower school tracks came from families who had to face increasing difficulties in making ends meet during the past five years. Most important for the perception of social change is whether families live in East or West Germany. East German adolescents and adults perceived an increasing uncertainty of the life situation to a greater extent than West Germans, who nonetheless also reported changes in the same direction. Furthermore, covering the expenses for basic goods such as rent and child care (Purchasing Power II) had become more difficult for East German families as compared to the time when in the former German Democratic Republic rents and child care had been highly subsidized. Consumer goods (Purchasing Power I), however, had become less difficult to buy given East German families' budgets. For West German families, on average, both kinds of expenses had not changed during the past five years. Taken together, the results showed that East and West German families currently lived under different macrosocial conditions.

Table 7.1 Means of Perceptions of Social Change by Residence, School Track, and Gender of Adolescent (N = 201)

| Variable | Place | | Gender | | School Track | |
	West Germany	East Germany	Male	Female	Low	High
Purchasing Power I	3.04	2.28	2.67	2.64	2.75	2.55
Purchasing Power II	2.95	3.60	3.23	3.31	3.40	3.13
Adolescents' Uncertainty	3.89	4.25	4.11	4.04	4.06	4.08
Mothers' Uncertainty	3.89	4.33	4.05	4.16	4.14	4.08
Fathers' Uncertainty	3.86	4.32	4.01	4.15	4.09	4.08

Variable	Place[a]	Gender	School	PxG	PxS	SxG	PxGxS
Purchasing Power I	***	ns	***	ns	ns	ns	ns
Purchasing Power II	***	ns	**	ns	+	ns	ns
Adolescents' Uncertainty	***	ns	ns	ns	ns	ns	ns
Mothers' Uncertainty	***	ns	ns	ns	ns	ns	ns
Fathers' Uncertainty	***	ns	ns	ns	ns	ns	*

[a] Results of ANOVAS: + $p < 0.10$; * $p < 0.05$; ** $p < 0.01$; *** $p < 0.001$; ns = nonsignificant.

Table 7.2 suggests that East and West German adolescents and adults on average showed rather low agreements with rightist attitudes as indicated by the means below the scale mean of 2.5. While place of living and gender of adolescent was of no relevance for the magnitude of rightist attitudes, school track was. Adolescents of both genders in East and West Germany who attended lower school tracks showed more pronounced antiforeigner and national-authoritarian attitudes than adolescents attending Gymnasium (the highest school track in the German school system). In the same vein, parents of lower-track students showed also more rightist orientations than parents of higher track students. The only exception were fathers in West Germany. Their national-authoritarian attitudes did not differ as a function of school track (M, low: 2.24; high: 2.11) whereas East German fathers' attitudes did (M, low: 2.41; high: 1.98) as indicated by the significant School x Place interaction effect.

Summarizing the results, we can state that although East German families experienced more social change on the global level and in parts of their family budgets they did not show more rightist attitudes. Instead, these political orientations seem especially typical overall of families with a lower educational background.

Rightist Attitudes, School Track, and Social Change

The effects of social change and parental attitudes on adolescents' rightist

Table 7.2 Means of Antiforeigner and National-authoritarian Attitudes by Residence, School Track, and Gender of Adolescent (N = 227)

Variable	Place		Gender		School Track	
	West Germany	East Germany	Male	Female	Low	High
Adolescents' Antiforeigner Attitudes	2.13	2.17	2.25	2.07	2.37	1.87
Mothers' Antiforeigner Attitudes	2.10	2.11	2.14	2.06	2.28	1.87
Fathers' Antiforeigner Attitudes	2.15	2.17	2.17	2.15	2.30	1.97
Adolescents' National-authoritarian Attitudes	2.14	2.21	2.24	2.13	2.30	2.02
Mothers' National-authoritarian Attitudes	2.14	2.18	2.24	2.10	2.28	2.00
Fathers' National-authoritarian Attitudes	2.18	2.25	2.24	2.19	2.33	2.06

(continued)

Table 7.2 *(continued)*

Variable	Place[a]	Gender	School	PxG	PxS	SxG	PxGxS
Adolescents' Antiforeigner Attitudes	ns	ns	***	ns	ns	ns	ns
Mothers' Antiforeigner Attitudes	ns	ns	***	ns	ns	ns	ns
Fathers' Antiforeigner Attitudes	ns	ns	***	ns	ns	ns	ns
Adolescents' National-authoritarian Attitudes	ns	ns	***	+	ns	ns	ns
Mothers' National-authoritarian Attitudes	ns	ns	***	ns	ns	ns	ns
Fathers' National-authoritarian Attitudes	ns	ns	***	ns	*	ns	ns

[a] Results of ANOVAS: $+ p < 0.10$; $* p < 0.05$; $** p < 0.01$; $*** p < 0.001$; ns = nonsignificant.

attitudes were analyzed by a series of multiple regression analyses. In the first step, school was entered as the control followed by Purchasing Power II (basic family needs) and Uncertainty as perceived by the adolescent in the second step, and rightist attitudes of both parents in the third step.

This selection of predictors was based on preliminary correlation analyses including all social change and rightist attitudes variables assessed in each family member, first, to have a rationale for selecting predictors for the regression analyses, and, second, to check how the variables within the different conceptual domains are interrelated. On the basis of these analyses Purchasing Power II was chosen as the only predictor reflecting financial problems in order to avoid collinearity effects with Purchasing Power I because of high intercorrelations in the West German sample ($r = 0.81$). Adolescents' uncertainty was picked because preliminary bivariate correlations had revealed that parents' perceptions of uncertainty were not substantially related to adolescents' rightist attitudes, whereas this was the case for at least West German adolescents' perceptions of uncertainty.

The correlation analyses also showed moderate correlations between antiforeigner and national-authoritarian attitudes of each family member in East and West ($rs = 0.44$ to 0.66), pointing to related but not identical concepts that might be influenced by third variables in different ways. Furthermore, East and West German fathers and mothers seemed to be rather similar to each other in their rightist attitudes (rs about 0.50). Regarding the relationship between experiences of social change and rightist

Table 7.3 Adolescents' Antiforeigner Attitudes as a Function of School Track, Families' Purchasing Power, Adolescents' Uncertainty, and Parents' Antiforeigner Attitudes

Predictor	West (N = 111) Germany				East (N = 112) Germany			
	r	Beta	R^2	R^2-Change	r	Beta	R^2	R^2-Change
1. Step								
School	–0.39***	–0.39***	0.15	0.15***	–0.28**	–0.28**	0.08	0.08**
2. Step								
School		–0.38***	0.30	0.15***		–0.25**	0.09	0.01
Purchasing Power II	0.26**	0.16+			0.12+	0.08		
Adolescents' Uncertainty	0.35***	0.31***			–0.12+	–0.11		
3. Step								
School		–0.32***	0.33	0.03+		–0.17+	0.18	0.08**
Purchasing Power II		0.15+				0.05		
Adolescents' Uncertainty		0.29***				–0.12		
Mothers' Antiforeigner Attitudes	0.34***	0.19*			0.21*	–0.01		
Fathers' Antiforeigner Attitudes	0.22**	–0.01			0.36***	0.31**		

+ p < 0.10; * p < 0.05; ** p < 0.01; *** p < 0.001.
Note: "Step" refers to the order in which the independent variables are entered into the regression model.

attitudes, the results revealed that the more financial strain in the family budget and the more uncertainty in the life situations the East and West German parents reported, the more they showed rightist attitudes. As will be shown in the regression analyses later on, their adolescent children reacted differentially to experiences of social change.

Preliminary regression analyses testing interaction terms of each predictor and place (West Germany versus East Germany) revealed significant effects for uncertainty, marginal effects for purchasing power, and marginal effects for mothers' national-authoritarian attitudes toward adolescents. Thus, results of regression analyses of political attitudes conducted separately for East and West German adolescents were reported.

Table 7.3 shows the results concerning adolescents' antiforeigner attitudes. The set of predictors was more relevant in the West German sample than in the East German sample as reflected by the different amount of explained variance (West 33 percent; East 18 percent). In West Germany, adolescents' antiforeigner attitudes were higher when they attended the lower track of the school system, when their parents reported more financial strain in the family budget, when they perceived increasing uncertainty in the living conditions, and when their mothers also expressed higher antiforeigner attitudes. Regression coefficients of lower magnitude than the respective bivariate correlations indicated that the predictors themselves were substantially intercorrelated. Antiforeigner attitudes of the father, for example, which were substantially correlated with adolescents' attitudes had no genuine effect in the regression analysis.

East German adolescents' antiforeigner attitudes could be best predicted by school track and fathers' antiforeigner attitudes. Similar to West Germans, adolescents from the lower school track with fathers expressing higher antiforeigner attitudes were more likely to agree with antiforeigner slogans than their agemates obtaining higher education and having more tolerant fathers. Contrary to West German adolescents, East German adolescents' resentments against foreigners were not influenced by experiences of social change.

The results for adolescents' antidemocratic attitudes are shown in Table 7.4. Again, our model explained more variance in the West German sample (25 percent) than in the East German sample (14 percent). In contrast to

Table 7.4 Adolescents' National-Authoritarian Attitudes as a Function of School Track, Families' Purchasing Power, Adolescents' Uncertainty, and Parents' National-authoritarian Attitudes

Predictors	West (N = 105) Germany				East (N = 103) Germany			
	r	Beta	R^2	R^2-Change	r	Beta	R^2	R^2-Change
1. Step								
School	−0.26**	−0.26**	0.07	0.07**	−0.27**	−0.27**	0.07	0.07**
2. Step								
School		−0.24*	0.13	0.06*		−0.27**	0.10	0.02
Purchasing								
Power II	0.22**	0.13			0.15+	0.11		
Adolescents'								
Uncertainty	0.29**	0.17+			0.07	0.10		

(continued)

Table 7.4 *(continued)*

Predictor	r	West (N = 105) Germany Beta	R^2	R^2-Change	r	East (N = 103) Germany Beta	R^2	R^2-Change
3. Step								
School		−0.13	0.25	0.12***		−0.19+	0.14	0.04+
Purchasing								
Power II		0.10				0.07		
Adolescents'								
Uncertainty		0.15				0.10		
Mothers'								
National-authoritarian								
Attitudes	0.44***	0.36**			0.17*	−0.01		
Fathers'								
National-authoritarian								
Attitudes	0.28**	0.03			0.31***	0.23+		

+ $p < 0.10$; * $p < 0.05$; ** $p < 0.01$; *** $p < 0.001$.
Note: "Step" refers to the order in which the independent variables are entered into the regression model.

the previous analyses, the final models only included parental national-authoritarian attitudes in the West sample as substantial predictors indicating that West German adolescents showed more national-authoritarian attitudes when their mothers did so, and that East German adolescents were, again, influenced most by their fathers in this respect. This result can be explained by the high intercorrelation between school track and parental authoritarian attitudes (adolescents in lower school track had more authoritarian parents), which reduced the effect of school track by about half after parental attitudes were included into the regression. Purchasing power also had no genuine influence on adolescents' authoritarian attitudes because of its high correlation with school track (adolescents in the lower school tracks experienced more strain in the family budget).

In both German subsamples the political attitudes of only one parent contributed to the explanation of adolescents' attitudes in the regression analyses while the correlational analyses showed no significant differences in the correlational relationships (according to Fisher Z-Tests) between the mother-adolescent dyad and the father-adolescent dyad. In East Germany, mothers' influence was mediated by fathers' attitudes while in West Germany, fathers' influence was mediated by mothers' attitudes. These results may be due to the fact that mothers' and fathers' attitudes were differentially related to other predictor variables and to the slightly but not significantly different correlation coefficients.

Longitudinal Effects on Rightist Orientations

In order to examine the direction of effects, such as whether social change or parental attitudes predict future changes in adolescents' rightist attitudes, longitudinal regression analyses were conducted. Criteria were adolescents' rightist attitudes at the second measurement point (Winter 1993), predictors were rightist attitudes at Time 1 (Winter 1992) entered in the first step, school-track at Time 1 entered second, Purchasing Power II and Uncertainty at Time 1 entered in the third step, and parental attitudes at Time 1 entered last.

The results in Tables 7.5 and 7.6 show that the stabilities of adolescents' rightist attitudes were rather high, ranging from 0.56 to 0.80 and indicating that the best predictor of future rightist attitudes were previous rightist attitudes. Fisher Z-Tests revealed that the stability of antiforeigner attitudes in the West German sample was significantly higher than

Table 7.5 Adolescents' Antiforeigner Attitudes at Year 2 as a Function of School Track, Families' Purchasing Power, Adolescents' Uncertainty, and Adolescents' and Parents' Antiforeigner Attitudes at Year 1

Predictor	West (N = 80) Germany				East (N = 82) Germany			
	r	Beta	R^2	R^2-change	r	Beta	R^2	R^2-change
1. Step								
Antiforeigner								
Attitudes T1	0.80***	0.80***	0.64	0.64***	0.56***	0.56***	0.31	0.31***
2. Step								
Antiforeigner								
Attitudes T1		0.72***	0.67	0.02*		0.49***	0.39	0.08**
School	−0.51***	−0.17*			−0.41***	−0.29**		
3. Step								
Antiforeigner								
Attitudes T1		0.68***	0.68	0.01		0.50***	0.40	0.01
School		−0.19*				−0.30**		
Purchasing								
Power II	0.21*	0.01			0.12	−0.01		
Adolescents'								
Uncertainty	0.33*	0.10			0.05	0.10		

(continued)

Table 7.5 *(continued)*

Predictor	r	West (N = 80) Germany Beta	R²	R²-change	r	East (N = 82) Germany Beta	R²	R²-change
4. Step								
Antiforeigner Attitudes T1		0.64***	0.68	0.00		0.45***	0.45	0.05*
School		–0.19*				–0.23*		
Purchasing Power II		0.00				–0.02		
Adolescents' Uncertainty		0.09				0.09		
Mothers' Antiforeigner Attitudes	0.46***	0.07			0.37***	0.15		
Fathers' Antiforeigner Attitudes	0.31**	0.05			0.41***	0.13		

+ p < 0.10; * p < 0.05; ** p < 0.01;*** p < 0.001.
Note: "Step" refers to the order in which the independent variables are entered into the regression model.

in the East German sample ($z = 2.91$, $p < 0.01$). The stabilities of national-authoritarian attitudes were not different in both subsamples. Additional mean comparisons between attitudes of the first and second measurement point showed no increase or decline in the agreement to antiforeigner and national-authoritarian statements.

The final models for East and West German adolescents included the stabilities and school track as significant predictors beyond the effects of Time 1 attitudes. Attending the lower school track at Time 1 was a risk factor for increases of antiforeigner orientations. Social change and parental attitudes at Time 1 did not predict change in antiforeigner attitudes. Their effects seemed to be mediated by the high stabilities of adolescents' attitudes. Table 7.6 shows that East and West German adolescents' national-authoritarian attitudes at Time 2 were best predicted by their attitudes at Time 1. In the West German sample, mothers' authoritarian attitudes and school track at Time 1 had effects beyond the stability. As was the case for antiforeigner attitudes, social change and parental attitudes seemed to exert influence on future authoritarian orientations through high cross-sectional correlations.

Table 7.6 Adolescents' National-authoritarian Attitudes at Year 2 as a Function of School Track, Families' Purchasing Power, Adolescents' Uncertainty, and Adolescents' and Parents' National-authoritarian Attitudes at Year 1

Predictor	West (N = 76) Germany				East (N = 76) Germany			
	r	Beta	R^2	R^2-change	r	Beta	R^2	R^2-change
1. Step								
National-authoritarian T1	0.69***	0.69***	0.47	0.49***	0.73***	0.73***	0.53	0.53***
2. Step								
National-authoritarian T1		0.62***	0.52	0.05**		0.69***	0.56	0.03*
School	−0.41***	−0.23**			−0.33**	−0.18*		
3. Step								
National-authoritarian T1	0.61***		0.52	0.00	0.68***		0.56	0.00
School		−0.23**				-0.18*		
Purchasing Power II	0.18+	0.03			0.14	0.01		
Adolescents' Uncertainty	0.14	0.04			0.07	0.02		
4. Step								
National-authoritarian T1	0.53***		0.56	0.04*	0.66***		0.59	0.03+
School		−0.21*				−0.12		
Purchasing Power II		0.04				0.00		
Adolescents' Uncertainty		0.01				0.01		
Mothers' National authoritarian Attitudes	0.51***	0.28*			0.25*	0.07		
Fathers' National-authoritarian Attitudes	0.28**	−0.13			0.39***	0.14		

+ p < 0.10; * p < 0.05; ** p < 0.01; *** p < 0.001.
Note: "Step" refers to the order in which the independent variables are entered into the regression model.

Discussion

The purpose of this chapter was to examine the impact of social change and parental political attitudes on adolescents' antiforeigner and national-authoritarian orientations. We wanted to integrate theoretical approaches focusing either mainly on macrosocial influences or on the immediate family context in attempts to explain adolescents' rightist attitudes. In contrast to previous research, which often assumed certain social groups of adolescents to be especially affected by social change without measuring the effect, we assessed social change by self-report. Furthermore, school track was considered as an important socialization context beyond the family and an indicator of educational and, thus, intellectual resources.

As discussed in the introductory section, current theories and research findings do not provide a unanimous picture as to which specific macrosocial processes affect adolescents' rightist orientations and how they do so. The macrosocial influences examined range from experiences of uncertainty of the life situation (e.g., Heitmeyer, 1988) to actual experiences of deprivation (e.g., W. Hopf, 1994). Our results show that the uncertainty as well as the deprivation hypotheses—when deprivation is captured in terms of economic disadvantage—seem to systematically contribute to the explanation of West German adolescents' antiforeigner and national-authoritarian attitudes. East German adolescents' rightist orientations, however, could be explained neither by experiences of uncertainty—as compared to West Germans' attitudes—nor, to a lesser degree, by economic deprivation. This finding is in line with Schröder and Melzer's (1992) finding that resentments against foreigners among fifteen- to twenty-four-year-old East German adolescents in the beginning of 1991 could not be explained by their perceptions of higher economic risk. Only among West German adolescents was the perception of higher economic risk related to negative attitudes toward foreigners. The authors also found that for East German adolescents, authoritarianism was an important basis for their antiforeigner attitudes. Together with our own results, Schröder and Melzer's findings seem to indicate that antiforeigner attitudes are differentially related to social change in East and West German adolescents.

How could these different reactions of East and West German adolescents be explained? Hofer and colleagues (1994) suggested an explanation referring to processes of social comparison. Even though East German adolescents perceive societal change to a much higher degree, they may interpret it as a normal side effect of the unification process that affects everybody, whereas West German adolescents may see themselves as being individually affected by societal changes and, therefore, especially disadvantaged, which could lead them to seek for scapegoats in foreigners.

Contrary to their offspring, East and West German adults were rather similar in their reactions to experiences of social change in that both showed more rightist attitudes when experiencing more change. It could be that in West German families, uncertainty in the life situation is shared by all family members and interpreted negatively in similar ways by parents and adolescents because they associate future loss of opportunities with it. Financial strain assessed in parents might be either directly noticed by Western adolescents because they personally have less money to purchase or indirectly by a strained family climate. In East German families it might be the case that social change mainly affects parents negatively. Although everybody is noticing increasing uncertainty, only parents may perceive it as a threat; for the younger generation it could mean a challenge, promising more opportunities in the future.

While social change had an impact on adolescents' rightist orientations in East and West Germany differently, the influence of school track and parental attitudes was similarly important in both subsamples. German parents in general seemed to have a strong influence in the socialization of their offspring's political orientations by creating a specific political climate in the family. This result supports some political commentators in Germany claiming that it is useless to intervene only on the side of rightist adolescents as long as adults approve of rightist attitudes and, thus, give the adolescents the feeling of having appropriate political attitudes.

The family effect was complemented by the effect of school track. In East and West Germany, attending a lower school track was associated with stronger rightist attitudes among adolescents and their parents. Because school track is a proxy for intellectual abilities, this result supports previous findings that rightist attitudes appeal to people who are not trained to think in complex terms—an ability needed to cope with the increasing complexity of societies. Moreover, school track is also associated with differential opportunities regarding future positions in society. Rightist attitudes of lower-track adolescents could, thus, reflect their fear of losing in the competition with other groups on the lower edge of society for securer positions. Our longitudinal results also point to a widening of the difference between lower and higher school tracks across the time of one year, with lower track adolescents increasing their intolerance.

The longitudinal analyses revealed significantly different stabilities in antiforeigner attitudes between East and West German adolescents, while national-authoritarian attitudes were of similarly high stability. This difference between adolescents from both parts of Germany could be due to different histories of contacts with foreigners and different histories of using foreigners as scapegoats for social and political difficulties. In West Germany, many more foreigners live and work as so-called guest workers (about 8 percent of the population) while in East Germany only about 1 percent of the population are foreigners.

Taken together, our study shows that it is important to consider influences from different socialization contexts when aiming at an appropriate explanation of adolescents' rightist attitudes. Aspects of social change as well as experiences in closer contexts seem to be influential. Furthermore, differences between East and West German families in their reactions to social change on the macrolevel and similarities in the importance of school track and parental attitudes for adolescents' rightist orientations point out that culture-specific as well as more general processes have to be considered when explaining adolescents' rightist attitudes.

Whether rightist attitudes are a problem in today's youth—not only in Germany—is no longer an open question. In many European countries right-extremist attitudes and violent acts are now common (e.g., Kirfel and Oswalt, 1991; Fend, 1994; Vollebergh, 1991). In order to gain more insight into culture-specific and more general processes in the development of adolescents' rightist attitudes, it would be necessary to have more cross-cultural studies addressing this question in different countries. What seems to be a common finding in the already existing research is that adolescents with poorer educational backgrounds and intolerant parents tend to show more rightist attitudes. Further research is badly needed in order to better understand the social and individual origins of intolerance and to adequately prepare young people for their lives in an increasingly complex world.

References

Adorno, T. W., Frenkel-Brunswik, E., Levinson, D. J., and Sanford, R. N. (1966). *The authoritarian personality*. New York: Plenum.

Bengston, V. L., and Troll, L. (1978). Youth and their parents: Feedback and intergenerational influence in socialization. In R. M. Lerner and G. B. Spanier (eds.), *Child influences on marital and family interaction* (pp. 215–240). New York: Plenum.

Bommes, M., and Scherr, A. (1992). Rechtsextremismus: Ein Angebot für ganz gewöhnliche Jugendliche [Right extremism: An offer for just normal adolescents]. In J. Mansel (ed.), *Reaktionen Jugendlicher auf gesellschaftliche Bedrohung* (pp. 210–227). Weinheim, Germany: Beltz.

Brown, B. B., Clasen, D., and Eicher, S. (1986). Perceptions of peer pressure, peer conformity dispositions, and self-reported behavior among adolescents. *Developmental Psychology*, *22*, 521–530.

Fend, H. (1991). *Identitätsentwicklung in der Adoleszenz* [Identity development in adolescence]. Bern: Huber.

Fend, H. (1994). Ausländerfeindlich-nationalistische Weltbilder und Aggressionsbereitschaft bei Jugendlichen in Deutschland und in der Schweiz: Kontextuelle und personale Antezedenzbedingungen [Antiforeigner and nationalist conceptions of the world and aggressive tendencies in German and Swiss adolescents: Contextual and personal antecedents]. *Zeitschrift für Sozialisationsforschung und Erziehungssoziologie, 14,* 131–162.

Heitmeyer, W. (1988). *Rechtsextremistische Orientierungen bei Jugendlichen: Empirische Ergebnisse und Erklärungsmuster einer Untersuchung zur politischen Sozialisation* [Rightist orientations among adolescents. Empirical results and explanations]. Weinheim, Germany: Juventa.

Hennig, E. (1982). Neonazistische Militanz und Rechtsextremismus unter Jugendlichen [Neonazi militance and right extremism among adolescents]. *Aus Politik und Zeitgeschichte, B23,* 23–37.

Hofer, M., Noack, P., Kracke, B., and Klein-Allermann, E. (September 1994). *Einflüsse des elterlichen Erziehungsstils auf politische Einstellungen und Gewaltbereitschaft Jugendlicher in Ost- und Westdeutschland* [Influences of parental child-rearing practices on adolescents' political attitudes and violence proneness in East and West Germany]. Paper presented at the Thirty-ninth Biennial Meetings of the German Society for Psychology, Hamburg.

Hopf, C. (1992). Eltern-Idealisierung und Autoritarismus: Kritische Überlegungen zu einigen sozialpsychologischen Annahmen [Idealization of parents and authoritarianism: Critical considerations concerning social-psychological assumptions]. *Zeitschrift für Sozialisationsforschung und Erziehungssoziologie, 12,* 52–65.

Hopf, C. (1993). Autoritäres Verhalten: Ansätze zur Interpretation rechtsextremer Tendenzen [Authoritarian behavior: Approaches to interpret rightist tendencies]. In H.-U. Otto, and R. Merten (eds.), *Rechtsradikale Gewalt im vereinigten Deutschland* (pp. 157–165). Opladen, Germany: Leske and Budrich.

Hopf, W. (1991). Familiale und schulische Bedingungen rechtsextremer Orientierungen von Jugendlichen [Family and school-related antecedents of adolescents' rightist orientations]. *Zeitschrift für Sozialisationsforschung und Erziehungssoziologie, 11,* 43–59.

Hopf, W. (1994). Rechtsextremismus von Jugendlichen: Kein Deprivationsproblem? [Adolescents' right extremism: No problem of deprivation?]. *Zeitschrift für Sozialisationsforschung und Erziehungssoziologie, 14,* 194–211.

Keiser, S. (1991). Die Familie als Faktor der politischen Sozialisation Jugendlicher in der DDR Ende der 80er Jahre [The family as a factor in the political socialization in the GDR at the end of the 1980s]. In W. Henning, and W. Friedrich (eds.), *Jugend in der DDR* (pp. 39–50). Weinheim, Germany: Juventa.

Khoshrung-Sefat, H., Hennige, U., Metz-Göckel, H., and Preiser, S. (1983). Sozialisationsbedingungen sozialen und politischen Engagements [Effects of socialization on social and political involvement]. In S. Preiser (ed.), *Soziales und politisches Engagement. Kognitive und soziale Bedingungen* (pp. 45–105). Weinheim, Germany: Beltz.

Kirfel, M., and Oswalt, W., eds. (1991). *Die Rückkehr der Führer: Modernisierter Rechtsradikalismus in Westeuropa.* [The return of the leaders: Modern right radicalism in Western Europe]. Vienna: Europa Verlag.

Klein-Allermann, E., Kracke, B., Noack, P., and Hofer. M. (1995). Micro- and macrosocial conditions of adolescents' aggressiveness and antiforeigner attitudes. In J. Youniss (ed.), *After the Wall: Family adaptations in East and West Germany* (pp. 71–83). *New Directions for Child Development, 70.* San Francisco: Jossey Bass.

Kracke, B., Noack, P., Hofer, M., and Klein-Allermann, E. (1993). Die rechte Gesinnung: Familiale Bedingungen autoritärer Orientierungen ost- und westdeutscher Jugendlicher [The right way of thinking: Family antecedents of authoritarian orientations among East and West German adolescents]. *Zeitschrift für Pädagogik, 39,* 971–988.

Krampen, G. (1991). *Entwicklung politischer Handlungsorientierungen im Jugendalter. Ergebnisse einer explorativen Längsschnittsequenz-Studie* [The development of politi-

cal behavior orientations in adolescence. Results of an explorative longitudinal study].
Göttingen, Germany: Hogrefe.

Mussen, P. (1984). Persönlichkeit und politische Einstellungen im Jugendalter [Personality and
political attitudes in adolescence]. In E. Olbrich and E. Todt (eds.), *Probleme des
Jugendalters* (pp. 317–332). Berlin: Springer.

Noack, P., Hofer, M., Kracke, B., and Klein-Allermann, E. (1995). Adolescents and their parents
facing social change: Families in East and West Germany after unification. In P. Noack,
M. Hofer, and J. Youniss (eds.), *Psychological responses to social change* (pp. 129–148).
Berlin: de Gruyter.

Noack, P., and Kracke, B. (1995). Jugendliche, Ausländer und Europa: Einstellungen in
Abhängigkeit von globalen Werthaltungen und Schultyp [Adolescents, foreigners, and
Europe: Attitudes as a function of global value orientations and school track]. *Psychologie
in Erziehung und Unterricht, 42,* 89–98.

Oswald, H., and Stuendel, R. (March 1990). *Adolescents between mothers, fathers, and peers:
Similarities in political attitudes in West Germany.* Paper presented at the 3rd Biennial
Meetings of the Society for Research on Adolescence, Atlanta, Georgia.

Schröder, H., and Melzer, W. (1992). Ökonomische Risiken und Verunsicherungspotentiale
Jugendlicher in Ost- und Westdeutschland: Vergleichende Befunde aus dem Jahr nach
der Wende [Economic risks and insecurities for adolescents in East and West Germany:
Comparisons in the year after reunion]. In J. Mansel (ed.), *Reaktionen Jugendlicher auf
gesellschaftliche Bedrohung* (S. 163–184). Weinheim, Germany: Juventa.

Schubarth, W., and Melzer, W. (1993). *Schule, Gewalt und Rechtsextremismus* [School, violence, and right extremism]. Opladen, Germany: Leske and Budrich.

Treibel, A. (1990). *Migration in modernen Gesellschaften* [Migration in modern societies].
Weinheim, Germany: Juventa.

Vollebergh, W. (1991). *The limits of tolerance.* Utrecht, Netherlands: Faculty of Social Sciences.

Wasmund, K. (1982). Sind Altersgruppen die modernen politischen Verführer? [Are peers the
modern political seducers?]. In B. Claussen, and K. Wasmund (eds.), *Handbuch der
politischen Sozialisation* (pp. 104–118). Braunschweig, Germany: Agentur für
wissenschaftliche Literatur.

Willems, H. (1993). Gewalt und Fremdenfeindlichkeit: Anmerkungen zum gegenwärtigen
Gewaltdiskurs [Violence and hostility against foreigners: Remarks on the current
discourse on violence]. In H.-U. Otto, and R. Merten (eds.), *Rechtsradikale Gewalt im
vereinigten Deutschland* (pp. 88–108). Opladen, Germany: Leske and Budrich.

Chapter Eight
Adolescents and Political Violence
The Case of Northern Ireland

Mícheál D. Roe and Ed Cairns

Introduction

The dominant image of an adolescent in Northern Ireland continues to be a youth with brick in hand facing riot police or armored military vehicles on a smoke-filled city street. Not only is this scene not representative of the country as a whole, it is relevant only to a short and early period in Northern Ireland's Troubles, as the current political violence is known. In reality, violent civil crime in Northern Ireland is lower than that experienced in other parts of the United Kingdom (England, Scotland, and Wales); in fact, it generally is below that experienced in any major city around the globe. A visitor to Northern Ireland is more likely to comment on the peace and quiet than on pervasive civil strife. On the other hand, Northern Ireland's population is only 1.5 million, and it is distributed among close-knit urban neighborhoods and rural communities. Consequently, in the twenty-five years of the Troubles, the more than 3,000 deaths and ten times that number of injuries, the 34,000 recorded shooting incidents and over 14,000 bombs planted, and the close to 16,000 charged with terrorist offenses, have touched the entire country (Gallagher, 1995).

This chapter reviews the literature on the psychosocial development of adolescents under such conditions of political violence in Northern Ireland. It provides multidimensional analyses of the dynamics of change in political conflicts over the past twenty-five years, the shift from rather pessimistic interest in short-term effects of traumatic events to more optimistic interest in long-term adolescent resilience, and the strengths and weaknesses of psychological research in Northern Ireland. Attempts also are made to show the importance of focusing on relationships between the social and political environments of Northern Ireland (e.g., economic instability, segregation, sectarian attitudes) and adolescent development.

The selection of topics for this chapter is a result both of what psychological research is available on Northern Irish adolescents, and the relevance of specific elements in that research to the peculiar context of political violence in that country. The chapter begins with brief characterizations of the Troubles and the evolution of psychological research performed during this period. Identity development in adolescence is next addressed, since ethnic or social identities are foundational to sectarian attitudes and behavior, including political violence. This is followed by a review of the effects of such violence on adolescent moral reasoning and behavior, and on social and religious values. Adolescent mental health and coping with the political violence follows, with the chapter closing on the small but growing literature focused on intervention programs and their evaluation.

Historical and Social Background

The current Troubles of Northern Ireland are a contemporary manifestation of centuries of conflict over what is now England's control of the people and resources of the island. Following its war of independence in the early twentieth century, Ireland was partitioned. This resulted in the creation of predominantly Protestant Northern Ireland as a part of the United Kingdom, and as a separate entity from the remainder of predominantly Catholic Ireland.

Since partition significant periods of political violence have broken out a number of times, with the Troubles of today beginning in the late 1960s. Street riots were the most common form of violence in the first two to three years of the Troubles, with large numbers of persons from both Protestant and Catholic urban, working-class communities affected. From then on the violence was primarily between paramilitary organizations and the security forces composed of the police and the British army. Also, over the years intimidation caused the relocation of tens of thousands of both Protestants and Catholics, resulting in a patchwork of increasingly segregated Protestant and Catholic working-class urban neighborhoods or rural towns (Boal and Douglas, 1982; Darby, 1986).

Currently, Northern Ireland is experiencing a cessation of armed conflict between paramilitary organizations and security forces, although I.R.A. bombings have resumed in London. Even though bullets and bombs have generally ceased, less lethal violence between the two communities still erupts. Recently a colleague of ours who works with adolescents in Belfast bemoaned some of the worst cross-community youth violence in years at an interface area between Catholic and Protestant working-class neighborhoods. The cessation of armed political violence does not mean the cessation of sectarian attitudes and relationships.

To describe these conflicts as "holy wars" would be inaccurate. Although *Protestant* and *Catholic* do describe religious denominations, the conflicts relate more to conflicting social identities associated with opposing political agendas than to religion. On the other hand, for some subgroups, religious belief is an element in sectarian attitudes and conflict (e.g., Bruce, 1986; Wright, 1973), and for many if not most, the exclusivity and apparent alien nature of religious practices of the other community perpetuate identity distinctiveness that is concretely demonstrated weekly in segregated worship. Although neither group is homogeneous, Protestants tend to be dominated by a "unionist" agenda, which aims to maintain Northern Ireland within the dominion of the United Kingdom, while Catholics tend to be dominated by a "nationalist" agenda whose goal is for Northern Ireland to become part of the Republic of Ireland. The more militant among unionists are termed loyalists, and their counterparts among nationalists are termed republicans. It is from among these militant elements that paramilitary violence arises (see Darby, 1995; D. Murray, 1995; Whyte, 1990).

Northern Irish Catholics and Protestants maintain their distinction as "ethnic" groups by selectively remembering, interpreting, and celebrating their shared history, resulting in distinct ethnic histories or ethnic memories (Falconer, 1988; Roe, Pegg, and Hodges, 1995; Wright, 1988). For example, historical events may be commemorated where one side triumphed over the other, as in the battlefield victory of Protestant William of Orange over Catholic King James II in 1690. Northern Irish Protestants, particularly from the working class, annually celebrate this event with bonfires and marches. Likewise, wall murals depicting a gallant William on a white charger are common in Protestant working-class neighborhoods. Similarly, Catholics celebrate their own triumphs and heroes.

It is within this social context that the youth of Northern Ireland must be understood. In addition to the backdrop of political violence, they experience segregated housing, education, and employment. Both formally and informally they are taught selective ethnic histories. Finally, for working-class adolescents in particular, they commemorate events of conflict, and they observe sectarian attitudes and behavior in the adults of their respective communities.

Psychological Research Emerging from the Troubles

The Troubles in Northern Ireland have provided a natural laboratory in which to examine effects of political violence on children and adolescents, and to test ideas about the psychosocial basis of intergroup conflict. Some of the first observations were made by local psychiatrists (e.g., Lyons, 1972; Fraser, 1974), psychologists from outside Northern Ireland (e.g., Russell, 1973; Jahoda and Harrison, 1975), and visiting academics from the United States (e.g., Coles 1980; Fields, 1973). Local psychologists began to make sporadic contributions by the early 1970s (e.g., Cairns and Duriez, 1976), leading to the first book devoted largely to the work of Northern Irish psychologists in 1980 (Harbison and Harbison, 1980). This was followed by other similar works over the next decade (Cairns, 1987, 1983; Harbison, 1983, 1989; Heskin, 1980). Overall these document the transformation of research with children and adolescents in Northern Ireland—from an interest in simple short-term effects of political violence, with a primary focus on stress, to a multidimensional approach to both causes and effects. These changes reflected the changing nature of the actual political conflict and the increasing dominance of local social scientists in structuring hypotheses and research designs. Research also moved from a rather pessimistic approach, in which psychopathology was the central focus, to a more optimistic one in which the resilience of children and adolescents tended to be emphasized (see Cairns and Toner, 1993).

In the late 1960s and early 1970s psychological explanations for intergroup conflict tended to be largely psychodynamic in content, and tested mostly by researchers from the United States. For psychologists in Northern Ireland these psychodynamic theories provided some particular problems, the most significant of which was that their primary explanation for intergroup conflict was *intra*personal. However, anyone who lived in Northern Ireland was aware that other factors such as religion, history, demography, politics, and economics also played a role. Consequently, when an alternative view of intergroup conflict emerged which focused on broader social contexts, Northern Irish psychologists moved from a North American to a more European perspective, and broadly adopted Tajfel's Social Identity Theory (SIT) (e.g., Tajfel and Turner, 1986).

Simply put, SIT posits that we derive our self-image in part from categorizing ourselves as members of various groups (i.e., our social identity), and that we have a need to evaluate ourselves positively through comparison with others who are not members of our own groups. Our social identity, then, leads to intergroup comparisons, which are not necessarily problematic. On the other hand, in circumstances where we find ourselves members of a group from which it is virtually impossible to leave, the only way to enhance our self-esteem may be to act so as to preserve or defend our group's interests *against* the interests of another group. Intergroup conflict may result and be maintained, as has been the case in Northern Ireland (Cairns, Wilson, Gallagher, and Trew, 1995).

The analyses which follow in this chapter reflect a social identity theoretical framework. In all fairness, it should be noted that SIT is not without its critics in Northern Ireland. In particular it has been suggested that the dominance of this model has resulted in research of limited scope as a result of studying a complex social issue from a rather singular theoretical perspective (Trew, 1992; Weinreich, 1992).

Psychosocial Development of Adolescents in Northern Ireland

Introduction

In addressing the psychological research on adolescents in Northern Ireland, one must begin by recognizing that interpretations are complicated by a number of variables related to social context, and by limitations in research methodology. To begin with, the patterns of violence varied across the 25 years of the Troubles, and these variations likely differentially affected adolescent responses. First, temporally, level of violence has not been constant, but rose rapidly in the first three years, then dropped over subsequent years to an average of below 100 fatalities annually (see Figure 8.1). Second, geographically, certain areas of Northern Ireland were more likely to be sites of political violence than others (see R. Murray, 1982). Belfast, Derry, and smaller towns near border crossings were particularly at risk. Even within a setting such as Belfast, political violence was more likely to occur in interface areas between Protestant and Catholic working-class area than in mixed middle-class neighborhoods. Consequently, daily reminders of the conflict in the form of heavily armed and armored security forces were more evident in those settings. Third, qualitatively, the type of violence changed from the widespread street riots with consequent dislocation of residents, that lasted for a number of hours or days, to bombings, specifically targeted assassinations, or plainly random sectarian killings, lasting only a few seconds. Similarly, tactics and weaponry changed, becoming increasingly more sophisticated (see Guelke, 1995).

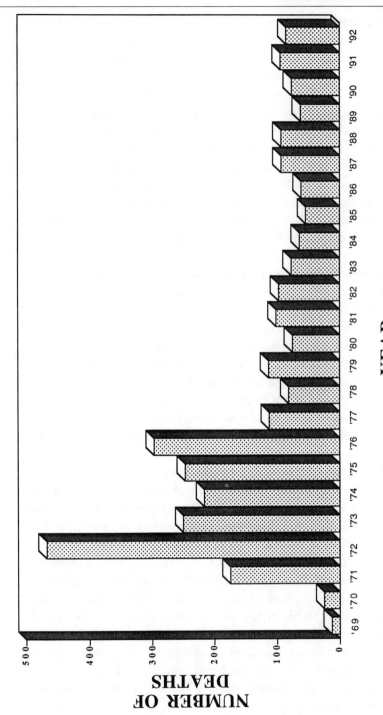

Figure 8.1. Northern Ireland: Deaths Due to Political Violence, 1969–1992

Socioeconomic variables also confound interpretations of adolescent development in Northern Ireland. Throughout the period of the Troubles, Northern Ireland has been the least affluent region of the United Kingdom, and is among the least prosperous areas within the European Community. A combination of large families, poor standards of health, high prices, low earnings, high unemployment, and poor housing all contributed to social stresses that can be detrimental to adolescent development, independent of political violence (see McWhirter, 1983). This is particularly problematic in Northern Ireland since those adolescents most likely to have experience with sectarian violence or its consequences live in economically depressed neighborhoods (e.g., McLachlan, 1981).

Methodological limitations in the research include lack of pre-Troubles psychological data to permit before-and-after comparisons, weaknesses in assessment techniques of adolescent outcomes, inadequate characterizations of what political violence was pertinent to the adolescents under study, and a general lack of theoretical grounding (Cairns and Cairns, 1995). Research performed by Northern Irish social scientists has benefited from insider understanding; however, it also has been hampered by the researchers' personal social identifications and their being identified by others with one or the other community (see Cairns and Toner, 1993; Cairns, 1994; Heskin, 1980; Taylor, 1988). Finally, few studies specifically targeted adolescents as a subject group. Much of the research in Northern Ireland focused on the category of "children," and either exclusively investigated children, or combined young adolescents with children in the interpretations.

Identity Development

In the context of Northern Ireland's political violence, a key dimension in adolescent identity development is the social identity associated with one's ethnic community. Ethnic categorization differs from racial categorization in that the cues are not perceptual, but stereotypic (i.e., oversimplified generalizations or beliefs). Mastering ethnic categorization appears to take longer than mastering racial categorization. In Northern Irish children, ethnic categorization emerges at about eleven years of age (Cairns, 1980, 1989; Jahoda and Harrison, 1975); thus, fully developed sectarian identity and attitudes first appear as an adolescent experience. That this is clearly a part of later adolescent identity was demonstrated in a study of close to 1,000 sixteen- to seventeen-year-olds. Cairns and Mercer (1984) found that only 3 percent of these adolescents failed to identify themselves as Catholic or Protestant, and that these denominational labels were ranked among the most important personal characteristics when describing themselves.

This polarization of adolescent denominational identities was roughly paralleled by adolescent preferences in national identities, although national identities were less stable. (National identities are associated with political boundaries and sovereignty, such as "Irish" with Ireland and "British" with the United Kingdom.) For example in a study of seventeen-year-old Protestant and Catholic adolescents, Waddell and Cairns (1991) demonstrated that the label "Northern Irish" was associated with "Irish" for Catholic youth, but with "British" and "Ulster" for Protestant youth. (Ulster is the name of the northern province in Ireland. The term generally is associated with the Protestant majority in Northern Ireland.) In line with the assumptions of SIT, Stringer and Cairns (1983) demonstrated with a sample of fourteen- to fifteen-year-olds that adolescents appear to possess positive social identities regarding their own community membership, and both Weinreich's (1982) and Cairns's (1983) data support a pressure in adolescent identity development to disassociate from the other group, which results in a tendency to exaggerate differences between the two groups or even to create differences.

Social categorization requires that Northern Irish adolescents ascertain to which of the two communities unknown persons belong. This they must do in a roundabout manner, since a direct inquiry would violate the socially taboo topics of politics and religion. A local dictum in Northern Ireland is "whatever you say, say nothing." Adolescents then must become proficient in a rather sophisticated social psychological process of "telling" (Burton, 1978); that is, indirectly discovering the community membership of strangers. Common cues used are location of residence, school attended, name, appearance, and speech. For example, one strategy applied by an inner-city Protestant gang to make judgments on the identity of unknown youths was to call out a name associated with the Catholic community. If reactions followed, then gang members assumed that the youths were Catholic, and they became legitimate targets for beatings (Burton, 1978). This process of telling can become even more complicated when adolescent subcultures are taken into account. For example, in Bell's (1990) data collected in the 1980s among working-class adolescents, in Derry the skinhead's style was adopted exclusively by Catholic adolescents and marked their group membership, whereas in Belfast, this same style was the subcultural property of Protestant adolescents. Confusion regularly resulted when adolescents from one city visited the other.

Sectarian social identities are expected to be particularly strong in settings of intergroup conflict such as Northern Ireland (Cairns, 1982). However, social identities are situational, and although Northern Irish adolescents are not likely to feel Catholic in one context and Protestant in another, variances in the degree of adherence to such exclusive identities certainly exist (see Gallagher, 1989; Waddell and Cairns, 1986). Trew (1983), for example, found that a notable portion of her sample of adolescents living in a peaceful and integrated setting were not strongly committed to either Irish or British national identities. Perhaps even more noteworthy are observations among working-class adolescents in segregated neighborhoods who regularly participate in cross-community violence. Friendly relations, including romantic ones, may exist between individual Protestant and Catholic youths. This is more likely to occur if the relations are not with members of geographically adjacent housing areas between which sectarian violence is common (e.g., Bell, 1990; Roe et al., 1995). Also, the presence of a superordinate identity can at least temporarily override the influence of the sectarian social identity. Again from observations of working-class adolescents, even in the midst of a sectarian riot, the arrival of the police may lead the two groups of battling adolescents to join forces and fight the police, only to return to fighting each other when the police leave. In the words of a Protestant adolescent girl (who happened to have a Catholic boyfriend),

At night they all come up from the shops lookin' for a fight, the ones from Irish Street. Then they [the kids from Gobsnascale] say, "To hell with that there, we're not taking that," and they come up and brick back. But. . .we usually join up at the end of the night and brick the cops. We all hate the cops. . .but then when they leave we'd just be brickin' each other again. (Bell, 1990, p. 136)

For nonacademic youths, sectarian symbolism and attitude can also be associated with a school counterculture identity (Bell, 1990; Jenkins, 1983). With little hope for class mobility, a sectarian social identity may be held onto tenaciously by these young people. This appears particularly so for loyalist youths, as a crisis in Protestant identity has emerged along with the Troubles. Politically the relationship of unionism to the British state has become less secure; economically, the Protestant privilege of previous decades has eroded, and working-class Protestants face high unemployment along with their Catholic counterparts. Loyalist street culture among youths (e.g., band parades, wall murals, curb painting, and Twelfth of July bonfires) is a response to this crisis (Bell, 1990).

Although the cessation of armed conflict is welcome, the social identities of both communities are less clear, and so it is not surprising that sectarian attitudes and clashes between the two communities remain to clarify identity boundaries. Adolescents from both communities are reticent to give up sectarian symbols and celebrations, and both continue to participate in clashes (Roe et al., 1995).

Moral Development

One of the first predictions made at the beginning of the present Troubles in Northern Ireland was that a new generation would emerge which would be morally scarred. It was suggested that this "truncation of the development of moral judgment in a whole generation of children" (Fields, 1973) would take two principal forms. One would be the development of anti-authority attitudes (Fraser, 1974). The other would be, according to a major church report, a "catastrophic and terrifying decline in respect for the sacredness of human life" (*Violence in Ireland,* 1976). Some twenty years later it is possible to say that there is virtually no empirical evidence to substantiate either of these dire predictions.

Moral Reasoning

Some early evidence did suggest that, compared to their peers in England or in the United States, Northern Irish young people were more likely to perform at a lower level on objective tests of moral reasoning. They did not, however, differ from their peers in the Republic of Ireland (Breslin, 1982; Cairns and Conlon, 1985; Kahn, 1982). These studies shared at least two methodological limitations. The samples were relatively small and unrepresentative, and it was not clear that the measures utilized were suitable for Irish contexts. In response, more recent research (e.g., Ferguson, McLernon, and Cairns, 1994) first established the psychometric qualities of a new measure, the Sociomoral Reflection Measure—Short Form (SRM-SF) (see also Gibbs, Basinger, and Fuller, 1992), and then went on to use this in a cross-national study (Ferguson, 1995). This study involved a stratified sample of some 600 adolescents aged thirteen to fourteen years from Scotland, the Republic of Ireland, and Northern Ireland. Preliminary analyses indicated that on average Irish children (whether from the Republic or

Northern Ireland) scored at a higher level than did their peers from Scotland. Further, the data from these studies suggested that children in Northern Ireland also were scoring at a higher level on the SRM-SF than same-aged adolescents from the United States.

As noted earlier, political violence in Northern Ireland has not had an equal impact on all young people. Therefore data that indicate that political violence has not influenced "overall levels" of moral reasoning do not mean that the violence has had no impact on any specific young person. Investigating this idea, Ferguson and Cairns (1996) compared 421 young people from areas which had experienced high or low levels of political violence. What this study suggested was that in the areas where political violence had been high, children and adolescents scored at a significantly lower level on the SRM-SF than their peers in less politically violent areas.

Moral Behavior

In the early days of the Troubles the amount of school absenteeism and juvenile crime among young people did rise slightly, but soon settled down to a level similar to that which has been experienced in other parts of the United Kingdom. Recently in Northern Ireland there has been a decline (by some 59 percent since 1983) in the number of young people appearing in court for both nonindictable and more serious, indictable offences (Jardine, 1995). Finally, the majority of these young people who appear in court have been limited to males charged with property offenses. Relatively few have been charged with crimes of violence.

Overall there is little evidence that political violence has impacted the young people of Northern Ireland in such a way as to lead to greater criminal behavior. This is true both during adolescence and when those adolescents grow into adulthood. As a result general crime levels tend to be low. For example, according to a government report (PPRU, 1984), when the Northern Ireland rate of offenses known to the police was compared in 1981 with twelve similar-sized areas, seven in England and Wales and five in the United States, Northern Ireland ranked tenth. Similarly in 1989, an International Victimization Survey found that a person in Northern Ireland was less likely to be the victim of crime compared to people living in any of the countries surveyed, with the exception of Japan (Jardine, 1995). It should be added that these figures do not take into account two important factors. First there is the phenomenon of unreported crime (e.g., Hamilton, et al., 1990; Jenkins, 1983). Second, there is the role of the paramilitary organizations in community policing, which has involved operating kangaroo courts, and handing out summary punishments such as beatings and "knee-capping" (i.e., shooting the offender in one or both knees) (e.g., Jenkins, 1983).

While the above evidence reveals a lower level of criminal behavior among young people in Northern Ireland than might have been expected, it should not be taken to indicate the complete absence of antisocial behavior among the young. To begin with there is some evidence involving acting-out, aggressive behavior in children immediately preceding their adolescence. This comes from a series of surveys, based mainly on teachers' ratings of children aged eleven years and spanning the period 1975–1983. Wilson and Cairns (1992), reviewing this work, suggested that there was evidence that "trends in measures of conduct disorder and acting-out, aggressive behavior in young people have paralleled variations in levels of political violence" (p. 52). Further, they pointed out that these trends were more apparent in boys, who in all samples showed higher mean levels of acting-out behavior than girls. Wilson and Cairns also noted that it was difficult to disentangle the relationship between behavioral disturbance, political violence in young people, and the confounding effects of socioeconomic disadvantage, given that these sources of stress tended to correlate.

Also among young people in Northern Ireland there is increasing evidence of the misuse of substances such as alcohol and drugs. From 1988 to 1994 the proportion of frequent drinkers among the eleven- to fifteen-year-old age group increased from 37 percent to 52 percent according to self-report evidence from a government-based survey (Craig, 1995). Similarly, illegal drug use, while never a major problem in Northern Ireland, has been steadily on the increase. As a result the number of those under twenty-one prosecuted for drug-related offenses has risen from 141 in 1989 to 446 in 1993. More recently, with the announcement of the cease-fires, some of the largest seizures ever of illegal drugs have taken place in Northern Ireland and all experts appear to agree that this is likely to be a major problem in the future.

Political Violence

Undoubtedly a certain amount of antisocial behavior has taken the form of cross-community violence, but probably much less than might have been expected. Part of the reason for this was suggested earlier; that is, street violence on any large scale was only a relatively short-lived phenomenon in Northern Ireland, common especially during the 1970s. During this period, the media were full of stories and pictures of children and adolescents participating in riots. However, according to more objective evidence, participation by young people in such activities was the exception rather than the rule. Lyons (1972), in a study involving over 1,500 people arrested during 1969–1971, reported that only about 15 percent were nineteen years or younger, and that the vast majority of these were males. However, this report, based on arrests, may well have underestimated the number of young people involved in rioting (see Mercer and Bunting, 1980).

More recent evidence has come from a series of anthropological studies of a suburb of Belfast (Jenkins, 1983), a public housing project in Derry (Bell, 1990), and three other small communities in Northern Ireland (Hamilton et al., 1990). Young people's involvement in street politics was only tangentially reported in these ethnographies. However, in at least one of the communities studied by Hamilton and colleagues, young men in their "teens" were reported to form a youth culture in which discussion about loyalist issues predominated. Similarly, both Jenkins and Bell described portions of the youth culture in the areas they studied as symbolizing militant loyalism and masculinity. Also, while the young people expressed no interest in formal politics, activities such as taking part in parades and demonstrations and writing political slogans on walls were common. It is also of interest to note that while some adults in particular had an undue political influence on the adolescents, more generally it was the adults who were acquiescing to the thinking of the young people. In another of the communities studied by Hamilton and colleagues, it was reported that while Catholic and Protestant relationships were "still reasonably tolerant," the younger generations "were described as being very bitter" (Hamilton et al., 1990, p. 47). It was proposed that this was due to the fact that these youth lacked knowledge of a time in their community when political violence did not predominate, and as a result a "very real and palpable hatred . . . had been burnt deeply" (p. 47) into those who had grown up during the Troubles.

While paramilitary support among young people has been relatively easy to gauge in Northern Ireland, actual paramilitary involvement is a more problematic topic. The obvious reason for this is that paramilitary organizations are secretive and therefore difficult to investigate. Usually the only members of paramilitary organizations available to researchers for interview are those who have been caught and imprisoned and/or reformed. Available evidence suggests that in the early days of the Troubles young people were indeed deeply involved. For example during the period 1975–1977, seven young men aged under sixteen years were charged with murder and six with attempted murder, while some forty-one were charged with firearms and/or explosives offenses. More recent evidence suggests that young people's involvement at this level of violence has diminished (see Cairns, 1987). Cairns (1987) also reported in detail a series of studies from the 1970s which investigated what type of young person became involved in paramilitary activities. In those studies young men charged with "political" offenses tended to emerge with a better profile when compared to "ordinary" young criminals. In particular they were more likely to be more intelligent, less aggressive and have better educational attainments, and they were less likely to have been referred to child psychiatrists prior to their arrests. One reason for this difference may have been that paramilitary organizations preferred to recruit and/or accept more intelligent young people.

Social and Religious Values
Social Attitudes

During the period of the Troubles, social attitudes of adolescents in Northern Ireland appear to have remained relatively stable and not to have been in marked conflict with their parents either in terms of moral standards or political behavior. For example Greer (1990), reported a series of virtually identical surveys carried out in 1968, 1978, and 1988 involving Protestant students about eighteen to nineteen years of age, in their last two years of secondary education. The survey probed moral attitudes to such issues as gambling, war, and suicide. Across these cohorts of adolescents, most responses either did not change, or indicated an increasingly conservative position. Only four out of more than twenty items produced trends which indicated the "rejection of traditional practice or moral judgment" (Greer, 1990). Utilizing a different methodology and sample, Cairns (1992) examined social attitudes through analyzing data obtained from a random sample survey of the population of Northern Ireland (The Northern Ireland Social Attitudes Survey). Specifically, Cairns compared young adults in the age range eighteen to thirty-four years (the oldest of whom would have been about twelve years of age when the Troubles began), middle-aged adults of thirty-five to fifty-four years (half of whom spent a portion of their adolescence in the Troubles), and older adults of fifty-five years and over. These analyses indicated that on most issues some generational differences existed, but these differences were not of sufficient magnitude to be labeled "generation gaps." For example, in the area of attitudes toward authority Protestants from all three generations were in almost complete agreement. Among Catholic respondents however, the data suggested that Catholic young people held less conservative views of authority when compared with their elders. Similarly, young Protestant adults were in agreement with the views of their elders in the area of political protest. All Protestants took a fairly conservative view on this issue. Among Catholics, however, there were again signs that this was an issue on which young adults were likely to hold more progressive views. Clear evidence for a generation gap was found only on attitudes toward premarital sexual intercourse. Almost 60 percent of the older adult sample believed this was "always wrong," while only around 10 percent of the youngest adults so believed.

Religious Attitudes, Beliefs, and Behaviors
In Northern Ireland, attendance and membership in churches have remained relatively high as compared to the rest of the United Kingdom or western Europe (Cairns, 1991; Morrow, 1995). In the 1991 census, 89 percent identified themselves as belonging to a specific Christian denomination, with 38.4 percent declaring as Roman Catholic and 50.6 percent declaring membership in one of a number of Protestant churches. Comparing 1989 data to findings from 1968 (Rose, 1971) and 1978 (Moxon-Brown, 1983), Cairns (1992) noted a slight drop in the number of people attending church each week and a somewhat steeper rise in the number never attending, with this latter finding most marked among Protestants. Cairns (1992) also noted that Catholics were more frequent in their church attendance than Protestants, and that their attendance was more consistent across generations and social class than it was for Protestants (see Table 8.1). Unfortunately, the youngest participants in the Cairns (1992)

Table 8.1 Church Attendance in Northern Ireland across Three Age Groups: Catholic and Protestant

Age	Church attendance	Catholic %	Protestant %
18–34 years	Weekly	77	26
	Never	4	22
35–54 years	Weekly	88	44
	Never	2	10
55 years or over	Weekly	91	49
	Never	3	16

analyses were eighteen years of age, and so for the most part *current* adolescent religious behavior was not addressed. On the other hand, the patterns described in the Cairns analyses were consonant with patterns reported both by Roe and colleagues (1995) in their small sample of Belfast working-class Catholic and Protestant adolescents, and by Greer (1990) in his study of Protestant adolescents.

Northern Irish adolescents were specifically assessed in two studies that investigated changes in religious behavior and belief during the period of the Troubles. Turner, Turner, and Reid (1980) studied Catholic and Protestant adolescent boys in 1969 and in 1979. Differences across this decade of relatively high levels of political violence were noted only in the Catholic samples, with the 1979 sample less favorable in religious attitudes than the 1969. Even so, religious attitudes were consistently more positive among Catholic youth than among Protestant youth at all ages and times of measurement. Despite their lower ratings, the Protestant youth still retained religious attitudes that were moderately favorable. In general, Turner and colleagues were impressed with the stability of these religious attitudes "during a period characterized by social and political unrest and by an intensification of endemic economic problems" (p. 51). Greer's (1990) study of Protestant adolescent boys and girls in 1968, 1978, and 1988 found a steady decrease in weekly church attendance, from 58 percent and 71 percent in 1968 to 43 percent and 60 percent in 1988 for boys and girls, respectively. In contrast to the attendance trends, Greer found evidence of no change or increased religious orthodoxy on a number of indices of religious belief. He also found that the 1988 sample of adolescent boys and girls as more inclined than its predecessor to express approval of religion in school.

More recently, Roe and colleagues (1995) applied scales of religiosity to Catholic and Protestant youth from working-class areas in Belfast, who had participated in cross-community violence and subsequently in reconciliation work. They found that the Catholic youths attended church more frequently and endorsed a higher level of religious orthodoxy than the Protestant youths; however, both groups generally agreed with credal elements of the Christian faith. In addition, Roe and colleagues found that these Catholic and Protestant youths were similar in the overall extrinsic nature (i.e., religion as a means to one's own ends) and intrinsic nature (i.e., religion as the end to be lived) of their religious experiences, although the two groups notably deviated from each other in magnitude and variability on specific items.

These studies taken together indicate that there has not been a rapid movement away from traditional social and religious values in Northern Ireland as a result of the political violence. Indeed, on a small number of issues Protestants in particular show remarkable uniformity across the generations.

Coping with the Troubles

The lack of mental health research that specifically targets adolescents in Northern Ireland is quite noteworthy. A few exceptions exist. For example, in a study of trait anxiety in children and young adolescents, no difference was found between Northern Irish and English fourteen-year-olds (McWhirter, 1983). In a study among Belfast children and adolescents, there was evidence of a heightened awareness of death, but there was no evidence of a preoccupation with violent death among the various age groups (McWhirter, 1988; McWhirter, Young, and Majury, 1983).

One strategy that provides some glimpses of adolescent responses is to extract relevant data from larger samples when possible; however, little confidence can be placed in their providing a profile of distinct adolescent reactions. For example, young adolescents (twelve and thirteen year olds) were among Fraser's (1974) "children" whose psychiatric symptoms were precipitated by violent events related to the urban riots early in the Troubles. Their reactions, along with those of older children, led Fraser to conclude that a child's (young adolescent's) vulnerability was contingent on the emotional climate provided by the immediate family and the child's individual style of coping with stress. In another example, adolescents between fourteen and seventeen years of age were among thirty-three victims referred for psychiatric evaluation following a devastating bombing. Their diagnoses ranged from acute reactions to stress (including the full symptomatology of Post Traumatic Stress Disorder—PTSD), through adjustment reactions, to anxiety and depressive neuroses (Curran et al.,1990).

Another strategy that provides indirect access to adolescent coping responses is to assume that younger adolescents are similar to older children, and older adolescents to adults. A number of relevant trends for adolescents can then be interpolated from the large child and adult research and clinical literature. From child psychiatric admission and referral data (McAuley and Troy, 1983), and from child clinical studies (e.g., Fraser, 1974; Lyons, 1974), it appears that little evidence exists for a direct link between rates of child psychiatric disorders and general level of political violence; however, for any individual child who has directly experienced a violent act such as a shooting or bombing, posttraumatic anxiety reactions certainly do occur. From community-based survey studies of children (Fee, 1980; McWhirter, 1983; McGrath and Wilson, 1985), it can be concluded that although a portion of Northern Irish children have had personal experience with political violence, and some feel anxiety symptoms as a result, most of these children appear able to cope and do not suffer serious psychological disorders, at least in terms of depression. On the other hand and as discussed earlier, there is evidence that political violence may be linked with aspects of antisocial and sociopathic behavior; that is, as assessed on teacher ratings or self-report personality and clinical measures.

Adult responses to political violence have been studied through correlational studies of psychiatric admission and referral rates, rates of suicide and attempted suicide, alcohol-related personal and social problems, psychotropic drug prescriptions, and community-based survey studies (for an extensive review, see Cairns and Wilson, 1993). Similar to the research on children, these adult studies indicate that only a very small portion of the adult population has suffered long-term psychiatric disturbance as a consequence of the Troubles. Most of the population has probably suffered some form of stress due to political violence, but this likely has been short-lived. In contrast, these adult studies indicate that other social problems of unemployment and general economic hardship may well have a greater impact than the political strife.

Coping strategies in children have been little studied in Northern Ireland; however, habituation has been proposed to explain the relatively low level of reported psychological problems (e.g., McWhirter, 1983). That is, with the constant presence of political violence in the background, children become less vulnerable to the trauma because they are desensitized to it. Wilson and Cairns (1992) noted the possibility that aggressive behavior may be a form of coping behavior for young people, particularly boys (see also Fee, 1980). This type of coping may be extended to those adolescents discussed earlier who identify with militant loyalist or republican youth subcultures, who participate in cross-community violence, or who join paramilitary organizations. Finally, the mediating effect of family stability/instability has been recognized (e.g., Fraser, 1974), with children surrounded by intact and supportive families being buffered to some extent from negative psychological consequences of traumatic events.

Habituation also has been implicated in adult coping strategies (e.g., Giles and Cairns, 1979; McWhirter, 1987), as have the defense mechanisms of denial and distancing, positive reappraisal (i.e., reinterpreting a violent event by finding some positive outcome in addition to the trauma), and seeking social support from family, church, or community (Cairns and Wilson, 1984, 1985, 1989). In addition, religion has been found to be relevant in the appraisal process and in the selection of coping strategies (Wilson and Cairns, in preparation; discussed in Wilson and Cairns, 1992).

Finally, an important element emerging from the adult research is that how an individual perceives the level of violence (e.g., Cairns and Wilson, 1989) or perceives the political ideological purpose of such violence (Loughrey and Curran, 1987) may interact with the selection and efficacy of coping strategies. It is reasonable to assume that as adolescents become more facile with abstract reasoning skills, this mediating role of appraisal becomes more relevant to their coping with political violence.

Promoting Peaceful Cross-Community Relations
Education
The most widely applied intervention technique for social change during the period of the Troubles has used education as its vehicle and has consisted of modifying curricula of existing segregated schools. The most recent program began in 1989 and consisted of a common curriculum for both Catholic and Protestant schools that included two cross-curricular themes, Education for Mutual Understanding (EMU) and Cultural Heritage (Smith, 1995). This common curriculum also included a community relations dimension. Under the banner of EMU, Protestant and Catholic schools have been encouraged, but not required, to establish contacts between their pupils.

Smith and Dunn (1990) carried out the first evaluation of the impact of such a program on secondary-level young people in one town in Northern Ireland, comparing contact with non-contact children. They found no evidence that the program eroded Catholic or Protestant youth's national identities. Also, where awareness of the other community was concerned, they found that this was related to the majority/minority balance in the group, with the minority developing a greater awareness of the majority. Finally they hinted at attitude change in the form of an emergence of "uncertainty," where previously issues had seemed simple and clear-cut.

An alternative intervention strategy that also uses education as its vehicle has been to focus on the composition of the students enrolled in the schools. According to Smith (1995), the "most dramatic development in education in Northern Ireland over the past twenty years has been the creation of integrated schools; that is, schools that are attended in roughly equal numbers by Protestants and Catholics" (p. 175). While it has grown steadily, the integrated school movement accounts only for about 1 percent of schoolchildren and adolescents, with most of these at the elementary level. The integrated schools share a common aim of reflecting both communities in their governing body, pupil, and staff compositions. In addition, they aspire to reflect cultural pluralism in their curricula.

Irwin (1991), an anthropologist, carried out an intensive study of one planned integrated secondary-level school in Northern Ireland. This study produced firm evidence that the school was successful in establishing positive intercommunity friendships among the adolescents who were its students. The study also claimed that there was preliminary evidence that youth attending the integrated school were beginning to develop a better understanding and possibly even a less confrontational acceptance of the politics of the youth from the other community. On the other hand, data from this study also indicated that the integrated secondary school was apparently having little effect on national identity. In other words, as in the adult community, most Catholic adolescents thought of themselves as Irish, while most Protestant adolescents thought of themselves as British.

Similar findings were reported by Cairns, Dunn, Morgan, and McClenahan (1992), who compared Catholic and Protestant adolescents attending a planned integrated school where the ratio was approximately 50:50, adolescents attending other unplanned integrated schools where the balance of Catholics and Protestants was less even, and adolescents from totally segregated schools. Preliminary results indicated that youth in both the planned and unplanned integrated schools were making friends on a cross-community basis; however, their national identities remained unchanged and polar.

Short-term Contact Programs

Short-term contact programs lie outside the formal educational structures and consist mainly of summer camps of various kinds. They are usually a few weeks in duration and either take place within Northern Ireland or more commonly outside Northern Ireland in countries such as Holland or the United States (Wilson and Tyrrell, 1995). These have been going on since the early days of the Troubles, with organizers in Europe and North America setting up programs designed to bring together Catholic and Protestant young people for short periods in a setting removed from the unrest of their homeland. Most of the schemes include as their rationale the simple belief that relations between members of conflicting groups can be improved by equal-status contact. (For an evaluation of this contact hypothesis, see Hewstone and Brown, 1986.)

As Trew (1989) noted in a review of work in this area, there is surprisingly little empirical research, and in particular there is a need for more systematic, longitudinal research. So far attempts to evaluate such programs have been limited, but suggest that few attitudinal changes occur. These few data indicate that although short-term contact schemes may help to improve young people's self-esteem, they appear to be of limited value in improving cross-community relations. One possible explanation may be that on many summer programs there were few actual attempts to bring all the young people together, and perhaps as a result the young people often did not know that there were peers from the other religious community in the program (Trew et al., 1985).

Another explanation for the apparent weak outcome may be the limited duration of the contact; after all, the more long-term contact of integrated school settings does appear to promote cross-community friendships. On the other hand, it appears that even such long-term contact may not radically alter young people's national identities. This can be regarded as a positive outcome if one sees the aim of such programs as achieving a pluralistic society in Northern Ireland with individuals able to tolerate differences. However, if one sees the aim as the building of a shared social identity between the two warring factions, then these results are not particularly encouraging.

Conclusions

In contrast to early predictions of a "lost generation" resulting from the backdrop of persistent political violence (e.g., Fields, 1973, 1979; Lyons, 1975), most evidence indicates that adolescents in Northern Ireland have coped well. Studies of their moral reasoning and behavior, and social and religious attitudes and practices, indicate that while changes in values and attitudes are taking place in Northern Ireland, these changes are occurring quite gradually, and appear to be more in line with a secular trend than as a consequence of civil strife. Likewise, although adolescents (and children and adults) undoubtedly have experienced short-term stress from political violence, there is little sign of serious or pervasive psychological disorder; in fact, unemployment and general financial hardship may actually be taking a greater toll.

Less positively, the polar national identities of adolescents from both communities have been rather resistant to change. In general, Catholic adolescents continue to identify with Ireland and Protestant adolescents with Britain. Working-class adolescents in particular are reticent to give up sectarian symbols and celebrations, and they continue to participate in cross-community violence. Intervention programs have succeeded in raising adolescent self-esteem, and in promoting cross-community friendships at the *individual* level. To date they do not appear to have had much impact on *group* social identities.

The current cessation of armed conflict certainly is providing the "social space" for the formation of a shared social identity between Catholic and Protestant, although what form or forms such an identity may take is unclear. This period of quiet also is providing the opportunity for increased economic development in Northern Ireland, which should contribute to lessened tensions between the communities. However, given past centuries of conflict, it is unrealistic to assume that even with a lasting cease-fire sectarian attitudes and behavior will disappear soon. That will have to be the experience of a future generation of adolescents.

Notes

At the time this chapter was initiated, Mícheál Roe was a Senior Visiting Research Fellow at the Centre for the Study of Conflict, University of Ulster at Coleraine.

References

Bell, D. (1990). *Acts of union: Youth culture and sectarianism in Northern Ireland.* Hampshire, England: MacMillan.

Boal, F. W., and Douglas, J. N. (1982). *Integration and division: Geographical perspectives on the Northern Ireland problem.* London: Academic Press.

Breslin, A. (1982) Tolerance and moral reasoning among adolescents in Ireland. *Journal of Moral Education, 11,* 112–127.

Bruce, S. (1986). *God save Ulster: The religion and politics of Paisleyism.* Oxford: Oxford University Press.

Burton, F. (1978). *The politics of legitimacy.* London: Routledge and Kegan Paul.

Cairns, E. (1980). The development of ethnic discrimination in young children in Northern Ireland. In J. Harbison and J. Harbison (eds.), *Children and young people in Northern Ireland: A society under stress* (pp. 115–127). Somerset, England: Open Books.

Cairns, E. (1982). Intergroup conflict in Northern Ireland. In H. Tajfel (ed.), *Social identity and intergroup relations* (pp. 277–297). Cambridge: Cambridge University Press.

Cairns, E. (1983). *The role of ethnic identity in the Northern Irish conflict.* Paper presented to the Sixth Annual Scientific Meeting of the International Society of Political Psychology, Oxford.

Cairns, E. (1987) *Caught in crossfire: Children and the Northern Ireland conflict.* Belfast and New York: Appletree Press and Syracuse University Press.

Cairns, E. (1989). Social identity and intergroup conflict: A developmental perspective. In J. Harbison (ed.), *Growing up in Northern Ireland* (pp. 115–130). Belfast: Stranmillis.

Cairns, E. (1991). Is Northern Ireland a conservative society? In P. Stringer and G. Robinson (eds.), *Social attitudes in Northern Ireland, 1990–1991 Edition* (pp. 142–156). Belfast: Blackstaff.

Cairns, E. (1992). Political violence, social values and the generation gap. In P. Stringer and G. Robinson (eds.), *Social attitudes in Northern Ireland: The second report 1991–1992* (pp. 149–160). Belfast: Blackstaff Press.

Cairns, E. (1994). Understanding conflict and promoting peace in Ireland: Psychology's contribution. *Irish Journal of Psychology, 15,* 480–493.

Cairns, E., and Cairns, T. (1995). Children and conflict: A psychological perspective. In S. Dunn (ed.), *Facets of the conflict in Northern Ireland* (pp. 97–113). London: Macmillan.

Cairns, E., and Conlon, L. (1985). *Children's moral reasoning and the Northern Irish violence.* Unpublished paper, University of Ulster at Coleraine, Northern Ireland.

Cairns, E., Dunn, S., Morgan, V., and McClenahan, C. (1992). *The impact of integrated schools in Northern Ireland on cultural values and social identity. Final Report to the Economic and Social Research Council* (UK).

Cairns, E., and Duriez, B. (1976). The influence of accent on the recall of Catholic and Protestant children in Northern Ireland. *British Journal of Social and Clinical Psychology, 15,* 441–442.

Cairns, E., and Mercer, G. W. (1984). Social identity in Northern Ireland. *Human Relations, 37,* 1095–1102.

Cairns, E., and Toner, I. J. (1993). Children and political violence in Northern Ireland: From riots to reconciliation. In L. A. Leavitt and N. A. Fox (eds.), *Psychological effects of war and violence on children* (pp. 215–230). New York: Erlbaum.

Cairns, E., and Wilson, R. (1984). The impact of political violence on mild psychiatric morbidity in Northern Ireland. *British Journal of Psychiatry, 145,* 631–635.

Cairns, E., and Wilson, R. (1985). Psychiatric aspects of violence in Northern Ireland. *Stress Medicine, 1,* 193.

Cairns, E., and Wilson, R. (1989). Coping with political violence in Northern Ireland. *Social Science and Medicine, 28,* 621–624.

Cairns, E., and Wilson, R. (1993). Stress, coping, and political violence in Northern Ireland. In J. P. Wilson and B. Raphael (eds.), *International handbook of traumatic stress syndromes* (pp. 365–376). New York: Plenum Press.

Cairns, E., Wilson, R., Gallagher, T., and Trew, K. (1995). Psychology's contribution to understanding conflict in Northern Ireland. *Peace and Conflict: Journal of Peace Psychology, 1,* 131–148.

Coles, R. (1980) Ulster's children: Waiting for the Prince of Peace. *Atlantic,* December, 33–44.

Craig, J. (1995). *The health behaviour of school children in Northern Ireland.* Belfast: The Health Promotion Agency.

Curran, P. S., Bell, P., Murray, A., Loughrey, G., Roddy, R., and Rocke, L. (1990). Psychological consequences of the Enniskillen bombing. *British Journal of Psychiatry, 156,* 479–482.

Darby, J. (1986). *Intimidation and the control of conflict in Northern Ireland.* Dublin: Gill and Macmillan.

Darby, J. (1995). Conflict in Northern Ireland: A background essay. In S. Dunn (ed.), *Facets of the conflict in Northern Ireland* (pp. 15–26). London: Macmillan.

Davies, J., and Turner, I. F. (1984). Friendship choices in an integrated primary school in Northern Ireland. *British Journal of Social Psychology, 23,* 185–186.

Falconer, A. D. (1988). The reconciling power of forgiveness. In A. D. Falconer (ed.), *Reconciling memories* (pp. 84–98). Blackrock, Co. Dublin: Columba Press.

Falconer, A. D. (1990). From theologies-in-opposition toward a theology-of-interdependence. *Life and Peace Review, 4,* 11–13.

Fee, F. (1980) Responses to a behavioral questionnaire of a group of Belfast children. In J. Harbison and J. Harbison (eds.), *A society under stress: Children and young people in Northern Ireland* (pp. 31–42). London: Open Books.

Ferguson, N. (1995). *Moral truncation in Northern Ireland: Myth or reality?* Unpublished Ph.D. thesis, University of Ulster, Coleraine, Northern Ireland.

Ferguson, N., and Cairns, E. (1996). Political violence and moral maturity. *Political Psychology, 17,* 713–725.

Ferguson, N., McLernon, F., and Cairns, E. (1994). The Sociomoral Reflection Measure—Short Form: An examination of its reliability and validity in a Northern Irish setting. *British Journal of Educational Psychology, 64,* 483–489.

Fields, R. (1973). *A society on the run: A psychology of Northern Ireland.* Middlesex, England: Penguin.

Fields, R. (1977). *Society under siege: A Psychology of Northern Ireland.* Philadelphia: Temple University Press.

Fields, R. (1979). Child terror victims and adult terrorists. *Journal of Psychohistory, 7,* 71–75.

Fraser, M. (1974). *Children in conflict.* New York: Basic Books.

Gallagher, A. M. (1989). Social identity and the Northern Ireland conflict. *Human Relations, 42,* 917–935.

Gallagher, A. M. (1992). Education in a divided society. *The Psychologist: Bulletin of the British Psychological Society, 5,* 341.

Gallagher, A. M. (1994). Political discourse in a divided society. In A. Guelke (ed.), *New perspectives on the Northern Ireland conflict* (pp. 28–45). Aldershot, England: Avebury.

Gallagher, A. M. (1995). The approach of government: Community relations and equity. In S. Dunn (ed.), *Facets of the conflict in Northern Ireland* (pp. 27–42). London: Macmillan.

Gibbs, J. C., Basinger, K. S., and Fuller, D. (1992). *Moral maturity: Measuring the development of sociomoral reflection.* Hillsdale, NJ: Erlbaum.

Giles, M., and Cairns, E. (1979). Colour naming of violence- related words in Northern Ireland. *British Journal of Clinical Psychology, 28,* 87–88.

Greer, J. (1990). The persistence of religion: A study of sixth-form pupils in Northern Ireland, 1968–1988. *Journal of Social Psychology, 130,* 573–581.

Guelke, A. (1995). Paramilitaries, republicans and loyalists. In S. Dunn (ed.), *Facets of the conflict in Northern Ireland* (pp. 114–130). London: Macmillan.

Hamilton, A., McCartney, C., Anderson, T., and Finn, A. (1990). *Violence and communities: The impact of political violence in Northern Ireland on intra-community, inter-community and community-state relationships.* Coleraine, Northern Ireland: Centre for the Study of Conflict.

Harbison, J., ed. (1983). *Children of the troubles: Children in Northern Ireland.* Belfast: Learning Resources Unit, Stranmillis College.

Harbison, J., ed. (1989). *Growing up in Northern Ireland.* Belfast: Learning Resources Unit, Stranmillis College.

Harbison, J. and Harbison, J., eds. (1980). *A society under stress: Children and Young People in Northern Ireland.* London: Open Books.

Heskin, K. (1980). *Northern Ireland: A psychological analysis.* Dublin: Gill and MacMillan.

Hewstone, M., and Brown, R. (1986). *Contact and conflict in intergroup encounters.* Oxford: Basil Blackwell.

Irwin, C. (1991). *Education and the development of social integration in divided societies.* Unpublished paper, Queen's University, Belfast, Northern Ireland.

Jahoda, G., and Harrison, S. (1975). Belfast children: Some effects of a conflict environment. *Irish Journal of Psychology, 3,* 1–19.

Jardine, E. (1995, April). *Growing through conflict: The impact of 25 years of violence on young people growing up in Northern Ireland.* Paper presented to the Conference of the International Association of Juvenile and Family Court Magistrates, Belfast.

Jenkins, R. (1983). *Lads, citizens and ordinary kids: Working-class youth life-styles in Belfast.* London: Routledge and Kegan Paul.

Kahn, J. V. (1982). Moral reasoning in Irish children and adolescents as measured by the Defining Issues Test. *Irish Journal of Psychology, 2,* 96–108.

Loughrey, G. C., and Curran, P. S. (1987). The psychopathology of civil disorder. In A. M. Dawson and G. M. Besser (eds.), *Recent advances in medicine* (pp. 1–17). Edinburgh: Churchill Livingstone.

Lyons, H. A. (1972). Depressive illness and aggression in Belfast. *British Medical Journal, 1,* 342–344.

Lyons, H. A. (1974). Terrorist bombing and the psychological sequelae. *Journal of the Irish Medical Association, 67,* 15.

Lyons, H. A. (1975). Legacy of violence in Northern Ireland. *International Journal of Offender Therapy and Comparative Criminology, 19,* 292–298.

McAuley, R., and Troy, M. (1983). The impact of urban conflict and violence on children referred to a child guidance clinic. In J. Harbison (ed.), *Children of the Troubles: Children in Northern Ireland* (pp. 33–43). Belfast: Learning Resources Unit, Stranmillis College.

McGrath, A., and Wilson, R. (1985). *Factors which influence the prevalence and variation of psychological problems in children in Northern Ireland.* Paper presented at the Annual Conference of the Developmental Section of the British Psychological Society, Belfast.

McLachlan, P. (1981). Teenage experiences in a violent society. *Journal of Adolescence, 4,* 285–294.

McSweeney, B. (1989). The religious dimension of the "Troubles" in Northern Ireland. In P. Badham (ed.), *Religion, state, and society in modern Britain* (pp. 67–83). Lampeter, Wales: Edwin Mellen Press.

McWhirter, L. (1983). Northern Ireland: Growing up with the "Troubles." In A. P. Goldstein and M. H. Segall (eds.), *Aggression in global perspective* (pp. 367–400). New York: Pergamon.

McWhirter, L. (1987). Psychological impact of violence in Northern Ireland: Recent research findings and issues. In N. Eisenberg and D. Glasgow (eds.), *Recent advances in clinical psychology.* London: Gower.

McWhirter, L. (1988). The meaning of violence for children of Northern Ireland. In E. J. Anthony and C. Chiland (eds.), *The child in his family. Volume 8, Perilous development: Child raising and identity formation under stress* (pp. 479–496). New York: John Wiley and Sons.

McWhirter, L., and Trew, K. (1982). Children in Northern Ireland: A lost generation. In E. Anthony and C. Chiland (eds.), *The child in his family. Volume 7, Children in turmoil: Tomorrow's parents* (pp. 69–82). New York: Wiley.

McWhirter, L., Young, V., and Majury, J. (1983). Belfast children's awareness of violent death. *British Journal of Social Psychology, 22,* 81–92.

Mercer, W. G., and Bunting, B. (1980). Some motivations of adolescent demonstrators in the Northern Ireland civil disturbances. In J. Harbison and J. Harbison (eds.), *A society Under Stress: Children and young people in Northern Ireland* (pp. 153–166). London: Open Books.

Morrow, D. (1995). Church and religion in the Ulster crisis. In S. Dunn (ed.), *Facets of the conflict in Northern Ireland* (pp. 151–167). London: Macmillan.

Moxon-Brown, E. P. (1983). *Nation, class and creed in Northern Ireland.* Aldershot, England: Gower.

Murray, D. (1995). Culture, religion and violence in Northern Ireland. In S. Dunn (ed.), *Facets of the conflict in Northern Ireland* (pp. 215–229). London: Macmillan.

Murray, R. (1982). Political violence in Northern Ireland 1969–1977. In F. W. Boal and J. N. H. Douglas (eds.), *Integration and division: Geographical perspectives on the Northern Ireland problem.* London: Academic Press.

PPRU (Policy Planning Research Unit) (1984) *Commentary on Northern Ireland crime statistics, 1969–1982. Policy Planning Research Unit Occasional Paper 5,* Belfast: Social Research Division, Policy, Planning and Research Unit, Department of Finance and Personnel.

Roe, M. D., Pegg, W., and Hodges, K. (June 1995). Reconciling ethnic memories in settings of political violence: Youth in Northern Ireland. In E. Frydenberg (chair), *The role of memories in conflict.* Symposium conducted at the Fourth International Symposium on the Contributions of Psychology to Peace. Sponsored by the Committee for the Psychological Study of Peace, International Union of Psychological Science, Cape Town, South Africa.

Rose, R. (1971). *Governing without consensus: An Irish perspective*. London: Faber and Faber.

Russell, J. (1973). Violence and the Ulster schoolboy. *New Society*, July, 204–206.

Smith, A. (1995). Education and the conflict in Northern Ireland. In S. Dunn (ed.), *Facets of the conflict in Northern Ireland* (pp. 168–186). New York: St. Martin's Press.

Smith, A., and Dunn, S. (1990). *Extending inter-school links*. Coleraine, Northern Ireland: Centre for the Study of Conflict.

Smyth, G. (1995). Sectarianism: Theology gone wrong? In T. Williams and A. Falconer (eds.), *Sectarianism* (pp. 52–76). Dublin: Dominican Publications.

Stringer, M., and Cairns, E. (1983). Catholic and Protestant young people's rating of stereotyped Protestant and Catholic faces. *British Journal of Social Psychology*, 22, 241–246.

Tajfel, H., and Turner, J. C. (1986). The Social Identity Theory of intergroup behavior. In S. Worchel and W. G. Austin (eds.), *Psychology of intergroup relations*, 2nd ed. (pp. 7–24). Chicago: Nelson-Hall.

Taylor, R. (1988). Social scientific research on the "Troubles" in Northern Ireland: The problem of objectivity. *The Economic and Social Review*, 19, 123–145.

Trew, K. (1983). A sense of national identity: Fact or artifact? *Irish Journal of Psychology*, 6, 28–36.

Trew, K. (1989). Evaluating the impact of contact schemes for Catholic and Protestant children. In J. Harbison (ed.), *Growing up in Northern Ireland* (pp. 131–159). Belfast: Learning Resources Unit, Stranmillis College.

Trew, K. (1992). Social psychological research on the conflict. *The Psychologist: Bulletin of the British Psychological Society*, 15, 342–344.

Trew, K., McWhirter, L., Maguire, A., and Hinds, J. (1985). *Irish children's summer program in Greensboro (NC): Evaluation 1984–1985*. Unpublished report, Queen's University, Belfast, Northern Ireland.

Turner, E. B., Turner, I. F., and Reid, A. (1980). Religious attitudes in two types of urban secondary schools: A decade of change. *Irish Journal of Education*, 14, 43–52.

Violence in Ireland: A report to the churches. (1976). Belfast: Christian Journals Ltd.

Waddell, N., and Cairns, E. (1986). Situational perspectives on social identity in Northern Ireland. *British Journal of Social Psychology*, 25, 25–31.

Waddell, N., and Cairns, E. (1991). Identity preference in Northern Ireland. *Political Psychology*, 12, 205–213.

Weinreich, P. (1982). *Identity development in Protestant and Roman Catholic adolescent boys and girls in Belfast*. Paper presented at the Tenth International Congress of the International Association for Child and Adolescent Psychiatry and Allied Professions, Dublin.

Weinreich, P. (1992). Socio-psychological maintenance of ethnicity in Northern Ireland: A commentary. *The Psychologist: Bulletin of the British Psychological Society*, 5, 345–346.

Whyte, J. (1990). *Interpreting Northern Ireland*. Oxford: Oxford University Press.

Wilson, D., and Tyrrell, J. (1995). Institutions for conciliation and mediation. In S. Dunn (ed.), *Facets of the conflict in Northern Ireland* (pp. 230–250). New York: St. Martin's Press.

Wilson, R., and Cairns, E. (1992). Psychosocial stress and the Northern Ireland troubles. *The Psychologist*, 5, 347–350.

Wright, F. (1973). Protestant ideology and politics in Ulster. *Archives of European Sociology*, 14, 213–280.

Wright, F. (1988). Reconciling the histories of Protestant and Catholic in Northern Ireland. In A. D. Falconer (ed.), *Reconciling memories* (pp. 68–83). Blackrock, Co. Dublin: Columba Press.

Part Three

Immigration, Acculturation, and Xenophobia

Chapter Nine
Acculturation and Adaptation
A Case of Vietnamese Children and Youths in Finland

Karmela Liebkind and Liisa Kosonen

Introduction

Since the Second World War, European countries have experienced a vast international movement of persons with a different cultural background than the indigenous population. The migrant population in Europe is steadily increasing. During the 1960s and early 1970s, there was a large-scale labor migration into the more industrialized countries of Europe (Westin, 1993). Since then, there has been an increasing inflow of other migrants such as family members and refugees. In addition, the unforeseen developments in central and eastern Europe are leading to the arrival of a new wave of immigrants in the countries of western Europe, in search of a better future not only for themselves, but, more importantly, for their children. European countries, therefore, are becoming increasingly multicultural and multiethnic societies (Marsella, 1994).

Immigrant children have in recent years come to constitute a significant and growing proportion of the total school enrollment in many European countries, and the proportion is particularly large in some cities. For instance, 31 percent of the total school enrollment in Paris are children of foreign background (Costa-Lascoux, 1989). In the United Kingdom, the immigrant population constitutes approximately 4.5 million or 8 percent of the national population. In London, immigrants represent approximately 15 percent of the population (United Nations Population Fund, 1993). It has also been estimated that by the year 2000, a third of the population under the age of thirty-five in urban Europe will have an immigrant background (Extra and Vallen, 1989). The second-generation immigrants have been called the "European time-bomb" (*Newsweek*, 1990).

Immigrant children are overrepresented among the clients of health workers in many schools (Aronowitz, 1984). The adaptation problems of immigrant children (including academic difficulties, delinquency, identity and generational conflicts) are linked to the gap between the child-rearing styles and educational values of the parents and those of the host society (Sam and Berry, 1995).

Research in this area has increased our knowledge of these phenomena, but in spite of their relevance, many of the studies have been characterized as sporadic, isolated, and cursory, which limits the possibility to draw generalized conclusions (Stein, 1986). Often studies in Europe have relied on theories coming from the traditional countries of immigration—North America and Australia—where the sociocultural context is different, especially regarding both the absolute and the relative number of immigrants. This calls for a thorough integration of existing theories and models, backed by empirical research rooted in appropriate sociocultural contexts (Ward and Kennedy, 1993).

Finland as a Host Society for the Vietnamese

Finland has a total population of about 5 million and has, for historical reasons, two official national languages, Finnish and Swedish. However, the Swedish-speakers today constitute only 6 percent of the population. In 1987 there were only 17,000 foreign citizens living in Finland, and the majority were from other European countries. In addition, many of them were return migrants coming from Sweden, North America, and Australia, over half of whom spoke Finnish or Swedish. Having adopted a very restrictive de facto immigration policy for a long time, Finland is, therefore, internationally far behind other Western countries in the scope of its immigration policy. In comparison Sweden, Finland's neighboring country, already had 700,000 foreign-born inhabitants in 1987 and an even greater number with a foreign background. (Jaakkola, 1994). Even today, the proportion of immigrants and refugees in Finland is the lowest in Europe, slightly over 1 percent (about 66,000 in 1995), and two-thirds of them still come from other European countries and the majority are Finnish return migrants.

The first group of quota refugees from southeast Asia, mainly Vietnam, in 1979 consisted of 100 persons. Before that, Finland had received only 182 refugees, from Chile, in 1973. Even now, the total number of refugees is only around 13,000 (about 0.2 percent of the total population), the second largest group still being the southeast Asians (about 2,500) and the largest group being the Somalians (about 3,500), who started arriving in 1991. The increase in refugee numbers has been very rapid, as only 900 refugees had been resettled in Finland by 1987. In comparison, almost 140,000 refugees had resettled in Sweden at that time.

The Vietnamese refugees in Finland form an ethnically heterogeneous (North, South, and Chinese Vietnamese) but socially rather homogeneous (predominantly lower-class) group. They have arrived in Finland from 1979 onward for reasons other than their own choice, and have, since 1987, been dispersed in small groups throughout the country (Matinheikki-Kokko, 1991; Liebkind, 1993). Finland has resettled refugees only on so-called humanitarian grounds, meaning that they have been in special need of resettlement because of illness or disability. Five ministries, the local municipalities, and the Red Cross are all responsible for some part of the resettlement process, which means an overlapping and unclear division of labor.

Although lip service is given to the principle of multiculturalism, in practice the term "adaptation" still stands for total assimilation (Matinheikki-Kokko, 1991, 1992, 1994), despite increasing awareness on the grassroots level of the importance of cultural sensitivity. In assimilative countries, the pressure in school for children and youth toward sameness and conformity seems to be considerably greater than in multicultural societies (Kosonen, 1994). About 2 percent of the school-age population in Finland comes from abroad, but in areas with a dense immigrant population (as in the capital area), this percentage often rises to 20–25 percent.

The relationship between the concrete acculturation experience of individuals and the resulting acculturative stress depends on a variety of moderating factors, including the nature of the host society (see Figure 9.1). Argument and some evidence exist that mental health problems may be fewer among immigrants and refugees in countries with multicultural ideologies (with attendant tolerance for cultural diversity) than countries with assimilationist ideologies (with pressures to conform to a single cultural standard) (Berry et al., 1987). The policy of refugee dispersal, applied also in Finland since 1987, has proved to be an especially serious mistake in several countries (Westermeyer, 1987; Liebkind, 1990, 1995a, 1995b; Dalglish, 1989). There is a significant inverse relationship between the density of any ethnic migrant group and the rate of mental illness in that group (Furnham and Bochner, 1990). Viewed in this perspective, the possibilities for the Vietnamese refugees in Finland to receive social and emotional support in their acculturation process are not the best possible.

Ethnocultural Identity and Acculturation
Studies in the change of ethnic identity have, within social psychology, been mostly elaborated in the field of ethnolinguistic identity (e.g., Clément

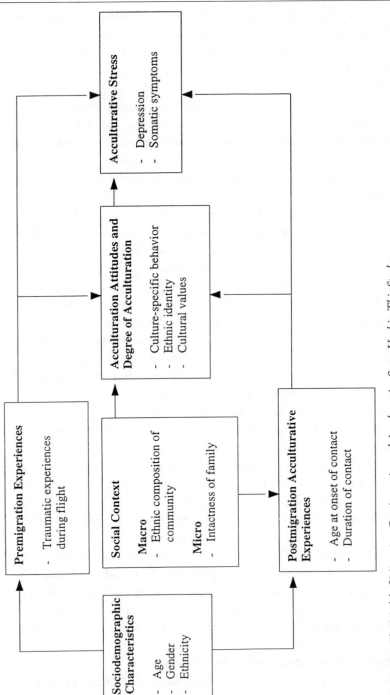

Figure 9.1. The Model of Migration Contingencies and Acculturative Stress Used in This Study

and Noels, 1992; Sachdev and Bourhis, 1990b). Traditional social psychological studies in the change of social identity are moving from a descriptive approach (e.g., Garza and Herringer, 1987) and an experimental approach (e.g., Tajfel, 1978) toward a greater acknowledgment of the multidimensionality, contextuality, and affectivity of social identity (e.g., Hinkle and Brown, 1990; Johnston and Hewstone, 1990; Hogg and Abrams, 1990; Sachdev and Bourhis, 1990a). However, social identity theorists have traditionally tended to ignore the larger literature on ethnicity and acculturation (Liebkind, 1992).

Within cross-cultural psychology there is an increasing interest in the psychological adaptations individuals make when they move between cultures. Changing identification patterns within and across ethnic boundaries modify the self-constructs and the value systems of individuals. For different ethnic groups, different features of their culture may contribute to their sense of ethnic identity (Liebkind, 1989, 1992; Weinreich, 1989; Phinney, 1990; Sue and Sue, 1990; Rosenthal and Feldman, 1992). In this context, culture can be conceptualized as shared patterns of belief and feeling toward issues such as child-rearing habits, family systems and ethical values or attitudes (Fernando, 1991).

The aim of this chapter is to describe some results of a study in which the relationship between acculturation and stress experienced by young refugees in a quite monocultural host society was investigated. Pre- and postmigration experiences and the concomitant acculturation attitudes and degree of acculturation are examined and related to acculturative stress (see Figure 9.1).

Acculturation is a key concept used in research that has dealt with groups in contact (Phinney, 1990). Psychological acculturation refers to the changes in identity, values, behavior, and attitudes that occur through contact with another culture. In principle, both cultural groups could influence each other equally, but in practice one tends to dominate the other (Berry et al., 1987; Berry, 1990). Acculturation is a multilinear process, a set of alternatives rather than a single dimension ending in assimilation or absorption in a dominant culture (Liebkind, 1984, 1989; Berry, 1990). The ways in which the ethnocultural minority wishes to relate to the dominant group have been termed acculturation attitudes (Berry et al., 1987; Berry, 1990). The two basic issues in the research on ethnocultural minorities are (a) whether they emphasize the value of maintaining their cultural identity and characteristics, and (b) whether they stress the value of maintaining relationships and contact with the dominant group (Berry et al., 1987).

Questions (a) and (b) (Berry et al, 1987; Berry, 1990) can be simplified into four types of acculturation attitudes. *Alienation/marginalization*
occurs if one rejects one's own culture but does not adopt the majority
culture. One is caught between two worlds and accepted by neither. *Assimilation* means rejection of one's own culture and adoption of the majority culture. Adolescents who, in their attempts to become "mainstream,"
reject skills necessary to interact with their own culture, are at particular
risk for maladjustment. *Separation* occurs when individuals emphasize their
own culture and withdraw from contact with the dominant culture. It
provides temporary protection but involves risks of maladjustment, if it
implies failure to learn how to interact in the mainstream context (Phinney,
Lochner, and Murphy, 1990).

There is some empirical evidence suggesting that the fourth option,
integration—maintaining both one's own ethnic traditions and contacts
with the majority culture—affords the best psychological outcomes
(Berry, et al., 1987; Rumbaut, 1991; Phinney et al., 1990; Sue and Sue,
1990). Berry (1990) emphasizes, however, that acculturation may be "un-
even" across domains of behavior and social life; for example, one may
seek economic assimilation (in work), linguistic integration (by way of
bilingualism), and marital separation (by endogamy).

The Ethnocultural Identity of Vietnamese Refugee Youths

As Nga Anh Nguyen (1992) has pointed out, puberty with its hormonal
upsurge and growth spurt is a well-established aspect of youth, but the uni-
versality of its psychological counterpart, adolescence, has been an ongoing
subject of controversy. For some, adolescence is a mere by-product of the
discontinuity of Western cultures, and, therefore, does not exist as such in
Eastern cultures typified by continuity. However, for Asian families who
resettle in Western countries, the existence of a developmental phase between childhood and adulthood—whether it is named adolescence or not—
undoubtedly becomes a harsh reality (Nga Anh Nguyen, 1992).

In adolescence, the child questions his or her own identity and his
or her identifications. In the Western world this is a normal process of
growing up, a process that can be turbulent for some, but that usually
leads to a new sense of self and belonging to society. For the adolescent
refugee this can be a very rough and lengthy period of identity search, for
he or she has lost all that is familiar and has been plunged into a new
environment with sociocultural norms different from his or her own
(Nguyen and Malapert, 1988). Refugee adolescents can sometimes be seen

desperately searching for models with which to identify—first in their own culture and then in the host culture, which, as Nguyen and Malapert note, does not lead to a harmonious blend of identification.

It is especially important for refugee children that they are able to maintain their relationships with other family members or, if this is not possible, with those who share their language, culture, and identity. Such social support systems are now known to be extremely important for all persons experiencing acculturation, no less so for a developing child (Berry, 1991; Knudsen, 1988).

According to Phinney and colleagues (1990), all minority individuals need to resolve two primary issues stemming from their minority status in society. These issues are (a) the existence of what is at best ignorance, and at worst stereotyping and prejudice toward themselves and their group, and (b) the existence of two different sets of norms and values, those of their own culture and those of the majority, which have varying degrees of impact on their lives. In attempting to face these issues and conflicts, minority youth may consciously weigh the various options open to them and make active decisions on how to cope, they may ignore them, or they may fail to deal consciously with these issues (Phinney et al., 1990).

Studies of generational differences in ethnic identity tend to show an erosion of ethnic identity in later generations of immigrants (Rosenthal and Feldman, 1992; Rick and Forward, 1992; Liebkind, 1993). Rick and Forward (1992) found that overall acculturation level was a significant predictor of the degree of intergenerational differences and conflicts perceived by Hmong refugee youths from Laos. Intergenerational conflicts within refugee families, in turn, are linked both to school problems and the mental health status of adolescent refugees (Lin, Masuda, and Tazuma, 1984; Nguyen and Williams, 1989).

These results are more understandable if one considers traditional Vietnamese family values and compares them to their Western counterparts. As has been pointed out by several authors (e.g., Chang, 1982; Rosenthal and Feldman, 1992; White and Marsella, 1989; Ho, 1987; Nidorf, 1985), the concept of self in the Eastern world is quite different from that in the Western world. For traditional southeast Asians, self and the family are integral, not separable concepts (Nguyen and Williams, 1989). The notion of family and filial piety is the single most important construct binding and organizing southeast Asian psychological experience and social reality (Nidorf, 1985).

Conflicting Cultural Norms and Adolescence

Western, and also Finnish, child rearing fosters autonomy and independence to help the child mature into a self-sufficient adult. In Finnish culture, children are taught early to make their own decisions. Dependence on other people has, for better or worse, traditionally been considered a sign of weakness or immaturity. In general, authority relations are downplayed and equality is the core value defining interpersonal and intergroup relations. In Finland, as in other Nordic countries, there is an especially strong emphasis in family child-rearing practices, official educational aims, national legislation, and working life on the principle of equality between the sexes; thus the position of women in Finland is traditionally strong inside and outside the home. In 1906, Finnish women were the first in Europe to gain the right to vote in national elections. Women constitute almost half (47.5 percent [*Yearbook of Population Research in Finland*, 1995]) of the workforce in Finland today, and their children are mostly cared for in municipal and private child-care facilities.

Vietnamese child rearing, on the other hand, places emphasis on interdependence, familial affiliation, and relatedness over individuality. In the light of the fundamental differences between Western and Eastern culture, some first-generation Vietnamese youths may suffer from major intergenerational conflicts and deep identity struggles, resulting in intense emotional turmoil (Nguyen, 1992).

The southeast Asian family is often multigenerational and characterized by tight boundaries. Family members are expected to be loyal to each other and to distrust outsiders. Hierarchical authority applies both to age and to gender. Regardless of what parents do, children are obligated to give respect and obedience; sibling rivalry and aggression is discouraged; and wives are expected to be the nurturant caretakers of both husbands and children. The energy and creativity of mothers are channeled primarily into taking care of their children, with whom they form strong emotional bonds (Ho, 1987). To such families, cultural transition is a severe blow. When relatives and close friends are no longer available for emotional support, the traditional hierarchical structure and rigidity of family roles make the expression and resolution of conflicts within the nuclear family very difficult, if not nearly impossible, leaving members with a high degree of vulnerability (Ho, 1987).

The warm familial affiliation and interrelatedness in the Eastern child-rearing system often shelters the individual from the alienation and self-estrangement plaguing some Western youths. However, self-negation entailing suppression of anger and ambivalence may have its own psychological price, with relief often found in somatization, a common form of psychopathology among Asians (Nguyen, 1992). For Asian youth in particular, therefore, the ambivalence arising from the existence of two different sets of cultural norms and values may be difficult to confront in the active manner advocated by Phinney and colleagues (1990).

Discrepancies in acculturation between husband and wife and between parents and children can have negative effects for the whole family. If the children adopt Western ways of assertiveness and freedom of choice and speech, the parents may feel threatened and demand even more respect and deference (Ho, 1987; Phinney, 1990). Considering the prevailing gender roles in the Nordic countries, emphasizing equal status and independence, the cultural gap experienced by the Vietnamese in Finland is considerable.

The Consequences of Acculturation

One of the most obvious and frequently reported consequences of acculturation is social disintegration, accompanied by personal crisis. However, these problems are not inevitable and depend on a variety of different factors (for reviews, see Minister of Supply and Services, Canada, 1988; Berry, 1990). Cultural isolation appears to be a major stressor, as does separation from family members. Several authors stress the supportive and protecting function of "ethnic enclaves," communities of conationals (Beiser, 1988, 1991; Westermeyer, 1987; Furnham and Bochner, 1990; Knudsen, 1988).

Of all kinds of acculturating groups, refugees are the most vulnerable (Berry et al., 1987; Berry, 1990). Refugees experience high levels of unpredictability, stress, and powerlessness, leading to higher incidences of depression, anxiety, and psychosomatic complaints (Furnham and Bochner, 1990). For refugees, the contrast between past, present, and future poses exceptionally great problems of continuity (Knudsen, 1990).

Recent literature has shown that refugees in general, and the Indochinese in particular, have experienced greater psychological distress and dysfunction than other immigrant or native-born groups (Liebkind, 1993; Rumbaut, 1991; Beiser, 1991; Minister of Supply and Services, Canada, 1988; Westermeyer, 1987). Factors especially relevant for refugee youths include the specific family histories of the flight (whether or not the children arrived together with their parents, before or after them) and the specific family structures (one- or two-parent families) (Krupinski and Burrows, 1986; Charron and Ness, 1981; Aronowitz, 1984).

Methods

Sample

The sample included 208 first-generation refugee children and youths, aged eight to nineteen, and 204 Finnish children and youths of the same age. The sample was divided into three age groups, eight-to-twelve-year-olds (N=76), thirteen-to-sixteen-year-olds (N=188) and seventeen-to-nineteen-year-olds (N=148). The number of Vietnamese and Finns was equivalent within each age group. The mean age in the total sample as well as in each ethnic group was fifteen years. The ratio of males to females was equivalent in the two ethnic groups (56 percent for the Vietnamese and 54 percent for the Finnish sample) and in each age group, as was the ratio of those living in the capital area to those living in other parts of the country (47 percent for the Vietnamese and 44 percent for the Finnish sample).

In empirical studies on the acculturation process, cross-sectional research, employing a time-related variable such as length of residence or age, is a common alternative to longitudinal research (Berry, 1990). In this study, both length of residence and age were used to assess the acculturation process. Of the Vietnamese in the sample, one-third had stayed in Finland two years or less, one-third had stayed three to four years, and one-third had stayed five years or more. Ethnically, the Vietnamese sample was quite homogeneous in that 78.4 percent were ethnic Vietnamese, 11.5 percent ethnic Chinese and 10.1 percent mixed Chinese-Vietnamese.

The total sample was composed from three separate subsamples of earlier studies. One of the studies (Liebkind, 1993, 1994, 1995a, 1996a) examined the mental health and ethnic identity of a nationwide sample of 159 Vietnamese refugees born between 1969 and 1976 who arrived in Finland in 1979–1989, and their parents and guardians (total N=280). In the second study (Saarinen, 1993), the depression and anxiety of 116 Finnish adolescents were examined using the same measures as in Liebkind's (1993) study. In order to study culture-specific expression of these symptoms, Saarinen's Finnish sample was compared with the Vietnamese sample of Liebkind's study. The third study (Kosonen, 1994) compared the mental health and school adaptation of a random nationwide sample of 97 Vietnamese students (aged eight to twenty) to 97 Finnish students of the same age in comprehensive school in 1992. All the Vietnamese and Finnish eight- to nineteen-year-olds of these three studies were combined to form the present sample.

In all three studies, permission to approach the families was obtained from the schools, and if the respondents were under the age of eighteen, parental permission for the interviews was also obtained. The interviews were conducted either in the homes of the respondents or in the schools.

Measurements

Single Item Variables

Single items with sufficient variability were used as predictors of acculturation and acculturative stress. These items concerned sociodemographic characteristics (age, gender, and ethnicity), premigration experiences (time spent in refugee camps, separation from family during flight), postmigration acculturation experiences (age on arrival, length of time in Finland) and aspects of the large-scale (macro) and the immediate (micro) social contexts. The former item concerned the density of co-ethnics in the residence area (ethnic composition of the community) and the latter the present composition of the family (intactness of family). Culture-specific behavior was also measured by single-item variables (celebration of Vietnamese holidays, reading Vietnamese books and magazines, and speaking Vietnamese with siblings) (see Figure 9.1).

Acculturative Stress

Acculturative stress was assessed with a depression scale that combines nine items from different instruments used with the three original samples combined for this study: two Western scales, the Children's Depression Inventory (CDI) (Kovacs, 1985) and the Hopkins Symptom Check List 25 (HSCL 25) (Mollica et al., 1987), and one culture-specific scale, the VDS (Vietnamese Depression Scale) (Kinzie et al., 1982). All original scales used were standardized and available in Vietnamese.

A maximum likelihood factor analysis of the combined measure was conducted in order to separate the more psychological symptoms of depression from the specifically somatic symptoms of fatigue and loss of appetite. A three-factor solution was adopted. The first factor measured fatigue (general reliability coefficient = 0.94); the second factor, poor appetite (general reliability coefficient =0.94); and the third factor, psychological depression (e.g. loneliness, crying, worry) (general reliability coefficient =.074). The three factors explained 42 percent of the total variance of the scale.

Degree of Acculturation

A twenty-nine-item questionnaire of traditional Vietnamese family values, developed and translated into Vietnamese by Nguyen and Williams (1989), was used to assess the actual degree of acculturation of the respondents. The statements in this questionnaire, called the Family Value Scale can be conceived of as a sample of the shared beliefs (and their opposites) of child rearing and family values endorsed within the Vietnamese culture.

The Family Value Scale was used as a three-factor solution extracted from an unweighted least squares factor analysis.

The *Family Solidarity* factor (general reliability coefficient = 0.89) included eleven items, for example, "family members should prefer to be with each other rather than with outsiders," "brothers and sisters should never be envious or jealous of one another," and "parents always know what is best." The *Children's Autonomy* factor (general reliability coefficient =0.87) included twelve items, for example, "when a girl reaches the age of sixteen, it is all right for her to decide whom to date and when to date," "it is all right for boys over eighteen to decide when to marry and whom to marry," and "it is all right for boys to choose their own career." The *Opposition to Equal Status* factor (general reliability coefficient =0.71) included six items, for example "boys should have more privileges than girls," "important family decisions should involve discussion among its members" (negative loading), and "older children should have more privileges than younger ones." The three factors explained 31 percent of the total variance of the scale.

Ethnic Self-Identification
Ethnic self-identification was assessed by asking the respondents to indicate whether they feel (1) totally Vietnamese, (2) both Vietnamese and Finnish, or (3) totally Finnish, the mid-option allowing for a balanced bicultural self-identification.

Results
Ethnic Identity and Acculturation: Changing Self-Identification and Family Values
The ethnic identity of the Vietnamese children and adolescents is in the process of acquiring Finnish elements. More than one-fourth of all the Vietnamese studied considered themselves to be both Finnish and Vietnamese, and more than one-tenth had already begun to speak only Finnish with their siblings. A two-way analysis of variance (age x gender, $F(5, 202)=5.10$, $p<0.001$) was conducted within the Vietnamese sample in order to determine the differences in ethnic identity (ethnic self-identi-

fication) between boys and girls on the one hand and the three age groups on the other. There was no main effect for gender, but there was one for age (F(4, 202)=6.18, p<0.001). No interaction effects were found. The youngest age group (eight to twelve years) considered itself significantly more Finnish than the two older age groups.

Ethnic self-identification does not, however, necessarily parallel the actual degree of acculturation (Liebkind, 1996a). Looking at the specific family values adopted by the Finnish and Vietnamese children and adolescents, the distinctive features of the Vietnamese culture become visible. If the Vietnamese and the Finnish samples are compared with each other on item of the Nguyen and Williams (1989) Family Value Scale (Table 9.1), the core differences between the family values in the two ethnic groups can be discerned.

As seen in Table 9.1, significantly more than their Finnish peers, the Vietnamese children and adolescents stress traditional gender and generation roles, the authority of grandparents and parents, and the necessity to obey them and seek their advice, especially for girls and for matters concerning dating and marriage. The Vietnamese strongly emphasize the inner harmony and exclusiveness of the family, the taboos against sibling rivalry, the desirability of sharing one's inner thoughts with other family members, and the protection of young children from bad news. Significantly more than the Vietnamese, the Finnish youngsters emphasize the obligation of parents to admit mistakes and the right to private thoughts within the family.

Table 9.1 Mean Differences between the Ethnic Groups in Agreement with Items concerning Cultural Values Response Scale: 1 (Disagree) to 5 (Agree)

	Vietnamese M	Finnish M	t
1. Family member should be preferred	4.38	3.09	−11.87***
2. Oldest girl should help at home	4.55	3.12	−13.15***
3. Parents always know best	4.47	2.79	−15.50***
4. Clear line of authority preferred	4.16	2.89	−9.96***
5. Grandparents should have great influence	3.87	1.77	−18.16***
6. Oldest boy should follow parents' wishes	3.41	1.87	−11.65***
7. Siblings should not be jealous	4.51	3.32	−9.72***
8. Family should eat together	4.43	3.94	−4.54***
9. Family should be together	4.46	4.15	−3.57***
10. Family members should share feelings	3.92	3.47	−3.97***

(continued)

Table 9.1 *(continued)*

	Vietnamese M	Finnish M	t
11. Anger should be made known	4.05	3.86	−1.66
12. Boy can decide about dating at 16	3.28	4.25	8.03***
13. Girl can decide about dating at 16	3.00	4.20	10.03***
14. Girl can decide about marriage at 18	3.65	4.59	8.48***
15. Boy can decide about marriage at 18	3.86	4.59	7.06***
16. Family members have right to private thoughts	4.29	4.82	6.39***
17. Girls can choose career	4.48	4.71	2.92**
18. Boys can choose career	4.60	4.64	0.49
19. Girls can leave home for studies or work	4.16	4.49	3.14**
20. Boys can leave home for studies or work	4.39	4.51	1.25
21. Problems should be told to children	2.96	3.79	6.35***
22. Parents should admit mistakes	3.92	4.81	8.67***
23. Crying openly is permitted	3.78	4.60	7.76***
24. Affection can be shown	4.31	4.01	−2.99**
25. Family decisions should be discussed	4.51	4.56	0.60
26. Boys should have more privileges than girls	2.69	1.91	−5.58***
27. Chores should be shared equally	4.20	4.15	−0.44
28. Older children should have more privileges	3.11	2.98	−0.93
29. Children may watch TV freely	2.71	2.54	−1.26

** $p<0.01$; *** $p<0.001$.

However, the acculturation of the Vietnamese adolescents is evident in a few similarities between the two ethnic groups. The difference in taboos against openly shown aggression is not statistically significant. In addition, the values of the Finnish and the Vietnamese youngsters do not differ from each other concerning the desirability of democratic discussions within the family and equally shared household chores, the freedom of children to watch TV, the undesirability of older children to have more privileges than the younger ones, and the right of boys to choose their career and of boys to leave home for studies or work. It seems that the traditional Vietnamese family values have remained more intact for girls than for boys.

Stress Symptoms among Vietnamese and Finnish Adolescents

A three-way analysis of variance (ethnicity x age x gender) was conducted for each of the three stress factors (psychological depression, fatigue, and poor appetite) in order to examine the differences between the sample groups related to age, gender, and ethnicity.

Concerning psychological depression, the main effect of ethnicity was not statistically significant in the three-way analysis of variance, although the Vietnamese tended to report more symptoms (see Table 9.2). In a one-way analysis of variance with fewer degrees of freedom than in the three-way analysis, ethnicity did show a main effect: The Vietnamese reported significantly more psychological depression than the Finnish children and adolescents (see Table 9.3). In the three-way analysis of variance (Table 9.2) there was a significant main effect for gender as well as for age; the girls and the oldest age group reported more depression symptoms in both ethnic groups. There was also a significant age x gender interaction: The oldest girls reported more symptoms than the other groups. The impact of ethnicity was evident in the comparison of the means between the sample groups: the Vietnamese boys reported more depression symptoms than the Finnish boys in the oldest age group ($t(80)=-2.26$, $p<0.05$), while in the youngest age group the Vietnamese girls reported significantly more psychological depression symptoms than the Finnish girls ($t(33)=-2.79$, $p<0.01$).

Table 9.2 Three-Way Analysis of Variance (Age x Ethnicity x Gender) of Psychological Depression

| | | Boys | | Girls | |
		Vietnamese	Finnish	Vietnamese	Finnish
Ages	M	0.02	−0.21	0.07	−0.45
8–12	SD	0.71	0.50	0.56	0.21
	N	23	18	16	19
Ages	M	0.07	−0.12	0.04	0.02
13–16	SD	0.79	0.84	1.00	0.80
	N	55	49	41	43
Ages	M	−0.09	−0.37	0.39	0.50
17–19	SD	0.69	0.45	1.02	0.90
	N	39	43	34	32

F-test for model: $F(11,400) = 3.45$, $p<0.001$.

Source	F	df
Ethnicity	1.56	6,400
Age	3.22*	8,400
Gender	5.26***	6,400
Ethnicity x Age	1.00	4,400
Ethnicity x Gender	1.18	3,400
Age x Gender	4.96**	4,400
Ethnicity x Age x Gender	1.19	2,400

*$p<0.05$; **$p<0.01$; ***$p<0.001$.

Table 9.3 Psychological Depression in the Vietnamese and Finnish
Samples

	Psychological Depression	
	Vietnamese	Finnish
M	0.02	–0.08
SD	0.84	0.76
N	208	204

One-way analysis of variance: F (1, 410)=4.41, p<0.05.

The three-way analysis of variance (ethnicity x age x gender) for fatigue (Table 9.4) showed a main effect for both ethnicity and age. The Finnish children and adolescents reported more fatigue than the Vietnamese, and the youngest children reported more fatigue than the older ones. The youngest age group (eight- to twelve-year olds), in particular, reported more fatigue than the middle age group (thirteen- to sixteen-year olds)

Table 9.4 Three-Way Analysis of Variance (Age x Ethnicity x Gender) of
Fatigue

		Boys		Girls	
		Vietnamese	Finnish	Vietnamese	Finnish
Ages	M	0.20	–0.33	0.18	–0.12
8–12	SD	1.27	0.57	1.05	0.72
	N	23	18	16	19
	M	–0.36	0.41	–0.21	0.01
13–16	SD	0.62	1.20	0.69	0.93
	N	55	49	41	43
	M	–0.12	0.22	–0.13	0.24
17–19	SD	0.90	1.04	0.89	1.47
	N	39	43	34	32

F-test for the model: F(11, 400) = 2.46, p<0.01.

Source	F	df
Ethnicity	4.27***	6,400
Age	2.09*	8,400
Gender	0.83	6,400
Ethnicity x Age	3.91**	4,400
Ethnicity x Gender	1.36	3,400
Age x Gender	0.94	4,400
Ethnicity x Age x Gender	1.49	2,400

*p<0.05; **p<0.01; ***p<0.001.

$(t(133)=-3.05, p<0.05)$. However, a significant ethnicity x age interaction effect indicated that the difference between the ethnic groups described above is significant only in the group aged thirteen to sixteen years (see Table 9.4). Strictly speaking, even in this age group, it was only the Finnish boys who were significantly more tired than the Vietnamese boys $(t(96)=2.31, p<0.05)$. There were no differences in poor appetite between any of the main sample groups.

Predictors of Acculturative Stress
A hierarchical regression analysis was conducted in order to determine the extent to which sociodemographic characteristics, pre- and postmigration experiences, contextual variables, and degree of acculturation predicted the three different factors of acculturative stress (psychological depression, fatigue and poor appetite) among Vietnamese children and adolescents (see Figure 9.1). For each of the stress factors, the predictive variables were entered into the equation in the order established by the theoretical model in Figure 9.1: premigration experiences were entered first, contextual variables (first macro, then micro) second, postmigration acculturative experiences third, and degree of acculturation fourth. Also, the three different classes of acculturation variables (culture-specific behavior, ethnic identity, and cultural values) were entered separately. The correlation coefficients between the predictors used in each regression analysis were all nonsignificant.

It was further assumed that age, and to some extent also gender, have to be considered when analyzing the predictors of the reported stress symptoms. Consequently, separate predictive models of acculturative stress were elicited for the different age groups and for the gender groups. Only one significant model resulted from the hierarchical regression analysis conducted for the gender groups: Fatigue among boys was best predicted by the combination of two different kinds of acculturation variables: culture-specific behavior (reading Vietnamese books or magazines) and ethnic identity (ethnic self-definition) (see Figure 9.1). Culture-specific behavior alone accounted for 4 percent of the fatigue reported by the boys (F_{change} $(1,115)=4.76, p<0.05$). Those boys who did not read Vietnamese books or magazines (beta=-0.20, $p<0.05$) reported more fatigue than those who did. Entering the ethnic identity variable (beta=0.22, $p<0.05$) increased the prediction of fatigue among the boys with another 5 percent (F_{change} $(1,115)=6.09, p<0.05$). The final explanatory model thus predicted 9 percent of the fatigue among the boys ($F(2, 114)=5.53, p<0.01$). This means that Vietnamese boys whose cultural behavior is more Finnish and those who identify themselves as more Finnish reported significantly more fatigue than other Vietnamese boys. In this respect they resemble the Finnish boys who reported more fatigue than the Vietnamese (Table 9.4).

For the girls, only one variable appeared as a significant predictor of depression, and that was the density of co-ethnics in the residence area (ethnic composition of the community). Those Vietnamese girls who lived in areas with at least some other Vietnamese families in the neighborhood reported significantly less psychological depression than those who lived in totally Finnish areas (R^2=.07, $F(1, 89)$=6.44, $p<0.01$ beta=–0.26, $p<0.01$).

Even more than gender, the age of the Vietnamese youth determined which factors were significant predictors of acculturative stress. Premigration traumatic experiences (notably separation from family during flight) predicted as much as 13 percent of the fatigue reported by the youngest age group ($F(1, 37)$=5.40, $p<0.05$, beta=.36, $p<0.05$). For this age group, culture-specific behavior seems to be important. Entering this variable (reading Vietnamese books or magazines) into the regression increased the prediction of fatigue in this age group another 9 percent ($F_{change}(1, 37)$=4.40, $p<0.05$, beta=–0.32, $p<0.05$). The final model thus explained 22 percent of the fatigue in the youngest age group ($F(2, 36)$=5.15, $p<0.05$). Those eight- to twelve-year-olds who arrived with intact families and who read Vietnamese books and magazines reported clearly less fatigue.

For the thirteen- to sixteen-year-olds, the immediate social context (present composition of the family) and culture-specific behavior (celebration of Vietnamese holidays) both turned out to be significant predictors of acculturative stress. The present composition of the family by itself predicted 8 percent of the psychological depression reported in this age group ($F(1, 94)$=7.85, $p<0.01$, beta=0.28, $p<0.01$). Entering a variable indicating culture-specific behavior (celebrating Vietnamese holidays) increased the prediction with another 4 percent ($F_{change}(1, 94)$=4.12, $p<0.01$, beta=–0.20, $p<0.05$). Those thirteen- to sixteen-year-olds who were now living in intact families and who celebrated Vietnamese holidays reported less psychological depression. This final explanatory model predicted 12 percent of the depression in this age group ($F(2, 93)$=6.11, $p<0.01$).

For psychological depression among the seventeen- to nineteen- year-olds, it was the combination of gender, postmigration experiences (the duration of contact with the majority), and degree of acculturation (Family Solidarity and Children's Autonomy factors) that provided the best explanatory model. Gender alone explained 7 percent of the psychological depression reported in this age group ($F_{change}(1, 71)=5.52$, $p<0.05$, beta=0.27, $p<.05$). Entering the duration of contact with the majority (i.e., the time spent in Finland) into the regression increased the prediction with another 8 percent ($F_{change}(1, 71)=6.01$, $p<0.05$, beta=0.27, $p<.05$). Entering next the degree of acculturation (the scores on the Family Solidarity and Children's Autonomy factors of the Family Value Scale) into the regression increased the prediction with an additional 8 percent ($F_{change}(2, 70)=3.69$, $p<0.05$, beta$_{Family\ Solidarity}=-0.22$, $p<0.05$, beta$_{Children's\ Autonomy}=0.26$, $p<0.05$).

In this age group, then, girls who had abandoned cultural values supporting family solidarity and hierarchy and adopted Western values supporting children's autonomy, and girls who, in addition, had stayed longer in Finland reported more psychological depression. The final model explained 23 percent of the psychological depression in this age group ($F(4, 68)=5.05$, $p<0.01$).

For poor appetite, the best model for the seventeen- to nineteen-year-olds combined gender, culture-specific behavior (speaking Vietnamese with siblings), and degree of acculturation (Opposition to Equal Status factor), although culture-specific behavior was not a significant predictor in and of itself. Gender alone explained 5 percent of the poor appetite reported in this age group ($F(1, 71)=4.10$, $p<0.05$, beta=0.23, $p<0.05$). Entering culture-specific behavior (speaking Vietnamese with siblings) did not increase the prediction significantly ($R^2_{change}=.05$, $F_{change}(1, 71)=3.82$, ns.), but the degree of acculturation (scores on the Opposition to Equal Status factor, beta=0.27, $p<0.05$) increased the prediction with 12 percent ($F_{change}(1, 71)=5.80$, $p<0.05$) together with the culture-specific behavior, the beta-value of which became significant (beta=0.26, $p<0.05$) in this final step. Consequently, girls who spoke Vietnamese with their siblings and those who had maintained family values opposing equal status more often reported having a poor appetite. The final model explained 17 percent of the poor appetite reported in this age group ($F(3, 69)=4.82$, $p<0.01$). Also in this age group, therefore, the acculturation variables remained the best predictors of acculturative stress.

Of the predictive variables included in the theoretical model, neither time spent in refugee camps nor age on arrival appeared as significant predictors in any of the explanatory models.

Summary and Discussion

Naturally, all the Vietnamese children and adolescents adhered more to traditional Vietnamese family values than did their Finnish peers. The main differences between the two groups concerned core values of filial obedience, harmony, and traditional gender roles, especially for females. However, some degree of acculturation had already occurred. The rights to openly shown aggression, democratic discussions, and equally shared chores within the family were emphasized as much as in the Finnish group.

In addition, the ethnic identity of the youngest Vietnamese was clearly more Finnish than that of the older ones, and one-tenth of all the Vietnamese studied spoke Finnish with their siblings. This rapid acculturation of the children can create a considerable generational gap between parents and children (see Liebkind, 1993, 1996a, 1996b). Consequently, at least some amount of acculturative stress is to be expected.

In accordance with this expectation, the Vietnamese reported more psychological depression than the Finns, but, surprisingly, less fatigue. In addition, those Vietnamese boys who reported the most fatigue had a more Finnish identity than the others. To what extent this reflects culture-specific symptom expression requires further study.

In this study, the Vietnamese girls reported more stress symptoms than the Vietnamese boys in the oldest age group. Also in previous studies on acculturative stress, females have frequently been noted to experience more stress (Berry et al., 1987; Berry, 1990; Liebkind, 1993). Whether this pattern really indicates greater female stress or, for example, a greater tendency to subscribe to symptom statements, is not always easy to judge. However, the more frequent stress symptoms among the girls in this study may be associated with the great discrepancy between Finnish and Vietnamese norms and values concerning female roles and behavior, in combination with a strong adherence among the Vietnamese studied to those traditional Vietnamese family values that concern girls. Vietnamese boys were more likely than girls to be allowed to behave like Finns.

This discrepancy in cultural values seems to create a special dilemma for the Vietnamese girls: Caught as they seem to be between "a rock and a hard place," both rapid acculturation (the adoption of Finnish norms concerning family solidarity and children's autonomy) and a failure to acculturate (the maintenance of traditional Vietnamese values opposing equal status) lead to stress symptoms in seventeen- to nineteen-year-old Vietnamese girls (psychological depression in the former and poor appetite in the latter case).

In general, the stress symptoms reported by the Vietnamese children and adolescents in this sample seem to be connected with postmigration contingencies, specifically attitudes toward and degree of acculturation, rather than premigration experiences. This confirms previous research results, which demonstrate that what happens to people after they enter a country of permanent settlement usually has a greater effect on their mental health than what happened to them before (Beiser, 1991). Generally, the more the youths had adopted Western values, the more they reported acculturative stress. Especially detrimental for the Vietnamese studied was the simultaneous adoption of Western family values favoring children's autonomy and rejection of tradition values supporting family solidarity and hierarchy; that is, the assimilation strategy (Berry, 1990).

Features of the social context were also significant predictors. The density of co-ethnics and the concomitant support of an ethnic community seems to be especially important for the girls, who expressed more symptoms of depression if an ethnic community was lacking. The Finnish dispersal policy in resettlement and the resulting lack of fellow Vietnamese going through the same acculturation process may have aggravated the acculturative stress of the Vietnamese girls in this study. This confirms the general finding that the density of any ethnic migrant group in an area is inversely related to the rate of mental illness in that group (Furnham and Bochner, 1990).

For the boys it was especially the abandonment of culture-specific behavior, like reading Vietnamese books and magazines, and the adoption of a more Finnish ethnic identity that increased reported fatigue. It appears that, both among the boys and among the girls studied, there were some difficulties in obtaining a truly bicultural identity; that is, integration (Berry, 1990; Sue and Sue, 1990).

The premigration experiences during flight had an impact only in the youngest age group (eight- to twelve-year-olds), where those children who had arrived in Finland with intact families reported less fatigue than those who had not. In combination with culture-specific behavior (reading Vietnamese books and magazines), the premigration experiences explained 22 percent of the stress symptoms in this age group.

For the thirteen- to sixteen-year-olds, the immediate social context and culture-specific behavior were both important factors in predicting acculturative stress. Living with intact families and celebrating Vietnamese holidays seemed to protect this age group from psychological depression.

The best regression model explained at the most 23 percent of the total variance of the stress symptoms in the oldest age group (seventeen- to nineteen-year-olds). In this age group, gender was a significant predictor:

girls reported more stress symptoms than boys. In addition, those who had stayed longer in Finland reported more psychological depression. The assumed psychological disadvantage of an assimilative orientation, simultaneous adoption of Western values, and rejection of traditional ones (Berry et al., 1987), seemed to be especially evident in this age group.

In general, the explained variance of the stress symptoms in the Vietnamese sample remained modest. Probably this is due to neglect of certain factors especially relevant for minority children. As the research literature suggests that intergenerational conflicts within refugee families are linked to various problems among refugee youths (Lin, Masuda, and Tazuma, 1984; Nguyen and Williams, 1989), assessment of the acculturation attitudes and degree of acculturation of the parents or guardians seems to be obligatory. Studies on refugee youths should also include their parents.

In this study, we are only beginning to reveal the complexity and multidimensionality of the subjective experience of exile and acculturation among youth. These experiences seem to depend, to a considerable degree, on age and gender, and they cannot be understood without close scrutiny of the particular cultural values clashing in the acculturation process.

National immigration policies are driven by a blend of self-interest and compassion. Research in this area springs from the same two motivations. Research has increased our understanding of the forces that can help prevent social exclusion among new settlers and of the factors that promote healthy adaptation and integration. Putting this knowledge to work in resettling refugees and immigrants is both expedient and moral (Beiser, 1991).

The fact is that substantial populations of different national or ethnic origins from those of the host society have come to live permanently in most of the member states of the European Union. Parts of these populations often find it difficult to become fully integrated into society, partly because of deliberate or unintended discrimination. The fear of massive immigration from third world countries and eastern Europe in the face of their soaring political and economic crises has also led to a revision of immigration policies, repatriation of illegal immigrants, and a general xenophobic atmosphere in Europe (*Newsweek*, 1994). Some groups of immigrants have been described as "inassimilable" because they have cultures that are incompatible with European culture (Suárez-Orozco, 1991).

In the area of immigrant adaptation, administrators and helping agencies are daily confronted with the problems immigrants face in their adaptation process, and are overwhelmed by the difficulties in catering to their needs and in offsetting maladaptive outcomes (Olowu, 1983; Williams, 1991). The Committee of Experts on Community Relations of the Council of Europe (1991) has emphasized the important role of the educational system, as it has a vital part to play in preparing the ground for better ethnic relations in the future, not only by means of specific measures to ensure that pupils of immigrant origin are enabled to achieve their full potential, but also by ensuring that all pupils are prepared for life in a multiethnic and multicultural society (Council of Europe, 1991, p. 65).

The results from this study seem to suggest that the society of resettlement should allow for a long-term process of adaptation and integration on the part of the refugees. In addition, the refugees themselves should also accept such a gradual melding of two differing sets of behavioral norms and expectations into a truly bicultural identity, instead of aiming at a very rapid pace of acculturation or even assimilation.

References

Aronowitz, M. (1984). The social and emotional adjustment of immigrant children: A review of the literature. *International Migration Review, 18,* 237–257.

Beiser, M. (1988). Influence of time, ethnicity and attachment on depression in Southeast Asian refugees. *American Journal of Psychiatry, 145,* 46–51.

Beiser, M. (1991). The mental health of refugees in resettlement countries. In H. Adelman (ed.), *Refugee policy: Canada and the United States* (pp. 425–442). Toronto: York Lanes Press.

Beiser, M., and Fleming, J. A. E. (1986). Measuring psychiatric disorder among Southeast Asian refugees. *Psychological Medicine, 16,* 627–639.

Berry, J. W. (1990). Psychology of acculturátion. In J. J. Berman (ed.), *Nebraska Symposium on Motivation. Vol. 37, Cross-cultural perspectives* (pp. 201–234). Lincoln: University of Nebraska Press.

Berry, J. W. (1991). Refugee adaptation in settlement countries: An overview with an emphasis on primary prevention. In F. Ahearn and J. Athey (eds.), *Refugee children: Theory, research, and services* (pp. 20–38). Baltimore: Johns Hopkins University Press.

Berry, J. W., Kim, U., Minde, T., and Mok, D. (1987). Comparative studies of acculturative stress. *International Migration Review, 21*(3), 491–511.

Chang, S. C. (1982). The self: A nodal issue in culture and psyche—An Eastern perspective. *American Journal of Psychotherapy, 36,* 67–81.

Charron, D. W., and Ness, R. C. (1981). Emotional distress among Vietnamese adolescents. *Journal of Refugee Settlement, 1,* 7- 15.

Clément, R., and Noels, K. A. (1992). Towards a situated approach to ethnolinguistic identity: The effects of status on individuals and groups. *Journal of Language and Social Psychology, 11,* 203–232.

Costa-Lascoux, J. (1989). Immigrant children in French schools: Equality or discrimination? In L. Eldering and J. Kloprogge (eds.), *Different cultures same school: Ethnic minority children in Europe* (pp. 61–84). Lisse, Netherlands: Swets and Zeitlinger.

Council of Europe. (1991). *Community and ethnic relations in Europe.* Final Report of the Community Relations Project of the Council of Europe. MG-CR (91) 1 final E. Brussels.

Dalglish, C. (1989). *Refugees from Vietnam.* London: Macmillan.

Draguns, J. G. (1990). Normal and abnormal behavior in cross-cultural perspective: Specifying the nature of the relationship. In J. J. Berman (ed.), *Nebraska Symposium on Motivation. Vol. 37, Cross-cultural perspectives* (pp. 235- 277). Lincoln: University of Nebraska Press.

Extra, G., and Vallen, T (1989). Second language acquisition in elementary school: A cross-national perspective on the Nederlands and Flanders, in the Federal Republic of Germany. In L. Eldering, and J. Kloprogge (eds.), *Different cultures same school: Ethnic minority children in Europe*, (pp. 61–84). Lisse, Netherlands: Swets and Zeitlinger.

Fernando, S. (1991). *Mental health, race and culture*. Hampshire, England: MacMillan.

Furnham, A., and Bochner, S. (1990). *Culture shock: Psychological reactions to unfamiliar environments*. London: Routledge.

Garza, R. T., and Herringer, L. G. (1987). Social identity: A multidimensional approach. *Journal of Social Psychology, 127*, 299–308.

Hinkle, S., and Brown, R. (1990). Intergroup comparisons and identity: Some links and lacunae. In D. Abrams and M. A. Hogg (eds.), *Social identity theory: Constructive and critical advances*, (pp. 48–70). New York: Harvester Wheatsheaf.

Ho, M. K. (1987). Family therapy with Asian/Pacific Americans. In M. K. Ho (ed.), *Therapy with ethnic minorities* (pp. 24- 68). Newbury Park, CA: Sage.

Hogg, M. A., and Abrams, D., eds. (1990). *Social identity theory: Constructive and critical advances*. New York: Harvester Wheatsheaf.

Jaakkola, M. (1994). Ulbamaalais asentelt Suomessa ja Rootsissa (Attitudes toward foreigners in Finland and Sweden). In K. Liebkind (ed.), *Maahanmuuttajat: Kulttuurien kohtaaminen Suomessa* [The immigrants: Cultural confrontation in Finland]. Helsinki: Gaudeamus.

Johnston, L., and Hewstone, M. (1990). Intergroup contact: Social identity and social cognition. In D. Abrams and M. A. Hogg (eds.), *Social identity theory: Constructive and critical advances*, (pp. 185–210). New York: Harvester Wheatsheaf.

Kinzie, J. D., Manson, M., Vinh, D. T. E., Tolan, N. T., Anh, B., and Pho, T. N. (1982). Development and validation of a Vietnamese language depression rating scale. *American Journal of Psychiatry, 139*, 1276–1281.

Kinzie, J. D., Tran, K. A., Breckenridge, A., and Bloom, J. D. (1980). An Indochinese refugee psychiatric clinic: Culturally accepted treatment approaches. *American Journal of Psychiatry, 137*, 1429–1432.

Kleinman, A. (1987). Anthropological psychiatry: The role of culture in cross-cultural research on illness. *British Journal of Psychiatry, 151*, 447–454.

Knudsen, J. C. (1988). *Vietnamese survivors: Processes involved in refugee coping and adaptation*. Bergen, Norway: University of Bergen.

Knudsen, J. C. (1990). Cognitive models in life histories, *Anthropological Quarterly, 63*, 122–133.

Kosonen, L. (1994). Vietnamilainen oppilas kahden kulttuurin välissä [The Vietnamese student between two cultures]. In K. Liebkind (ed.), *Maahanmuuttajat: Kulttuurien kohtaaminen Suomessa* [The immigrants: Cultural confrontation in Finland] (pp. 192–223). Helsinki: Gaudeamus.

Kovacs, M. (1985). The Children's Depression Inventory (CDI). *Psychopharmacology Bulletin, 21*, 995–998.

Krupinski J., and Burrows G. (1986). *The price of freedom: Young Indochinese refugees in Australia*. Sydney, Australia: Pergamon Press.

Liebkind, K. (1984). Minority identity and identification processes: A social psychological study. Maintenance and reconstruction of ethnolinguistic identity in multiple group allegiance. *Commentationes Scientiarum Socialium (Monographs of the Finnish Society of Sciences and Letters) 22*. Helsinki: The Finnish Society of Science and Letters.

Liebkind, K. (1989). Conceptual approaches to ethnic identity. In K. Liebkind (ed.), *New identities in Europe: Immigrant ancestry and the ethnic identity of youth* (pp. 25–40). Aldershot, England: Gower Press.

Liebkind, K. (1990). Pakolaisten mielenterveys ja identiteetti [Mental health and identity of refugees]. *Suomen Lääkärilehti, 45*, 3211–3216.

Liebkind, K. (1992). Ethnic identity: Challenging the boundaries of social psychology. In G. Breakwell (ed.), *Social psychology of identity and the self concept* (pp. 147–185). Surrey, England: Surrey University Press/Academic Press.

Liebkind, K. (1993). Self-reported ethnic identity, depression and anxiety among young Vietnamese refugees and their parents. *Journal of Refugee Studies, 6*, 25–39.

Liebkind, K., ed. (1994) *Maahanmuuttajat: Kulttuurien kohtaaminen Suomessa* [The immigrants: Cultural confrontation in Finland]. Helsinki: Gaudeamus.

Liebkind, K. (1995a). Ethnic identity and acculturative stress—Vietnamese refugees in Finland. *Migration, 23–24*, 155–177. (appeared in 1995).

Liebkind, K. (1995b). Dispersal, xenophobia and acculturative stress: Refugees in Finland. In J. Hjarnö (ed.), *Multiculturalism in the Nordic societies*, 261–273. Copenhagen: Nordic Council of Ministers.

Liebkind, K. (1996a). Acculturation and stress: Vietnamese refugees in Finland. *Journal of Cross-Cultural Psychology, 27*, 160–181.

Liebkind, K. (1996b). Vietnamese refugees in Finland: Changing cultural identity. In G. Breakwell and E. Lyons (eds.), *Changing European identities: Social-psychological analyses of social change*, pp. 227–240. Oxford: Pergamon Press.

Lin, K.- M., Masuda, M., and Tazuma, L. (1984). Problems of Eastern refugees and immigrants: Adaptational problems of Vietnamese refugees. Part IV. *Psychiatric Journal of the University of Ottawa, 9*, 79–84.

Marsella, A. J. (1994). Ethnocultural diversity and international refugees: Challenges for the global community. In A. J. Marsella, T. Bornemann, S. Ekblad, and J. Orley (eds.). *Amidst peril and pain. The mental health and well-being of the world's refugees.* Washington, D.C.: American Psychological Association.

Marsella, A. J., and White, G. M., eds. (1989). *Cultural conceptions of mental health and therapy.* Dordrecht, Netherlands: D. Reidel.

Matinheikki-Kokko, K. (1991). *Pakolaisten vastaanotto ja hyvinvoinnin turvaaminen Suomessa* [The resettlement and social welfare of refugees in Finland]. Sosiaali-ja terveyshallituksen raportti nro. 40. Helsinki: National Board of Health and Social Welfare.

Matinheikki-Kokko, K. (1992). *Pakolaiset kunnassa: Kenen ehdoilla?* [Refugees in the municipality: On whose conditions?]. Sosiaali-ja terveyshallituksen raportti nro. 69. Helsinki: National Board of Health and Social Welfare.

Matinheikki-Kokko, K. (1994). Suomen pakolaisvastaanotto: Periaatteet ja käytäntö [Refugee resettlement in Finland: Principles and practice]. In K. Liebkind (ed.), *Maahanmuuttajat: Kulttuurien kohtaaminen Suomessa* [The immigrants: Cultural confrontation in Finland] (pp. 82- 122). Helsinki: Gaudeamus.

Minister of Supply and Services, Canada. (1988). *Canadian task force on mental health issues affecting immigrants and refugees.*

Mollica, R. F., and Lavelle, J. (1988). Southeast Asian refugees. In L. Comas-Diaz and E. E. H. Griffith (eds.), *Clinical guidelines in cross-cultural mental health* (pp. 262–303). New York: John Wiley and Sons.

Mollica, R. F., Wyshak, G., de Marneffe, D., Khuon, F., and Lavelle, J. (1987). Indochinese versions of the Hopkins Symptom Checklist–25: A screening instrument for the psychiatric care of refugees. *American Journal of Psychiatry, 144*, 497–500.

Newsweek (1990). A lost generation. *Newsweek International. February 5*, 28.

Newsweek. (1994). Europe's new iron curtain. *Newsweek International, February 5*, 28.

Nidorf, J. F. (1985). Mental health and refugee youths: A model for diagnostic training. In T. C. Owan (ed.), *Southeast Asian mental health: Treatment, prevention, services, training and research* (pp. 391–429). Rockville, MD: National Institute of Mental Health.

Nguyen, B. T., and Malapert, B. (1988). The psychological consequences for children of war trauma and migration. In D. Miserez (ed.), *Refugees: The trauma of exile* (pp. 248–286). Dordrecht, The Netherlands: Martinus Nijhoff.

Nguyen, N. A. (1992). Living between two cultures: Treating first-generation Asian Americans. In L. A. Vargas and J. D. Koss-Chioino (eds.), *Working with culture* (pp. 204–222). San Francisco: Jossey-Bass.

Nguyen, N. A., and Williams, H. L. (1989). Transition from East to West: Vietnamese adolescents and their parents. *Journal of the American Academy of Child and Adolescent Psychiatry, 28*, 505–515.

Olowu, A. A. (1983). Counselling needs of immigrant children. *New Community, 10*, 263–274.

Phinney, J. S. (1990). Ethnic identity in adolescents and adults: Review of research. *Psychological Bulletin, 38*, 499–514.

Phinney, J. S., Lochner, B. T., and Murphy, R. (1990). Ethnic identity development and psychological adjustment in adolescence. In A. R. Stiffman and L. E. Davis (eds.), *Ethnic issues in adolescent mental health* (pp. 53–72). Newbury Park, CA: Sage.

Rick, K., and Forward, J. (1992). Acculturation and perceived intergenerational differences among Hmong youth. *Journal of Cross-Cultural Psychology, 23,* 85–94.

Rosenthal, D. A., and Feldman, S. S. (1992). The nature and stability of ethnic identity in Chinese youth. *Journal of Cross-Cultural Psychology, 23,* 214–227.

Rumbaut, G. (1991). Migration, adaptation and mental health. In H. Adelman (ed.), *Refugee policy: Canada and the United States* (pp. 381–424). Toronto: York Lanes Press.

Saarinen, M. (1993). *Masennuksen ja ahdistuksen ilmaisemisen kulttuurisidonnaisuus. Kahden kyselymittarin tarkastelua Suomessa asuvilla vietnamilaisilla pakolaisilla ja suomalaisilla* [The expression of depression and anxiety using a universal and a culture-specific scale: Comparing Vietnamese refugees to native Finns]. Unpublished master's thesis, University of Helsinki, Finland.

Sachdev, I., and Bourhis, R. Y. (1990a). Bilinguality and multilinguality. In H. Giles and W.P. Robinson (eds.), *Handbook of language and social psychology* (pp. 293–308). Chichester, England: John Wiley and Sons.

Sachdev, I., and Bourhis, R. Y. (1990b). Language and social identification. In D. Abrams and M. A. Hogg (eds.), *Social identity theory: Constructive and critical advances,* (pp. 211–229). New York: Harvester Wheatsheaf.

Sam, D. L., and Berry, J. W. (1995). Acculturative stress among young immigrants in Norway. *Scandinavian Journal of Psychology, 36,* 10–24.

Stein, B. N. (1986). The experience of being a refugee: Insights from the research literature. In C. L. Williams and J. Westermeyer (eds.), *Refugee mental health in resettlement countries* (pp. 5–23). Washington, D.C.: Hemisphere.

Suárez-Orozco, M. M. (1991). Migration, minority status and education: European dilemmas and responses in the 1990s. *Anthropological and Education Quarterly, 22,* 99–120.

Sue, D. W., and Sue, D. (1990). *Counseling the culturally different: Theory and practice.* New York: John Wiley and Sons.

Tajfel, H., ed. (1978). *Differentiation between social groups: Studies in the social psychology of intergroup relations.* (European Monographs in Social Psychology No. 14). London: Academic Press.

United Nations Population Fund. (1993). *The state of world population 1993.* New York: United Nations.

Ward, C., and Kennedy, A. (1993). Psychological and socio-cultural adjustment during cross-cultural transitions: A comparison of secondary students overseas and at home. *International Journal of Psychology, 28,* 129–147.

Weinreich, P. (1989). Variations in ethnic identity: Identity structure analysis. In K. Liebkind (ed.), *New identities in Europe, immigrant ancestry and the ethnic identity of youth,* (pp. 41–76). Aldershot, England: Gower Press.

Westermeyer, J. (1987). Prevention of mental disorder among Hmong refugees in the U.S.: Lessons from the period 1976–1986. *Social Science and Medicine, 25,* 941–947.

Westin, C. (1993). Immigration into Sweden 1940–1990 and the response of public opinion. *Migration, 18,* 143–170.

White, G. M., and Marsella, A. J. (1989). Introduction: Cultural conceptions of mental health research and practice. In A. J. Marsella and G. M. White (eds.), *Cultural conceptions of mental health and therapy,* (pp. 11–37). Dordrecht, The Netherlands: D. Reidel.

Williams, C. L. (1991). Toward the development of preventive interventions for youth traumatized by war and refugee flight. In F. L. Ahearn and J. L. Athey (eds.), *Refugee Children: Theory, Research and Services,* (pp. 201–217). Baltimore: Johns Hopkins University Press.

Yearbook of Population Research in Finland. (1995). Nr. 32 (1994–1995). The Population Research Institute, Helsinki, Finland.

Yu, E. S. H., and Liu, W. T. (1986). Methodological problems and policy implications in Vietnamese refugee research. *International Migration Review, 20,* 483–501.

Chapter Ten
Immigration, Xenophobia, and Youthful Opinion

Charles Westin

Introduction

In recent years the incidence of militant racist actions has escalated in most of western Europe (Björgo and Witte, 1993). This is also the impression disseminated by the media (Baumgartl and Favell, 1995). Political concern about these developments is reflected in the many initiatives to counteract xenophobia and racism (United Nations Centre for Human Rights, 1991; Council of Europe, 1991; European Communities Parliament, 1991; Commission of the European Communities, 1993; World Council of Churches, 1994; UNESCO, 1995). Whereas recent election results in some countries show that protest parties to the extreme right have been fairly successful in attracting new voters (for instance, in France and Italy) this is not true of all Europe (Baumgartl and Favell, 1995). Many journalists, politicians and molders of opinion assume that the rise in reported actions of racist violence reflects a public opinion that is increasingly hostile to immigrants and refugees. Intensifying political activity of the extreme right, however, does not automatically imply that public opinion is also geared to the right. Polarization of public opinion is an equally likely outcome (Westin 1993). Marxist-inspired sociological theory attributes the rise of xenophobic sentiments to unemployment, economic decline, and competition over scarce resources (Schierup, 1990). An abundance of literature on stereotypes, prejudice, and attitude formation exists (Lange and Westin, 1981; Liebkind, 1989; Breakwell, 1992) but surprisingly few attempts to explain the dynamics of public opinion shifts (Lippmann, 1922; Westin, 1987).

Over the years the Eurobarometer surveys have included some items on people's views on immigration and immigration policy. However, the restricted scope of these surveys does not permit analyses of identity or xenophobia variables. National public opinion polls are regularly carried out in countries of western Europe. However, they are seldom coordinated in terms of research problems, objectives, or instruments. Moreover, they are primarily carried out for commercial and political reasons, not in the service of social research. Besides some work in the Nordic countries (Jaakkola, 1995; Körmendi, 1986; Lange and Westin, 1993), very few systematic studies of public opinion on immigrants and integration policies based on national samples have been carried out in Europe. In this context the available Swedish data are important, since they provide an option to examine changes in the attitude climate in western Europe over the past decades.

Earlier Research

Views on immigration policy and immigrants in Swedish society have been researched for more than twenty-five years. A series of four comparable national attitude surveys, based on representative samples and carried out at regular intervals, provides a unique source of data. The first major study of Swedish attitudes to immigration was carried out in 1969, at a time when labor migration peaked. Unfavorable views on immigration and immigrants were found to be more frequent among sections of the population with little formal education, mainly among the elderly and among those who identified themselves as belonging to the working class. The young held the most favorable views on immigration (Trankell, 1974).

Twelve years later, 1981, a second national survey of attitudes was carried out. The findings of the 1969 survey were verified. Counter to general expectations, however, public opinion had *not* changed for the worse since 1969. The finding that many respondents were convinced that relations between immigrants and Swedes were deteriorating was hypothesized to be partly due to a negative selection of information about ethnic relations within the media and among the authorities (Westin, 1984).

During the latter part of the 1980s, molders of opinion once again called attention to rises in the level of overt racism. Moreover, refugee reception programs were not operating according to plan. The flow of asylum seekers grew year by year (5,000 in 1982, 20,000 in 1987, 80,000 in 1992). A third national attitude survey in 1987 confirmed the 1981 findings. The hypothesis that xenophobia was spreading in society was not supported by the survey data this time either. However, one striking difference was that the youngest respondents were more critical of immigration policy this time than the corresponding age groups had been in 1981 (Westin, 1987).

In recent years the problem of racist violence has hit Sweden as it has other European states. Refugee centers have been repeatedly attacked since 1990. One of the leading Swedish newspapers (*Svenska Dagbladet,* 1995) recently listed 107 acts of racist violence (among them three murders) during a period of twelve months from October 1994 to September 1995. Invariably the perpetrators were young men in their late teens and early twenties.

The Position of Young People

In Western countries, young people are well educated. Many currently popular ideals regarding life-style, taste, dress, music, and beauty focus on the concept of youth, almost to the extent of turning into a youth cult. Today's youth lack powerful interest organizations, and as unemployment rises young people are hard hit.

In Sweden the youth unemployment rates are not particularly high in comparison to the situation in several other European countries. Yet unemployment among young people in the mid-1990s is higher than ever for the past fifty years (19.2 percent for sixteen- to nineteen-year-olds, 18.1 percent for twenty- to twenty-four-year-olds as compared to 8.4 percent for twenty-five- to forty-four-year-olds in 1993). Young people compete for work and housing with refugees who are being resettled. In major cities there is a shortage of small, inexpensive apartments. Normally young people are not a category to which politicians give first priority. Although youth issues are recognized as being politically important, they are not constantly at the forefront of the political debate.

Young people in their late teens are preparing themselves for their future identity as adults. Part of this process involves testing attitudes and political opinions. Consequently, critical opinions that many young people voice may be part of a provocative jargon and an expression of young people's need to test the limits of what is socially acceptable.

For several decades, reference groups have existed with which young people identify and compare themselves, and of which they aspire to become members. The names of these groups differ, as do their markers, dress, and musical preferences, but the psychosocial functions these groups serve have been pretty much the same over the years. Nowadays the identities provided for by these reference groups seem to be more important to young people than they used to be some twenty or thirty years ago. This may be seen in the readiness for militant action that is manifested whenever social identities are asserted by one group against another. One reason why the relatively transitory social identities provided for by peer groups have grown in importance for young people as compared to the situation a generation back is because more stable group memberships and identities in society are harder to attain for the young of today than they were for their parents.

In many Western welfare states generational segregation has become commonplace (Atkinson and Rein, 1993). Often young people are well into their twenties before they find regular employment. It may take years before they think of themselves in terms of a professional identity. Professional identity, an essential cornerstone of adult life, implies responsibility, independence, esteem, and the pride in knowing a trade. Employment facilitates economic independence, which is essential to self-esteem. Changes in marital patterns (Visher and Visher, 1979) also contribute to the difficulties that young people face in their transitions to adult life.

Political Developments
A number of dramatic political events have taken place since the late 1980s on the domestic as well as international scene. Immigration and the future of multicultural societies in Europe have been at the forefront of public debate more than ever before. The role of the media in conveying images of the political process has become increasingly obvious. From our sitting-room armchairs we have witnessed brawls between skinheads and antiracists in the streets of European cities.

Political changes in eastern Europe have lead to an increasing migration pressure on western Europe. New routes to the West have opened up from the third world through eastern Europe and Russia (Blaschke, 1992). Ethnic and nationalistic conflicts are brewing in many of the territories formerly controlled by the Soviet Union. The war in Bosnia has driven hundreds of thousands from their homes.

During the early 1980s the immigration of refugees to western Europe was rather insignificant (King, 1993). In Sweden the refugee reception system was reorganized in 1985. Refugees were directed to municipalities where they were to stay throughout the course of an introductory program. Then, however, the number of asylum seekers started to increase year by year. One temporary camp after another was set up.

This development in Sweden led also to the opposition at the local level. For example, in the small rural community of Sjöbo, the municipal council refused to accept refugees for local resettlement. A local referendum was held in 1988 in which an overwhelming majority of the Sjöbo residents were opposed to receiving refugees.

Sjöbo was important for the discourse on racism. The small town was turned into an arena where opponents and advocates of refugee reception argued in front of the rolling cameras. The lesson of Sjöbo was that refugee reception, its size and organization, its objectives and costs, were issues that shouldn't be discussed openly. Those who dared question the refugee reception program were branded as racists. Less than fifteen months later, however, the government introduced a change of policy that in principle was the very course of action that the anti-immigration side had campaigned for. Since then it no longer is improper to express critical views on immigration policy, or to question refugee immigration. Young people, in the process of establishing their adult identities, are more impressionable to these kinds of debates than their elders.

Aims of the Study

The general aims of the national attitude survey were

1. to assess public opinion on immigration and integration policies in Sweden,

2. to assess changes in the attitude climate by comparing results with data from 1987 and 1993, and in cohort analyses also from 1981 and 1969,

3. to focus in particular upon the attitudes of young people 18-23 years of age.

The Survey

The 1993 study is the fourth national survey of views on immigrants and immigration policies in Sweden. A random sample of 1,800 persons was drawn according to the same criteria as in the three preceding studies. Requirements for being accepted were Swedish citizenship and age between eighteen and seventy-one. The sample was increased by an additional 300 Swedish adolescents between eighteen and twenty-three. The overall rate of nonresponse was 23.2 percent. For the age category eighteen to twenty-three years it was 22.0 percent.

Data were collected through structured interviews, normally conducted in the respondents' homes by interviewers employed by Statistics Sweden. The questionnaire included items measuring background variables, attitudes to immigrants and migration policies, identity and self conceptions, values, and social and cultural distance scales. The mean completion time was seventy-five minutes. Data collection was carried out between March 19 and June 16, 1993.

Table 10.1 Responses concerning Immigration among Swedish 18- to 23-Year-Olds, 1987 vs. 1993: Distribution by Percentage

Question	Year	More	Same as now	Fewer	No response	Chi²
1. A number of people come to Sweden every year for political reasons. Do you think we should accept more, about the same number as today, or fewer for these reasons?	1987	19	40	34	7	
	1993	14	44	40	2	9.95 $p < 0.05$
2. A number of people come to Sweden every year for work. Do you think we should accept more, about the same number as today, or fewer for these reasons?	1987	4	39	52	8	
	1993	7	35	57	1	8.93 $p < 0.05$
3. A number of people come to Sweden every year through family reunification. Do you think we should accept more, about the same number as today, or fewer for these reasons?	1987	12	44	40	5	
	1993	14	47	38	2	n.s.
4. Every year a number of children are adopted from other countries by Swedes. Do you think we should accept more, about the same number as today or fewer for these reasons?	1987	39	45	10	6	
	1993	37	56	7	1	12.52 $p < 0.01$
5. Do you think the regulations on immigration to Sweden should be (a) stricter, (b) unchanged, or (c) lightened? No response (d).		(a)	(b)	(c)	(d)	
	1987	44	39	10	8	
	1993	61	26	10	2	21.11 $p < 0.01$

(continued)

Table 10.1 *(continued)*

Question	Year	More	Same as now	Fewer	No response	Chi^2
6. A number of people come to Sweden every year to escape poverty and famine. Do you think we should accept more, about the same number as today, or fewer for these reasons?	1993 only	42	39	15	4	ns
7. A number of people come to Sweden every year to escape war conditions. Do you think we should accept more, about the same number as today, or fewer for these reasons?	1993 only	42	36	18	4	ns

Note: n = 147 for 1987; *n* = 394 for 1993; ns = nonsignificant.

Results

The most important finding was that the general public 1993 was more decisively in favor of restrictive immigration policies than in 1987. The measurements employed, however, do not indicate significant changes in the levels of manifest xenophobia. The views of young people (18–23 years) do not deviate from this general tendency. A majority of the young were opposed to the then-current volume of immigration and they disapproved of the immigration policy in force. Statistically significant differences are found for four of the five comparative questions given in Table 10.1.

Similar trends are evident in Table 10.2. As for the items that directly or indirectly bear upon immigration, young people commended restrictiveness to a much larger extent than in 1987. One item pertaining to foreigners' criminal activity is an obvious example. More than 80 percent of the respondents accepted the idea that foreigners who commit criminal offenses in Sweden should be expelled. In 1987 the rate was 50 percent.

Lange and Westin (1993) carried out a factor analysis of these items that led to the construction of three scales: *xenophobia* (seven items), *immigration attitudes* (four items), and *assimilation attitudes* (five items).

Table 10.2 Responses to Items Concerning Immigration among Swedish 18- to 23-Year-Olds, 1987 vs. 1993: Distribution by Percentage

Statement	Year	Agree entirely	Agree partly	Disagree partly	Disagree entirely	Chi^2
1. We should not permit more immigrants to settle in Sweden.	1987	12	24	24	40	13.93
	1993	13	28	25	34	$p<0.01$
2. It was wrong to accept all those immigrants in the past.	1987	25	16	29	30	30.35
	1993	27	30	21	21	$p<0.01$
3. Any one wishing to settle and work in Sweden should be permitted to do so.	1987	9	20	28	43	10.08
	1993	8	21	39	32	$p<0.05$
4. But for the past immigration, our standard of living would have been much lower than it is today.	1987	20	36	22	22	ns
	1993	21	44	22	13	
5. It's only fair that Swedes, who have built this country, should reap the economic benefits.	1987	31	37	19	12	ns
	1993	22	43	19	16	
6. Unemployment has increased because immigrants are taking jobs from the Swedes.	1987	7	22	30	40	8.59
	1993	4	27	26	43	$p<0.05$
7. Many foreigners come to Sweden merely to benefit from our social security system.	1987	22	40	18	18	ns
	1993	15	38	27	20	

(continued)

Table 10.2 *(continued)*

Statement	Year	Agree entirely	Agree partly	Disagree partly	Disagree entirely	Chi²
8. The less salient foreigners are in Sweden, the better it is.	1987	15	13	23	49	ns
	1993	9	19	26	30	
9. If unemployment increases, some of the foreigners should be forced to leave Sweden.	1987	6	13	28	53	ns
	1993	6	15	24	55	
10. First of all Swedes themselves should be employed.	1987	66	23	7	4	87.38
	1993	28	31	22	18	$p < 0.01$
11. Swedes have a greater sense of responsibility for their work than foreigners who come to Sweden.	1987	6	16	22	56	ns
	1993	6	18	32	44	
12. Society should make it possible for those immigrants who wish to maintain their language and cultural traditions to do so.	1987	27	30	25	18	11.61
	1993	21	44	20	14	$p < 0.01$
13. It is a good thing if immigrants who come to Sweden maintain their language and teach it to their children.	1987	30	23	26	21	ns
	1993	21	36	24	19	
14. Immigrants who intend to stay in Sweden should in their own interest become as Swedish as possible.	1987	30	36	21	13	ns
	1993	26	42	22	10	
15. Right from the very start immigrant children should be taught that Swedish is their mother tongue.	1987	30	21	32	17	8.90
	1993	23	34	22	21	$p < 0.05$

(continued)

Table 10.2 *(continued)*

Statement	Year	Agree entirely	Agree partly	Disagree partly	Disagree entirely	Chi^2
16. Only immigrants who speak Swedish at home and train their children in Swedish should be permitted to become Swedish citizens.	1987	11	12	28	49	
	1993	11	20	20	49	9.77 $p < 0.05$
17. All foreigners committing crimes in Sweden should be deported from the country.	1987	26	25	29	20	
	1993	51	29	12	7	89.03 $p < 0.01$

Note: n = 147 for 1987; n = 394 for 1993, ns = nonsignificant.

High values represented xenophobic attitudes, critical views on immigration, and views in favor of cultural assimilation. The results showed that the means of the xenophobia scale were generally lower than those of the other scales. The response patterns of young people were slightly more xenophobic than those of the middle-aged, but nowhere near as xenophobic as the elderly. Moreover, among the younger age groups, women have gave voice to less xenophobic views than men. Women also thought more favorably about immigration. Working-class as compared to middle-class background gave higher values on all three scales. The most

Table 10.3 Means for the Xenophobia, Immigration Attitudes, and Assimilation Attitudes Scales for 1987 and 1993 among Swedish 18- to 23-Year-Olds and 24- to 29-Year-Olds

Variable	Year	Ages 18-23	Ages 24-29
Xenophobia	1987	2.34	2.17
	1993	2.19	2.14
Immigration attitudes	1987	2.51	2.42
	1993	2.76	2.84
Assimilation attitudes	1987	2.41	2.28
	1993	2.41	2.39

Table 10.4 Assessment by Swedes of Similarity of Various Nationalities and Ethnic Minorities. Comparison of 1987 and 1993 Responses for 18- to 23-Year-Olds

| | 1987 | | 1993 | |
	Response Mean	Degree of Similarity Rank	Response Mean	Degree of Similarity Rank
Norwegians	1.4	1	1.6	1
Finns	1.9	2	2.2	2
English	2.6	4	2.4	3
Germans	2.6	5	2.7	4
Samis*	2.5	3	2.8	5
Jews	4.3	7	4.0	6
Poles	4.2	6	4.3	7
Greeks	5.1	8	4.8	8
Chinese	5.3	9	5.1	9
Turks	5.5	10	5.4	10
Ethiopians	5.7	11	5.6	11
Gypsies	6.0	12	5.7	12
Total	3.9		3.9	

Note: n = 147 for 1987; n = 394 for 1993.
* Samis: the indigenous reindeer-herding people of northern Scandinavia and Finland. The term Lapps, used earlier, is now regarded as derogatory.

unfavorable views on immigration among the young, as well as the highest levels of xenophobia, were found among working-class males.

Table 10.3 presents cohort data based upon the scales' means. The results showed that the xenophobia index decreased from 1987 to 1993 among eighteen- to twenty-three-year olds. However, no change was found among twenty-four- to twenty-nine-year-olds. The corresponding data for the immigration attitudes index show increases from 1987 to 1993 for both age groups. Finally, the assimilation attitudes have not changed at all.

In general, people cherishing racist convictions are expected to side against immigration. This tendency is obvious in our data. We have shown elsewhere, analyzing data from the same sample, that xenophobia correlates strongly with negative attitudes toward immigration (Lange and Westin, 1993).

Table 10.4 presents data on people's perceptions of the degree of similarity between themselves (as Swedes) and a number of nationalities and ethnic minorities. It is a seven-grade scale (1 corresponds to similarity/closeness, 7 to dissimilarity/distance) using "myself" as anchor. The resulting

Table 10.5 Perceptions of the Consequences of Immigration in the 1993
Survey by Percentage among Swedish 18- to 23-Year-Olds

	Not at all worried	Somewhat worried	Quite worried	Very worried	No answer
1. Immigrants get the worst jobs and constitute a new underclass.	38	30	16	7	8
2. Immigrants are subjected to racism.	9	27	28	34	2
3. Swedish culture is threatened.	42	24	18	15	2
4. The societal costs are much too high.	12	29	27	29	3
5. Immigrants lose their own culture.	62	23	8	2	5
6. The Swedish population will become too mixed with other races.	67	17	7	5	5
7. The sending countries will become impoverished.	38	22	15	8	17

Note: n = 394.

rank order in the 1993 data hardly differs at all from the one in 1987. The
average "distance" to groups showed that groups from Northern Europe
are seen as most close or similar (exemplified by "Norwegians" and
"Finns") to Sweden. However, this "distance" has increased since 1987. In
turn, ethnic and national groups from southern and eastern Europe, as
well as those of non-European origin, are considered to differ considerably
from Swedes. However, they were not conceived to be as different as they
were thought to be merely a few years ago. This finding is yet another
indication that extreme xenophobia and racism are not gaining ground
among the young.

By way of summary, then, the assumption that xenophobia is on the increase among young people is not founded in our data. This is also reflected in Table 10.5, which gives the data on how people have responded to questions about the possible consequences of immigration. These data confirm the impression given by the preceding tables that there is a growing discontent with immigration policy and immigration rates. However, although people are concerned about immigration and immigration policy, those concerns seem not to reflect xenophobic attitudes.

Discussion

The findings reported here showed that young people are opposed to the volume of immigration and commend stricter regulations (Tables 10.1 and 10.2). However, they do not appear to object to the immigration policy out of sheer racist convictions. Responses to the items on the immigration of children for adoption depart from the general trend (Table 10.1). The percentage advocating a reduction of children for adoption has decreased since 1987. Obviously young people do not view adoption as comparable to other kinds of immigration. An overwhelming majority, 87 percent, maintained that Sweden should accept at least as many adopted children as today. Since most of the foreign adoptees come from Africa, Asia, and Latin America, it may be argued that purely racial considerations have not come to mind when respondents favor restrictiveness and reductions with regard to the other categories of immigration. Thus, the response pattern to this particular item does not support the hypothesis that a blatant manifest phenotypical racism is on the increase. Were Swedes to found their positions on purely racial criteria, they would also oppose the immigration of nonwhite children for adoption.

Political persecution and family reunification are, officially, the only valid grounds for non-Nordic and non-European Union citizens to obtain residential permits in Sweden. Manpower is no longer recruited from abroad. Young people reject the "official" grounds for immigration. Surprisingly many, however, have accepted war, poverty, and famine as valid reasons for allowing people to stay in Sweden (Table 10.1).

The racist segments of the population hardly account for the currently widespread discontent with immigration (Tables 10.2 and 10.3). This was also evident in the study of Lange and Westin (1993), showing that negative attitudes towards immigration correspond even to fairly low levels of xenophobia. Data on cultural similarity/closeness also support this point (Table 10.4).

It is not easy to estimate the size of the racist segment of the population. Figures in Table 10.5 and previous surveys suggest that approximately 5 percent of the population is an estimation that may be defended. Only a very small proportion of this segment would be prepared to engage in direct racist violence. An additional 10 to 20 percent of the population may definitely feel uneasy about the immigrant presence in society without, however, voicing their discontent in racial or derogatory terms.

Increasingly immigration is criticized for reasons other than purely racist motives (Table 10.5). A substantial number of people are worried about escalating social conflicts and racism. In more general terms these apprehensions may be put down as a concern that the social system cannot stand up to the tensions that will arise from integrating refugees into mainstream society. Many people are concerned about the costs of the refugee reception program, some even about degradation, discrimination, and racism that immigrants may meet with. Consequently, it would be a mistake to regard critical views on immigration policy as expressions of racism and xenophobia. The results of this survey—a clear dissatisfaction with the current rate of immigration but yet a clear rejection of typically prejudicial and ethnocentric items—is typical of an attitude that the Norwegian sociologist Brox (1991) has pointed out: "I am not racist, but . . ."

Among the young, working-class males is embodied the most adverse opinion to immigrants. This is understandable because they are the most exposed to competition against immigrants for such scarce resources as jobs and housing. They also compete for available young Swedish women.

How should we interpret these findings? One explanation may be related to the fact that young people, preoccupied as they are by the task of forming their adult roles, are more sensitive to current fashions and modes of opinion than people who are approaching midlife and established their adult identities many years back. According to this view, youthful opinion mirrors currently popular attitudes and values. These attitudes need not necessarily coincide with those of the majority.

Although it is likely that young people's opinions change as they grow older, there is an apparent danger, that young people who actively subscribe to xenophobic views may cling to these values even later on in life.

According to Noelle-Neumann's (1984) theory of the spiral of silence, public opinion represents convictions that outspoken people are prepared to defend in public against other points of view. At any specific time a dominating point of view on a certain issue may be identified, which, however, need not necessarily correspond to the views held by the majority. The spiral of silence implies that those who do not go along with the dominant view retreat into silence, feeling reluctant to express their convictions in public. The media function as reinforcers and magnifiers of this dominating point of view. As discussed earlier, young people may be more easily influenced by the currently dominant views than their elders are.

In recent years, the dominant Swedish opinion (in Noelle-Neumann's terms) about immigration has been one of misgivings about its overall costs, social problems, and cultural consequences. The dominant view has been to reduce the immigration intake. Many people have been justifiably worried about the rate of immigration to Sweden. In the late 1980s and early 1990s the heavy flow of asylum seekers coincided with a deep economic recession and problems of a rapidly increasing budget deficit. In general, media coverage of questions related to immigration has brought out a one-sided, negative image. Until the late 1980s it was considered improper to discuss the unwanted impacts of immigration upon society. People suspected that journalists weren't rendering the true picture of the problems. However, since the Sjöbo referendum it has become acceptable to discuss the negative effects of immigration openly. Ever since, questions dealing with immigration have been debated intensely. It is hardly surprising, then, that many of the critical views that are voiced in the debate may have influenced the opinions of young people. One reason for this is that youths represent a formative period of life when personal views are grounded.

Conclusions

The developments in Sweden with regard to immigration, public opinion and the difficult transition for the young to adulthood represent a European development. Many Western countries are turning into multicultural societies as a result of immigration. In most of these countries, opposition has risen to these trends in aggressive anti-immigration movements. The Swedish data suggest, however, that there is no rise in levels of xenophobia within the general public of young people, as opposed to the images presented by the media, which are accepted by many politicians. It remains to be seen if this observation also applies more generally in Europe.

In Sweden, as undoubtedly in many Western countries, there is a definite rise in the incidence of racially motivated crimes such as assault or arson. The perpetrators are often affiliated to or sympathize with and try to qualify for membership in neo-Nazi and racist organizations. Although these organizations have grown considerably in recent years, the activists and passive sympathizers are not numerous enough to make any significant difference to a statistically national sample. On the other hand, however, their crimes are given much media coverage and are a legitimate cause of national concern.

The difficulties of young people in establishing themselves in the adult world are much the same all over western Europe. Unemployment rates among the young are high in most countries. Family structures are also in the process of change. Generational differences, to the point of age segregation, are another common denominator in most western countries. The interpretation offered in this article is that rises in racist actions among certain youth groups, and the more general criticism of immigration, is largely a by-product of the problems of the young in integrating into the adult world. The media play an important role in setting this stage. If European societies are to counteract xenophobic tendencies among certain youth categories, youth-related issues will have to play a more central role in politics. In everyday life it is important for adults to be close at hand for young people and to grasp the mass culture that directly targets the young. Most important of all will be to do something about the segregation, age and ethnic, that we have gotten without really asking for it.

References

Alsmark, G. (1990). *Att möta främlingar* (Meeting foreigners). Lund, Sweden: Studentlitteratur.

Atkinson, A. B., and Rein, M., eds. (1993). *Age, work and social security.* New York: St. Martin's Press.

Baumgartl, B., and Favell, A., eds. (1995). *New xenophobia in Europe.* London: Kluwer Law International.

Björgo, T., and Witte, R., eds. (1993). *Racist violence in Europe.* New York: St. Martin's Press.

Blaschke, J., (1992). *East-West migration in Europe and international aid as a means to reduce the need for emigration.* Geneva: United Nations High Commissioner for Refugees.

Breakwell, G., ed. (1992). *Social psychology of identity and the self concept.* London: Academic Press.

Brox, O. (1991). *Jeg er ikke rasist, men . . .* (I am not a racist, but . . .). Oslo: Gyldendal.

Commission of the European Communities. (1989). *Eurobarometer—Racism, xenophobia and intolerance.* Luxembourg: European Omnibus Survey.

Commission of the European Communities. (1993). *Legal instruments to combat racism and xenophobia.* Luxembourg: Office for the Official Publications of the European Communities.

Council of Europe. (1991). *Action to Combat Intolerance and Xenophobia.* Strasbourg: Council of Europe.

European Communities Parliament. (1991). *Report drawn up on behalf of the Committee of Inquiry into Racism and Xenophobia on the findings of the Committee of Inquiry.* Strasbourg: European Community.

Jaakkola, M. (1995). *Suomalaisten kiristyvät ulkomaalasiasenteet* (Finns' changing attitudes toward foreigners). Helsinki: Työministeriö.

King, R., ed. (1993). *Mass migration in Europe. The legacy and the future.* London: Belhaven Press.

Körmendi, E. (1986). *Os og andre. Danskernes holdninger til indvandrere og flygtninge* (Us and others. Danes' attitudes toward immigrants and refugees). Copenhagen: Socialforskningsinstituttet.

Lange, A., and Westin, C. (1981). *Etnisk diskriminering och social identitet* (Ethnic discrimination and social identity). Stockholm: Liber.

Lange, A., and Westin, C. (1991). *The generative mode of explanation.* Stockholm: Ceifo.

Lange, A., and Westin, C. (1993). *Den mångtydiga toleransen* (The inarticulate tolerance). Stockholm: Ceifo.

Liebkind, K., ed. (1989). *New identities in Europe.* Aldershot, England: Gower.

Lippmann, W. (1922). *Public opinion.* New York: Harcourt Brace.

Noelle-Neumann, E. (1984). *The spiral of silence.* Chicago: University of Chicago Press.

Schierup, C.-U. (1990). *Migration, socialism, and the international division of labour.* Aldershot, England: Avebury.

Svenska Dagbladet. 107 rasistiska våldsdåd på ett år (September 29, 1995): 8–9.

Trankell, A. (1974). *Svenskars fördomar mot invandrare* (Swedes' prejudice toward immigrants). Stockholm: The National Commission on Immigration.

UNESCO. (1995). *Management of cultural pluralism in Europe.* Stockholm: Ceifo.

United Nations Centre for Human Rights. (1991). *The Committee on the Elimination of Racial Discrimination.* Geneva: United Nations.

Visher, E. B., and Visher, J. S. (1979). *Stepfamilies.* New York: Brunner/Mazel.

Westin, C. (1984). *Majoritet om minoritet* (Majority on minority). Stockholm: Liber.

Westin, C. (1987). *Den toleranta opinionen* (The tolerant opinion). Stockholm: Deifo.

Westin, C. (1993). Immigration to Sweden 1940–90 and the response of public opinion. *Migration, 18,* 143–170.

World Council of Churches. (1994). *Combating racism in Europe.* Briefing paper No. 16. Geneva: World Council of Churches.

Chapter Eleven
Conclusions and Perspectives

Jari-Erik Nurmi

Introduction

The chapters in this book provide perspectives on adolescent diversity in contemporary Europe. Although variations in institutional transitions, social change, political history, cultural values, and immigrant status seem be associated with differences in adolescent thinking, well-being, career interests, political attitudes, control beliefs, and social behavior, young people are usually found to be successful in finding adaptive ways of coping, even with the most dramatic changes in their developmental environments. Overall, these findings fit well with the notion that adolescent development consists of a complex interaction between individual characteristics and the options, challenges, and demands of sociocultural environments. This interaction might be best described as a negotiation process between two active agents: one is the adolescent who makes an effort to direct his or her development, and the other is the society or culture that also acts as a collective agent to reproduce the values, belief systems, and even political interests shared by its members. Because most of the research on adolescence has concentrated on examining individual development, the issues dealt with in this volume may increase our understanding of how the diversity of options, challenges, and problems adolescents are facing influence their development in modern societies.

Similarities in Adolescence across Different Contexts

Although the aim of this book was to examine diversity in adolescent development, several similarities were also found. For example, Grob reported results suggesting that adolescents conceptualize well-being in similar ways across Europe. Similarly, Motola, Sinisalo, and Guichard and Hakvoort, Hägglund, and Oppenheimer showed that gender plays an important role in orienting adolescents' thinking in different developmental environments, such as career interests and conceptualizations of societal issues. Moreover, as was shown by Silbereisen and Schwarz, the timing of physiological maturation and the number of stressful life events during earlier life seem to have a similar impact on adolescent development in different contexts. Family and parental attitudes were also found to be important for adolescents' beliefs and opinions. At an even more macrosocial level, Kracke, Oepke, Wild, and Noack, as well as Westin suggested that levels of education, socioeconomic status, and economic disadvantage seem to provide a basis for the ways in which young people view various social issues.

Differences in Adolescents' Thinking and Development
However, diversity in developmental environments was also found to provide a basis for the differences in adolescents' thinking, interests, and well-being. First, variations in the age-graded institutional transitions, related opportunity structures, and cultural beliefs were found to be associated with the differences in how adolescents direct their future lives. For example, Motola, Sinisalo, and Guichard showed that the ways in which education is structured in terms of tracking and streaming orient future plans and career interests. Second, differences in cultural beliefs originating from the history of the nation seem to provide a basis for how young people view various political issues. According to Hakvoort, Hägglund, and Oppenheimer, the political history of a country, such as being involved in international conflicts, seems to be associated with the ways in which young people conceptualize the issues of peace and war.

Social Change
The findings reported in this volume also suggest that historical events, which also continue to provide a basis for future developments and conflicts, do influence adolescents' thinking, social identity, and well-being in several ways. For example, Grob pointed out that adolescents living in former socialist countries, which have recently faced the change to a market economy, showed more negative attitudes toward life and a lower level of self-esteem than youths living in western Europe. The results of Botcheva's longitudinal study provide a more detailed view of this process. Although adolescents started to value more active modes of behavior during the change from socialism to a market economy, they simultaneously began to identify themselves as having less control over their lives. This development was associated with a decrease in their well-being. Kracke, Oepke, Wild, and Noack further found that social change in terms of economic

disadvantage and experience of uncertainty also seems to influence adolescents' political attitudes in stable Western types of society. Finally, Roe and Cairns suggest that adolescent development in terms of social identity formation may play an important role in maintaining sectarian identities among different groups in the context of political conflicts.

The findings also provide a basis for another type of interpretation. Overall, adolescents seem to be able to cope successfully with even the most dramatic changes, problems, and adversities in their developmental environments. The impact of social change, and even of political violence, was found to be less dramatic than might have been expected. For example, according to Roe and Cairns, there is little evidence of any systematic serious psychological disorders among adolescents growing up in the contexts of political violence in Northern Ireland. Similarly, Grob found that young people from eastern Europe who have been facing rapid social change are still relatively optimistic about their futures.

An important finding from several studies was also that positive family relationships seem to act as a buffer against the negative developments caused by social change and political violence. The suggestion that adolescents are successful in coping with even the most dramatic changes in their sociocultural environments may arise because most of them are supported by their families and nearby communities.

However, some of the results sound a note of caution against making too simple, or empirically unverified, conclusions about the impact of social change on adolescent development. Against their expectations, Kracke, Oepke, Wild, and Noack found that social change in terms of economic disadvantage seems to provide a basis for rightist attitudes among young people in a society with considerable stability, but not in an environment of substantial social change. Moreover, Botcheva found that although the establishment of parliamentary democracy and free markets is usually considered a positive development, related changes in adolescent thinking may be negative, at least during the first years.

Implications for Policy Issues

Although there are good reasons for not drawing oversimplified conclusions, it is nevertheless possible to gain some insight into how to deal with some current social problems and how to develop interventions. For example, Roe and Cairns's review suggests that interventions that increase interpersonal contacts at an individual level in societies with political and cultural tensions may be effective. Kracke and colleagues' and Westin's findings suggest that efforts to decrease economic disadvantage among adolescents may help some youths to feel less threatened, and may therefore decrease their tendency to label some minority groups as "the enemy" in the process of social identity formation. Interestingly, some of the findings also suggest that rapid acculturation to the values of a host society is not always the best way for immigrant youths to adapt. For example, the findings of Liebkind and Kosonen showed that close contact with the co-ethnic group and parental family may provide a buffer against problems of adaptation.

Perspectives for Future Research

The aim of this book was to provide examples of how diversity in adolescents' developmental environments such as sociocultural transitions, social change and tensions in society, might be investigated. The issues raised in this book should be understood as a starting point for investigating adolescent development in changing environments, rather than as a systematic and complete review of these processes. To conclude, I would like to provide a few perspectives for future research.

1. It has been shown that there is substantial variation in the timing and sequencing of various transitions adolescents face across contemporary Europe. Although this diversity may cause some problems in interpreting research results concerning cross-national differences in adolescents' thinking, it also provides a natural setting for studies on the impact of this diversity. It can be assumed, for example, that research on the effects of educational structure (in terms of tracking and streaming) on adolescent well-being, later development, and entry into the social hierarchy would serve several purposes. It would have implications for planning educational curricula, decreasing problem behavior among certain groups of adolescents, and encouraging their positive development. Variation in the levels of youth unemployment across different contexts would also provide a basis for examining some of its developmental consequences. Furthermore, comparison of the impact of differences in transitions related to interpersonal relationships and the family would also provide useful information about socialization into adulthood roles.

2. Although there have been dramatic political changes in Europe recently, as this volume is being published, there are several signs of decreasing political tension and violence in Europe, especially in former Yugoslavia. However, it may be too optimistic to think that others will not arise. Current political changes typically provide a basis for future ones.

For example, the unification of Europe and the differences in the standard of living between European countries are likely to cause substantial changes in the future as well. These changes provide three types of challenge for researchers into adolescence. The first is to be ready to step in whenever changes begin to happen, and not to throw away the opportunity to investigate these "natural experiments." Second, although researchers usually do not have the means to prevent conflicts, they may at least put forward some ideas for decreasing tensions between different cultural groups. Third, adolescents growing up in the middle of political violence and war may have gone through traumatic experiences and may benefit from some counseling. Consequently, there is an evident need for research on the efficiency of different counseling methods in these contexts.

3. It seems that the immigrant population in Europe is continuously growing. Although a considerable amount of research has been carried out on the acculturation process, and on related adaptation to host societies, nonetheless diversity in the cultural background of various immigrant groups, the lengths of their residencies, and diversity in the host countries (cultural homogeneity, and language and cultural habits), all strongly suggest that there is an evident need to continue this type of research. It may provide some tools for how to promote well-being and adaptation among these groups in contemporary Europe.

4. The chapters in this book concerned several challenges and problems adolescents face when growing up in contemporary Europe. However, several important issues remain open for discussion in future volumes. One is the drug problem and how it relates to adolescent socialization. Although the major metropolitan cities of Europe have been facing this problem for the past two or three decades, there are reasons to assume drug abuse will become an even more serious problem in the next few years, or at least it will be more widely spread in different regions of Europe. This development is mainly due to slacker border controls in the context of European unification. There are some other social issues, too, that are in the pipeline for discussion. One is the presumed association between drug abuse and criminality. Another is the high unemployment rate, particularly in the periphery of European Union countries, which may cause serious problems for adolescents socializing into major adulthood roles.

Index